Critical Theory and Practice: A Coursebook

Critical Theory and Practice: A Coursebook is an accessible, up-to-date and clear introduction to literary theory. Each chapter contains guiding commentary, examples from literary and critical works, and a variety of exercises to provoke and engage. The chapters each have their own glossary and annotated selection of suggested further reading, and the book also contains a full bibliography.

All the key issues and debates which the student of literary theory is likely to confront are covered here. The reader has the opportunity to approach selected literary texts newly equipped with a knowledge of the methodology and assisted by suggested questions.

Critical Theory and Practice: A Coursebook is a challenging yet approachable textbook which not only clearly explains the terminology, but also stimulates the reader to engage with the theory and apply it in practice.

Keith Green is Senior Lecturer in English Studies at Sheffield Hallam University. He has published articles on a variety of linguistic and literary topics.

Jill LeBihan is Lecturer in English Studies and Women's Studies at Sheffield Hallam University. She has published articles on subjects including the position of women in the study of literary theory.

In collaboration, Keith Green and Jill LeBihan have written on the subjects of literature and psychoanalysis and poetics.

ROUTLEDGE

LONDON AND NEW YORK

Critical Theory and Practice: A Coursebook

- Keith Green and Jill LeBihan

First published 1996
by Routledge
11 New Fetter Lane, London EC4P 4EE

Simultaneously published in the USA
and Canada
by Routledge
29 West 35th Street, New York,
NY 10001

Typeset in Sabon and Futura by
J&L Composition Ltd, Filey,
North Yorkshire

Printed and bound in Great Britain by
Biddles Ltd, Guildford and
King's Lynn

*British Library Cataloguing in
Publication Data*
A catalogue record for this book is
available from the British Library

*Library of Congress Cataloguing in
Publication Data*
Green, Keith
Critical Theory and Practice/
Keith Green and Jill LeBihan.
p. cm.
Includes bibliographical references
and index.
1. Criticism. 2. Critical
Theory. 3. Language and languages.
I. LeBihan, Jill II. Title
PN98.S6G735 1995
801'.95–dc20 95–3558

ISBN 0–415–11438–1 (hbk)
ISBN 0–415–11439–X (pbk)

Contents

Acknowledgements

We are grateful to the Humanities Research Centre at Sheffield Hallam University for buying us some time to write this book.

Jules LeBihan and Margaret Smith transferred whole chapters from our old word-processing programme on to the new one for no financial gain – thank you both. Thanks also to Judy Bottrill, who typed the prototype version of this book some years ago, and has been tolerant of us making use of her office, computers and printers ever since.

Text permissions

The authors gratefully acknowledge permission to reprint material from the following sources:

Ashcroft, B., Griffiths, G. and Tiffin, H. *The Empire Writes Back*, Routledge;
Atwood, M. *Surfacing*, André Deutsch Ltd;
Atwood, M. from *Language in Her Eye*, Coach House Press, 1990, Ⓤ Margaret Atwood, reprinted by permission of Coach House Press;
Barrell, J. *Poetry, Language and Politics*, Manchester University Press;
Barthes, R. *Image/Music/Text*, HarperCollins Publishers Ltd;
Belsey, C. and Moore, J. *The Feminist Reader: Essays in Gender and the Politics of Literary Criticism*, Macmillan Press Ltd and Basil Blackwell Inc. (USA);
Best, G. *Mid-Victorian Britain 1851–1875*, Weidenfeld and Nicholson;
Blonsky, M. *On Signs*, Blackwell Publishers;

ACKNOWLEDGEMENTS

Butler, J. and Scott, J. *Feminists Theorize the Political*, Routledge;

Carr, E.H. *What is History?*, Macmillan Ltd;

Chomsky, N. *Syntactic Structures*, Mouton de Gruyter;

Christian, B. *Black Feminist Criticism*, Teachers College Press;

Cixous, H. 'The Laugh of the Medusa', *Signs* 1:4 (1975), © The University of Chicago Press;

Cixous, H. *The Newly-Born Woman*, Manchester University Press;

Crystal and Davy *Investigating English Style*, Longman Group Ltd;

Culler, J. *In Pursuit of Signs: Semiotics, Literature and Deconstruction*, Routledge 1981 (UK); Cornell University Press (USA);

Culler, J. *On Deconstruction*, Routledge 1983 (UK); Cornell University Press (USA);

Derrida, J. *Margins of Philosopy*, © The University of Chicago (1982);

Derrida, J. *Writing and Difference*, Routledge 1978 (UK and Commonwealth), © 1978 by The University of Chicago (World);

di Michele, M. from *Language in Her Eye*, Coach House Press, 1990, © Mary di Michele, reprinted by permission of Coach House Press;

Dollimore, J. and Sinfield, A. *Political Shakespeare*, Manchester University Press;

Eagleton, T. *Criticism and Ideology* Verso/New Left Books (1976);

Eliot, T.S. *The Selected Prose of T.S. Eliot*, ed. Frank Kermode, Faber and Faber Ltd;

Felman, S. *Literature and Psychoanalysis: The Question of Reading Otherwise*, The Johns Hopkins University Press;

Foucault, M. *The Foucault Reader*, ed. Paul Rabinow, reprinted by permission of Georges Borchardt Inc. Extract from 'Nietzsche, Genealogy, History from *Language, Counter-Memory, Practice*, © Basil Blackwell Publishers;

Fowler, R. *Linguistic Criticism* (1986), by permission of Oxford University Press;

Fowles, J. *The Magus*, Jonathan Cape Ltd;

Frye, N. *Anatomy of Criticism*, Princeton University Press;

Fuss, D. *Essentially Speaking*, Routledge;

Gates Jnr, H.L. 'Writing "Race" and the Difference It Makes', *'Race', Writing and Difference*, ed. Henry Louis Gates, © 1985, 1986 The University of Chicago Press;

Gearhart, S., excerpt from *The Wanderground* by Sally Miller Gearhart, © 1979 Sally Miller Gearhart, published in Great Britain by The Women's Press Ltd (London). U.S. edition by Alyson Publications, Inc. (Boston), reprinted by permission of Alyson Publications, Inc;

Genette, G. *Figures of Literary Discourse*, translated by A. Sheridan. ©

1982 Columbia University Press, reprinted by permission of the publisher;

Greene, G. and Kahn, C. *Changing Subjects: The Making of Feminist Literary Criticism*, Routledge;

Jefferson, A. and Robey, D. *Modern Literary Theory: A Comparative Introduction*, B.T. Batsford Ltd;

Kaplan, C. *Sea Changes: Culture and Feminisim*, Verso/New Left Books (1986);

Kermode, F., excerpt from *The Selected Prose of T.S. Eliot*, ed. Frank Kermode, © 1975 Valerie Eliot, reprinted by permission of Harcourt Brace & Company;

Krupat, A. *Ethnocriticism: Ethnography, History, Literature*, © 1992 The Regents of the University of California;

Lacan, J. *Écrits: A Selection*, trans. Alan Sheridan, Tavistock Publications;

Larkin, P. 'The Winter Palace' from *Collected Poems*, ed. Anthony Thwaite, Faber and Faber Ltd (UK); Farrar, Straus & Giroux, Inc. (USA);

Laurence, M., excerpt from *The Diviners* by Margaret Laurence, used by permission of the Canadian publishers, McClelland & Stewart, Toronto; Virago (UK and Commonwealth), © 1974 by Margaret Laurence, reprinted by permission of New End Inc;

Leech and Short *Style in Fiction*, Longman Group Ltd;

Lemon, Lee T. and Reis, J. Marion *Russian Formalist Criticism*, University of Nebraska Press;

Lodge, D. *Nice Work*, Martin Secker & Warburg Ltd; Curtis Brown Literary Agents;

Macherey, P. *A Theory of Literary Production*, Routledge (1966);

Mair, G.H. (1969) *English Literature 1450–1900*, by permission of Oxford University Press;

Maracle, L. from *Language in Her Eye*, Coach House Press, © Lee Maracle, reprinted by permission of Coach House Press;

Miller, J. *Seductions*, Virago Press (UK), reprinted by permission of the publishers from *Seductions: Studies in Reading and Culture* by Jane Miller, Cambridge, Mass.: Harvard University Press, © 1990 by Jane Miller;

Moi, T. *Sexual/Textual Politics*, Methuen & Co;

Morgan, S. *My Place*, Virago Press (UK), first published in 1987 by Fremantle Arts Centre Press, Fremantle, Western Australia;

Mülhäusler and Harre, *Pronouns and People*, Blackwell Publishers;

Naylor, G. *Mama Day*, Hutchinson, and Peters Fraser Dunlop (USA & Canada);

Perkins, D. *Is Literary History Possible?*, The Johns Hopkins University Press;

Phillips, A. *On Kissing, Tickling and Being Bored*, Faber and Faber Ltd (British Commonwealth excluding Canada only), reprinted by permission of the publishers from *On Kissing, Tickling and Being Bored: Psychoanalytic Essays on the Unexamined Life* by Adam Phillips, Cambridge, Mass.: Harvard University Press, © 1993 by Adam Phillips;

Piaget, J. *Structuralism*, Routledge (1971);

Reynolds, M. *The Penguin Book of Lesbian Short Stories*, courtesy of M. Reynolds;

Rimmon-Kennan, S. *Narrative Fiction: Contemporary Poetics*, Methuen & Co;

Rose, J. *The Case of Peter Pan or The Impossibility of Children's Fiction*, © Jacqueline Rose 1984, reprinted by permission of Macmillan Ltd;

Russ, J. The extract from *How to Suppress Women's Writing* by Joanna Russ, published in Great Britain by The Women's Press Ltd, 1984, 34 Great Sutton Street, London EC1V 0DX, reprinted on/page 231 is used by permission of The Women's Press Ltd;

Said, E. *Culture and Imperialism*, Chatto & Windus; © 1994 by Edward Said, reprinted with the permission of Wylie, Aitken and Stone, Inc;

Seidler, V. *Men, Sex and Relationships: Writings from Achilles Heel*, Routledge;

Showalter, E. *The New Feminist Criticism*, Virago Press (UK), Pantheon Books (USA);

Smith, P. *Discerning the Subject*, © 1988 the Regents of the University of Minnesota, reprinted from *Discerning the Subject* by Paul Smith, published by the University of Minnesota Press;

Smith, P., reprinted from *Men in Feminism* (1987), by permission of the publisher, Routledge, New York;

Spivak, G.C. *The Post-Colonial Critic*, Routledge;

Todorov, T. *Introduction to Poetics*, Harvester Wheatsheaf;

Turner, L. *The Love of Dugan Magee*, © 1992 by Linda Turner, all rights reserved, reproduction with the permission of the publisher, Harlequin Books S.A.;

Van Herk, A. *No Fixed Address*, permission granted courtesy of Abner Stein agency, © Aritha Van Herk 1986;

Veeser, H. Aram *The New Historicism*, Routledge.

Wales, K. *A Dictionary of Stylistics*, Longman Group Ltd;

Warhol, R. and Price Herndl, D. (eds) *Feminisms: An Anthology of Literary Theory and Criticism*, Macmillan Press Ltd; © 1991 Rutgers, The State University;

Weedon, C. *Feminist Practice and Post-Structualist Theory*, Blackwell Publishers;

White, H. *Metahistory: The Historical Imagination in Nineteenth Century Europe*, The Johns Hopkins University Press;

Widdowson, H.G. *Stylistics and the Teaching of Literature*, Longman Group Ltd;

Williams, P. and Chrisman, L. *Colonial Discourse and Post-Colonial Theory*, Harvester Wheatsheaf;

Wolf, N. *Fire With Fire*, Chatto & Windus (UK), and Brockman Inc. (USA & Canada);

Zimmerman, B. 'What Has Never Been: An Overview of Lesbian Feminist Literary Criticism'. This excerpt is reprinted from *Feminist Studies*, Volume 7, number 3 (Fall 1981): 451–75, by permission of the publisher, *Feminist Studies*, Inc., c/o Women's Studies Program, University of Maryland, College Park, MD 20742, USA.

Introduction

THIS BOOK HAS EVOLVED as a result of our own practice of teaching critical theory to undergraduates on English Studies degrees. It has been produced to meet the needs of students and teachers who are involved in the now standard practice of including a compulsory 'theory' course on most literature degree programmes. There are many introductions to literary theory available, not to mention introductory collections of essays, and criticism workbooks, but we wanted to produce a text which both deals with the complex problems of contemporary literary theory and gives students and teachers material to engage with in the seminar room or in private study.

Our experience of teaching theory suggests that students need more guidance on reading and assessing critical issues, rather than learning a fixed set of 'isms'. We are constantly being asked for a single volume that exposes students to theoretical

discourses and gives some assistance without simply replacing the original theory with a summary that is reproduced in class essays *ad infinitum*. From the mass of theories and accompanying textbooks appearing in the 1980s and 1990s, it has been hard for both the student and teacher to cut a coherent path. One of the main problems associated with the teaching of modern critical theory is that it requires, or seems to require, such vast areas of knowledge (including methodologies) which do not suggest a coherent, single discipline. Modern English students (or students of Literature or Cultural Studies) encounter complex rereadings and interpretations based on the implicit or explicit use of historical theory, philosophy, Marxism, psychoanalysis, linguistics, cultural theory, feminism, post-colonial theory and discourse theory. In an age of competition for resources and simultaneous expansion in higher education, this is extremely demanding for both student and teacher.

A note on postmodernism

In recent critical writing, particularly that coming from North America, it has become commonplace to make no distinction between postmodern practices and post-structuralist ones. Throughout this book we will maintain a distinction between the two areas, and we do not attempt to address the question of postmodernism, just as we have not attempted any detailed examination of any other cultural eras or modes. Susan Bordo points out how the confusion of postmodernism with post-structuralism occurs: 'There are those academics in literature and philosophy who, conflating theory with all of culture, identify the postmodern solely in terms of particular post-structuralist authors and the schools of thought they have spawned' (Bordo 1992: 160). Whilst it is not always easy, necessary or desirable to make clear-cut distinctions between examples of theoretical writing and other cultural artefacts, such as novels, architecture, films and so on, the very different evolution of the two discourses of the postmodern and of post-structuralism, and their uses, is not insignificant. It could be argued that the cultural practices which characterise the postmodern may be best approached through post-structuralist critical methodologies, but to collapse one into the other seems to us unhelpful.

The area of postmodern culture, as well as the critiques it has produced, is an enormous one, and it is far beyond the scope of this book to attempt an introduction. We deal with related issues in our sections on New Historicism (Chapter 3), Lacanian Psychoanalysis (Chapter 4), Deconstruction (Chapter 5) and Post-feminism (Chapter 6). In addition, there are many excellent introductions to this field including: Linda Hutcheon's *A Poetics of Postmodernism: History, Theory, Fiction* (1988); Brenda Marshall's *Teaching the Postmodern: Fiction and Theory* (1992); and Brian McHale's *Postmodernist Fiction* (1987).

How to use this book

Each chapter is designed to be self-contained, but cross-references are made where appropriate. Theory itself is not self-contained, so the divisions are personal ones to a great extent. The chapters are divided into sub-sections, each of which contains guiding commentary, examples from both literary and critical works, and a variety of questions and exercises. Where they are more abstract, these questions are partially answered, to give the reader a starting point. At the end of each chapter there is a glossary of key terms used. There is also a select, annotated bibliography, to give guidance on further reading. The critical bibliographies are not supposed to be representative; rather they include texts that we have found useful for ourselves or for our students. A full bibliography of works cited appears at the end of the book.

Each chapter contains roughly the same number of sections and includes exposition, analysis, questions and exercises. We have avoided a rigid question-and-answer format because this would run counter to the spirit of the book. Where appropriate we have given guidance in response to a particular question, but the questions themselves have various objectives: some call for a quick, intuitive response, others more detailed expositions. Others still are largely rhetorical or might call for more lengthy consideration. We have not been formulaic in our presentation of these questions, but the sections themselves are manageable enough for them to be worked through appropriately, either in private study or within a seminar.

This book assumes that the reader brings with her/him a certain amount of knowledge about how to approach texts. We don't give any explanations of the more traditional areas of literary study, such as rhetorical tropes, use of thematic devices, rhyme, metre, and so on. A useful introduction to some of these aspects of critical analysis can be found in *Ways of Reading* (Montgomery *et al.* 1992). Each chapter deals with a different collection of issues, so the amount of commentary and explanation in relation to extracts and exercises varies. The following should give a map of what to expect, and provides a brief overview to help you know where you need to begin.

1 Language, linguistics and literature

The focus of this chapter is the analysis and description of language and the relation between linguistics and literature. Despite the proliferation of linguistics-based theories in modern criticism, many students have not developed a working knowledge of their own language, and for this reason we include a basic grammar course. This can be used in conjunction with stylistic analyses as well as the material on structures in Chapter 2. We discuss recent developments in linguistics and stylistics, including speech act theory and pragmatics, and this is linked to earlier material on the nature of discourse and the analyses of style and stylistics. Again, building on the grammar and other linguistic elements, we investigate the relation between language and gender, looking particularly at the notion of gendered syntax. The final section begins with cognitive linguistics, particularly in the work of George Lakoff, and the relation between language and 'reality'. There is an extended discussion of an extract from Daphne Marlatt's *Salvage* (1991) to conclude the section, bringing together much of the material from the chapter as a whole. This chapter contains material that will be of use later in the book, particularly in Chapters 2 and 5. The aim is to provide a basic tool kit of linguistics and language issues that the student will be able to draw on when confronting other critical issues.

2 Structures of literature

Discussion of literary structuralism begins with the influential language theories of Ferdinand de Saussure. The conception of language as a system can be explored at a number of levels: at the smallest level of the sign, at the level of the system of signs, or at the wider structural level, which is built on a framework of sign-systems. The understanding of basic linguistic structures has been developed by literary theorists into a formula for analysing narrative structures. We include a folk-tale as an example of a simple narrative, and explain how to go about producing a structuralist analysis of such a text. Structuralist criticism has made its greatest impact in the fields of narratology and popular culture. In narratology, the morphological approach developed from Propp has provided insights into the essential structure of texts. In popular culture, semiotics has had considerable success and is a familiar methodology for approaching all kinds of texts, its most well-known incarnation is in the decoding of advertisements. We examine a number of examples and discuss not only the successes but also the failures of semiotics.

3 Literature and history

In this chapter we discuss the relation between the methodologies of historical analysis and literary analysis. We examine the notion of 'truth' and its relation to both history and literature, and assess the extent to which 'history' is part of literary study. The differences between aesthetic, ahistorical criticism and historical approaches become apparent in the consideration of 'literary histories'. The classifying and homogenising impulse of historical methodologies is fractured and subverted in modern historicist approaches, and this is explored with reference to the nature of historical and literary discourse. Key figures in the so-called 'New Historicism' are discussed in relation to New Historicist practices – the foregrounding of peripheral material, such as anecdotes, over more central 'facts', for example, problematises the notion of truth and highlights the relation between 'fact' and 'text'. The concluding section focuses on the concept of 'ideology', its function in and relation to literary texts, and as it figures in Marxist criticism. The concept of ideology is presented in various ways, through the work of major Marxist thinkers, and juxtaposed with analyses of literary extracts.

4 Subjectivity, psychoanalysis and criticism

The term 'subjectivity' has a wide range of definitions, and so we include a number of explanations from linguists, semioticians, discourse theorists and feminists, all of which can be debated. The main discussion of the chapter centres on the area of psychoanalysis, which is crucial to contemporary understanding of subjectivity, and is also quite widely incorporated in many literary critical practices, although not always explicitly. We begin with an introduction to the schematic relationship between literature and psychoanalysis, and the parallel relationship between the critic and the psychoanalyst.

The discussion of specific psychoanalytic theories is confined to the work of Sigmund Freud and Jacques Lacan, as these are the theorists who have written in a way that is most relevant to literary study. The explanation of the work of Freud includes his basic concepts: the id, ego and super-ego; the dream work, and the way it can be applied to literature. There is also commentary on Freud's famous explanation of the development of sexual identity, the Oedipus complex. Lacanian psychoanalysis provides a revision of many Freudian concepts, and offers us the possibility of reading Freud metaphorically rather than literally. The examination of Lacan's work is connected to other areas of literary criticism, such as feminism and deconstruction, and it is worth making these cross-references within this volume. The basic

Lacanian concepts explain the importance of language and gender in the construction of the subject, and we discuss some of his most well-known structures: the Imaginary and the Symbolic, the *nom du père* and the Mirror Stage.

5 Reading, writing and reception

This chapter focuses on the role of the reader in the construction of textual meaning. Phenomenology suggests that external 'reality' is always mediated through consciousness, and that the experience of reading literature is a process of interaction between text and that consciousness. Other theories, such as that expounded in the early work of Stanley Fish, posit the reader alone as having responsibility for the construction and production of meaning. The idea of reader bringing meaning to a text is explored in relation to theories of reading and identity and the construction of gestalten. How readers construct a unified text and reach a particular interpretation is shown through analyses from the micro-level of sentences to the macro-levels of texts and culture. Various conceptions of the reader are presented: the 'actual' reader, the implied reader, Fish's hybrid reader, the reader in a particular community, and Eco's 'model reader'. The section concludes with an extended discussion of a theory of interpretative trauma: deconstruction.

6 Feminism, literature and criticism

Feminism has established itself within literary studies in universities with extraordinary success. This has resulted in a proliferation of different kinds of feminist criticism, so we begin by offering a few definitions. We then chart the progress of academic feminism, beginning with its most familiar form in analysis of literary representations of women, and critiques of misogynist stereotypes.

Although earlier feminist literary criticism concentrated on representations of women, later developments concentrate more on form than content. This concentration on form begins by paying attention to the generic constraints that govern women's writing. Some female writers conform to traditional expectations about what women should write and produce romantic fiction; others go out of their way to subvert previously male-dominated spheres (such as the genre of detective fiction).

The concentration of forms of fiction is developed further by the feminist focus on gender and language (which is explored in Chapter 1), and on gender and subjectivity (which is examined in Chapter 4). These two areas are brought together under the heading of *écriture féminine*, which argues for a total transformation of language and other symbolic systems on the grounds that the feminine cannot be adequately represented by a masculine system of meaning.

The lack of adequate representation of women by fiction or by language generally is emphasised in the instance of lesbian experience. Lesbian feminism argues for an increase in the representation of relationships between women (not just sexual ones). Lesbian feminism begins with an examination of stereotyped representations or exclusions of lesbians from canonical literature. Lesbian discourse also raises the problem of the exclusivity of heterosexual feminism, which does not represent the interests of all women.

Lesbian feminism introduces the risk of essence that is faced by much feminist discourse, and which is challenged by many post-structuralist feminists. There is a struggle in contemporary feminist theory between the need to reject definitions of women that have been produced, whilst still needing some recognition that women as a category face discrimination. Finally, the success of feminism has resulted in its adoption or co-option by men for a variety of ends, not always worthy. The problem of men's relation to feminism, and many women's rejection of it as unhelpful, is explored in the final section of this chapter.

The crucial issue of the position of black women in feminism is not dealt with in this chapter. Like lesbians, many women of colour have felt ignored and excluded by academic feminism. Their contributions to the feminist movement have been substantial, but, perhaps controversially, we decided to include their work in the subsequent chapter on cultural identity. The inclusion of the work of black women critics under feminism would privilege their gender, whilst inclusion under the 'Cultural identity' chapter necessarily focuses on issues of race, and this should perhaps be borne in mind by the reader.

7 Cultural identity, literature and criticism

The issue of how literary canons exclude certain writers, and how the canonical hierarchy influences critical practice, is not only a problem for writers of colour; clearly it has significance across the spectrum of literary production. However, we illustrate the operation of the canon and the kind of reading practices it produces with the example of cultural identity, and show how readers are often not taught to be aware of the issues that cultural difference might make.

The canon is subverted, or perhaps reclaimed for different ends, by the practice of writing back. Many post-colonial authors rewrite classic works of English Literature as a process of regaining ideological control after imperial domination. Rewriting also shows how to reread the 'classics' with an eye to cultural identity. We use a case-study of Shakespeare's *The Tempest*, and a variety of extracts from a series of post-colonial revisions of the text, to illustrate how the writing-back process can transform the literature of empire.

The problem of how cultural identity might be established has connections with issues explored elsewhere relating to subjectivity (Chapters 4 and 6). There is a contemporary debate raging about how 'race' might be represented: is it an essential biological quality, or is it a cultural construction? The issues of identity politics that are crucial to feminism in a post-structuralist age are also of huge importance in discussions of 'race' and literature.

Post-colonial literary theory is a heavily contested area. Exactly what texts might be included, and precisely what kinds of critical processes it might involve, remains open to debate. We try to give some idea of the problems of the study of these critical discourses and literatures by examining how they have been integrated into the Western academic institutions, and with what compromises. Post-colonial literatures pose a threat to the whole notion of 'English' degrees, and so their presence on the scene is not universally welcomed. If they are to be incorporated into literary study, what changes must take place within the Academy? And what changes within the area of post-colonial discourse? One answer to these questions concerns that of tokenism. In order to dilute the threat of these new literatures and counter-discourses, many literature degrees incorporate token 'black' texts and assume that their work has been done. We examine the issue of tokenism and the ways in which counter-discourses can be appropriated by the mainstream.

Finally, we examine the issue of gender and cultural identity. This conjuncture is a particularly complex one in an age where identity of any kind is so fraught. The ways in which women of colour have been represented, and the ways in which they represent themselves, provide discursive issues which have an impact on all areas of understanding of self and self-representation.

Chapter 1

Language, linguistics and literature

1 Basic relations

THE RELATION BETWEEN linguistics and literature is complex, but here we wish to distinguish between linguistics as a metalanguage (a language *about* language), used 'practically' for the analysis and description of literary texts, and linguistics as metaphor for such analysis and description. Literary criticism has sought to use linguistics rather eclectically: sometimes enlisting its language and methodologies for the purposes of 'practical' criticism (a rather curious term); and sometimes enlisting its theory in order to attempt to gain an overview of literary textual phenomena, for instance, to find a 'grammar' (a system of rules and conventions) of the literary text.

Linguistics and linguistic models have occupied an important, but not dominant, place within literary criticism during the twentieth century, but a paradox has recently emerged. Despite the proliferation of linguistics or language-based theories which now form the core of any theory course taught at undergraduate and postgraduate levels, students' formal knowledge of English has weakened. This point brings us to a key issue: knowledge about language. The title of this chapter is not simply 'Linguistics and literature'; a third term, 'language', is at its head. We shall make basic distinctions here, but these will ultimately need to be questioned:

Literature   = a textual form, an object of study
Language   = the 'medium' of texts, an object of study
Linguistics   = the metalanguage; language used about language

In this chapter we are not going to discuss those aspects of literary and cultural criticism which have taken linguistics as a metaphor for their analyses and methodologies. The concern is rather with the relation of literature to language and of literature to linguistics on a primarily practical level, although we shall see that this is often a spurious distinction.

It might be argued that any literary text is by definition made *of* and *by* language, so the obvious tools for analysis are the tools of the linguist. But many critics suggest that literature has a special status or quality not accessible through the application of the metalanguage of linguistics. This issue is central to the debate, and we shall return to it. First, however, it is worthwhile noting two terms used in the above commentary which are crucial to our views about linguistics. We have talked about the 'application' of linguistics and the 'tools' of linguistics. These terms betray a commonsensical, empirical and practical view of the relations which might exist between language, linguistics and literature. This is not the only view. How else might linguistics be viewed? The title of the chapter could contain another term, which we are implicitly discussing: *criticism*. This is how Katie Wales in *A Dictionary of Stylistics* defines the term 'linguistic criticism':

> **linguistic criticism**
> Particularly associated in the 1980s with the work of Roger Fowler . . . to refer to the application of linguistic theory and ideas to literature for the purposes of analysis and INTERPRETATION . . . Fowler's own approach is in essence a linguistic complement to PRACTICAL CRITICISM.
>
> (Wales 1989: 277)

In the 1960s and 1970s the linguist Fowler and a literary critic, F. W. Bateson, conducted a fierce debate on the issue of the relation of linguistics to literature (see Select Bibliography at the end of the chapter). Fowler insisted that linguistic methods and tools were necessary for the proper and detailed analysis of literary texts. Bateson objected vehemently, declaring that literary texts had an 'ineradicable subjective core' that was simply not amenable to linguistic analysis. In other words, there is something in literary texts that cannot be discovered objectively and that therefore cannot be described by the linguist. To what extent would you agree with Bateson that literary texts have such a core? What aspects of literary texts would necessarily evade the linguistic critic?

In his introduction to *Linguistic Criticism* (1986) Roger Fowler states:

> By the time I went to university . . . , it was well accepted that commentary on language was a normal and essential practice within literary criticism: essential for coaxing out the complexity of literary texts.
>
> (Fowler 1986: 2)

But this kind of focus on 'commentary on language' is quite different from the linguistic poetics proposed by Roman Jakobson, the Russian formalists and the Prague School of linguists in the early and middle part of the century. Jakobson focused on the fundamental workings of language and developed theories that specifically applied to literature. The most important of these derived from the Swiss linguist Ferdinand de Saussure, whose ideas are explored in greater detail in Chapter 3. Language is produced along two axes, the *syntagmatic*, or horizontal, and the *paradigmatic*, or vertical. The syntagmatic axis represents combination: linguistic elements are combined in sequence with other elements. The paradigmatic axis represents selection or choice: each element is selected from a number of possible choices. In the sentence 'the sky is blue', for instance, the items 'the', 'sky', 'is' and 'blue' combine in sequence; yet for each item that appears something else might be substituted. For 'the' we might have 'this', 'that' or 'yonder'; for 'sky' we could have any from a massive number of nouns. For 'is' we could have further variations on the verb form – 'was', 'could have been', 'will be', etc. 'Blue' could be replaced by any other colour, or any other adjective. Some of the items, therefore, have a great number of possible substitutions, some much less so. Each substitution will determine what will be acceptable in the following element. Thus syntagmatic and paradigmatic elements are intimately related, and can be seen at every level of discourse. For instance, at the level of the individual word, letters or sounds combine in sequence. At a higher level, sentences combine in sequence to form texts. At each point within each level, a number of possible elements can be realised.

This idea of syntagmatic and paradigmatic relations has been enormously influential in language study, and Jakobson used it in his theory of literary language. In one of the most-often quoted but least-understood pronouncements in criticism he stated that: 'The poetic function projects the principle of equivalence from the axis of selection into the axis of combination' (Jakobson 1967: 303).

Jakobson means that elements of poetry that are similar in some way, whether in sound or sense or some other aspect, are combined in sequence. The paradigmatic is projected on to the syntagmatic. But this does not only occur in poetry, for the poetic function is potentially present in all kinds of discourse. In poetry, however, the function is at its most evident. The projection of selection on to combination is made in both of the following texts:

> More reasons to shop at Morrison's (chain-store slogan)
> The force that through the green fuse drives the flower
> (Dylan Thomas)

Similar sounds are thus combined in sequence to make the reader infer some other relationship between the items, for example 'necessity to shop' and 'Morrison's'. Here is another literary example:

> Desire may grow more circumstantial and less circumspect
> (Thom Gunn: 'Carnal Knowledge')

The words 'circumstantial' and 'circumspect' form a paradigm of similarity (they have similar forms) through being combined along the syntagmatic axis. The linear, syntagmatic relationship between the two words is thus projected on to a paradigmatic, vertical relationship: a similarity of form.

Syntagmatic and paradigmatic relations are part of the essential elements of language. No distinction in *kind* is made between literary and non-literary texts here, only a distinction of *degree*. But is literary language different from 'ordinary language', and are the goals of literary criticism distinct from that of literary criticism?

5

Consider the following quotations:

The novelist's medium is language: whatever he does, *qua* novelist, he does in and through language.

(Lodge 1966: ix)

Linguistics is an independent discipline, quite distinct . . . from literary criticism with its own goals and criteria.

(Fowler 1986: 3)

In linguistics . . . deliberate attempts have been made to appear as objective, rigorous etc. as possible . . . not because the resultant practices are necessarily more appropriate than others, but because they bring with them an enhanced position in the academic community.

(Cameron 1985: 11)

a linguist deaf to the poetic function of language and a literary scholar indifferent to linguistic problems and unconversant with linguistic methods are equally flagrant anachronisms.

(Jakobson 1967: 322)

In the first quotation, Lodge suggests that language is the medium in which the novelist works inasmuch as content is seen as prior to form. Ideas are worked *in* language, but ultimately *through* it. Language is that which enables an idea to be partly realised: there are elements which come before language, and elements which come after it.

i) What kind of criticism would this give rise to?

Language is only one aspect of the literary experience, albeit an important one. Criticism would have to develop methods of integrating linguistic analysis with other aspects of texts such as context (historical, social, situational).

In the second extract, Fowler makes a clear distinction between linguistics and literary criticism.

ii) Make a list of the 'goals' of literary criticism. Can you speculate as to the goals of linguistics at this stage?

In the third excerpt Cameron insists that linguists hide behind a mask of objectivity that serves no methodological purpose. In stressing its scientific nature linguists have sought to protect linguistics from radical movements. In the last extract, Jakobson proposes a link between linguists and literary critics. This seems commonsensical. But why is it that the linguistic analysis of literary texts is by no means the methodological norm? To repeat the question, surely, as literary texts are made of language, the proper analyst is the linguist? Can you defend any other kind of readings of literary texts?

2 Texts, grammars, discourses

Fowler and Jakobson (above) talk about 'linguistics' and 'linguistic methods'. It is at this point we should consider the formal elements which make up any text. According to certain grammars, notably the scale-and-category grammar developed by J.R. Firth and M.A.K. Halliday, the linguistic units which comprise a sentence can be seen as ranking from the smallest to the largest (although it should be stated immediately that the notion of size in relation to the ranking elements is far from straightforward). For example:

Phoneme	/b/
Morpheme	walk / ed (walked)
Word	Hello
Group	The man in the bowler hat
Clause	While I was writing / I had a beer
Sentence	The kitchen was dark

Formal linguistics stops at the sentence. It has been assumed that most of what can be said of language can be said of the maximal descriptive unit, the sentence. However, there are elements which function beyond sentence level, and this draws our attention to the phenomenon of *texts*.

Consider the following text:

Wash and core six apples. Put them in a bowl.

This example, similar to those discussed by Halliday and Hasan in their book *Cohesion in English* (1976), is recognisable as coming from a cookery book. The sentences are subjectless, being imperatives (telling us to do something). The 'them' in the second sentence relates to the apples of the first. This is an example of cohesive relations existing across sentence boundaries.

The term 'text' is quite difficult to define. The word is based on the Latin *textere* 'to weave', and suggests a coherent, integrated collection of sentences, but this is not really the case. A text is a stretch of language, complete or partial, which comprises one or more units of meaning. A *text* can therefore be Tolstoy's *War and Peace*, or a road sign saying 'STOP'. However, a text can be a jumble of unrelated sentences.

Consider the following text:

Sheffield Wednesday for the cup. Is there a God? My auntie keeps goats.

This is a text in that it is a collection of (presumably) unrelated sentences; it is a stretch of language, but it is not coherent. As sense-making creatures, humans strive to understand texts, to make them coherent, but the above text would hardly be realised in any knowable context, apart (perhaps) from a surrealist novel. When a text is realised in a knowable context, when it is coherent for the reader or addressee in this way, it is a *discourse*. Discourse, according to the Russian theorist Bakhtin, is language in its 'concrete living totality'. A *text* is transformed into *discourse* when it forms a coherent whole (even if it is a fragment). We now need to look at those elements which form texts and discourses. It is beyond the scope of this chapter to discuss the individual ranked elements here. However, we shall take a simple sentence and point out some simple relations. The sentence is taken from Aritha Van Herk's *No Fixed Address* (1989).

> Arachne is particularly fond of graveyards; they are her ideal picnic grounds.
>
> (Van Herk 1989: 16)

This sentence is decontextualised: it is removed from further text which surrounds and accompanies it. We shall have more to say about context shortly. Our purpose here is to describe essential formal elements, so any sentence would do. We are going to use the grammatical terms developed by M.A.K. Halliday, often referred to as 'systemic' grammar. There are other grammars available (such as 'transformational' grammar, based on the work of Noam Chomsky), but systemic grammar has the advantage of being fairly simple in its descriptions and readily applicable to literary texts.

Phonemes

A phoneme is a *speech sound*, and is to be differentiated from *letter* by virtue of that sound. For example the letters 'c' and 'h' in the word 'character' form the same speech sound as the letter 'c' in the word car: /k/. *Phonology* is the study of how speech sounds contribute to meaning. There are twenty-six letters in the English alphabet, but forty-five phonemes in the English phonetic alphabet (although this is a rather arbitrary figure, and not fixed in the way the alphabet is). Phonologically, there is nothing remarkable about the above sentence, or at least nothing to comment about in terms of *stylistic effects*.

Morphemes

The morpheme has been described by Bloomfield as the 'minimum grammatical unit'. Words are often composed of parts of other words that recur and have the same kind of function or meaning across the words. Although the relationship between morphemes and any stretch of language is more complex than this, it is

9

sufficient to say that in English there are elements which, though below the rank of words, nevertheless contribute to some aspect of the meaning. For example, the word 'graveyards' comprises three morphemes: 'grave', 'yard' and 's'. The first two are *free* morphemes, because they can stand as words on their own. The third is simply one letter and one phoneme, 's'. It cannot occur as a separate word and is thus a *bound* morpheme. In this word as in many others, the 's' is the morpheme of plurality. In a word such as 'bus' the 's' has no such function. 'Arachne' is thus one morpheme (being a proper name); 'is' is one; 'particularly' is two: 'particular' and the adverbial morpheme 'ly'; 'fond' is one morpheme; 'of' is one'; 'graveyards' is three, and so on. Not all morphemes are 'realised' in a word. The word 'sheep', for instance is one single morpheme when used to refer to a single sheep and appears to be the same when used to refer to more than one. The plurality of more than one 'sheep' is not realised morphemically.

Words

The word is not as easy to define or as stable an element as we might at first think. Linguists tend to prefer the term *lexical item* (or variations upon that term). Some traditional definitions of the word do not hold for all cases. For instance, one could view the word as a 'minimum free form' (Bloomfield 1935: 158–69) – an item of language with a space before and after it, and one that can be used on its own ('Wait!'). However, the word 'the' would not conform to this definition, as 'the' is never *used* on its own. Similarly, an expression such as 'cats and dogs' in the sentence 'It's raining cats and dogs' can be said to be one *lexical item* as it is a substitution for another item such as 'heavily' and is not 'about' cats and dogs.

Groups

The group is easier to define, and corresponds roughly to the more traditional 'phrase'. There are four syntactic groups (relating to clause and sentence structure) in English:

Nominal
Verbal
Prepositional
Adverbial

Nominal groups generally (and one must be mindful of the enormous variations possible) encode subjects and agents. Thus in our sentence 'Arachne is particularly fond of graveyards', 'Arachne' is the subject, and is a nominal group. A group can therefore be a single lexical item. It can also be considerably greater than a single word, as in:

> The woman with the fast car that shot through the lights was in a great hurry.

Here the nominal group (in subject position) is 'the woman with the fast car who drove through the lights'. The verbal group follows, and again this comprises a single word, *is*. This verb is called a *copula* verb. The copula has little independent meaning, but serves to relate the subject to other parts of the sentence, notably the complement. Because 'is' is a copula verb, what follows is an *intensive complement* (C^i) comprising a group with an adjective at its head. The complement comprises the items 'particularly fond'; the adjective 'fond' is preceded by an intensifier, 'particularly'. This kind of complement, the intensive, is quite different from the *extensive* complement (C^e, or *object* in traditional grammars) which occur if the verb were not a copula. Compare:

a) She became ill
b) She kicked the football

In a) the complement 'ill' is in direct relation to the subject; there are not two things, a 'she' and an 'ill'. In b) 'she' and the 'football' exist independently, hence the older term for this element, 'object'. Further, a) cannot be transformed into a passive construction, whereas b) can ('The football was kicked by her', but not, 'Ill became by her' *, where * = an unacceptable or ungrammatical construction). Became, therefore, is a copula verb like 'is'.

The element 'of graveyards' in the original sentence is a prepositional group. Prepositions, which usually begin these groups, semantically indicate possession, place and direction.

Clauses

The clause is the syntactic unit above the group, and usually contains a subject (S), which is often a nominal (noun-based) group, and a predicator (P), which is a verbal group. Sometimes a clause will take a complement (C) and an adjunct (A). The adjunct contains both the adverbial and the prepositional groups. In a declarative sentence, the smallest clause unit would be something like 'He cried' – with just the subject (S) and predicator (P). There are seven basic main clause types (in declarative sentences – that is, statements such as 'He cried'). Examples are:

She / cried
S   P
She / walked / in the garden
S   P   A
She / kicked / the ball
S   P C^e
She / became / ill
S   P C^i
She / considered / the teacher / a fool
S   P C^e C^i
She / gave / the child / a kiss
S   P C^{e1} C^{e2}
She / put / the cat / on the landing
S   P C^e A

Clauses can be independent (main) or dependent (subordinate). A subordinate clause cannot stand on its own, but needs a further syntactic unit to 'complete' it. For instance, in the sentence:

> While I was walking down the street, I found a ten pound note.

there are two clauses. The first, 'while I was walking down the street' is dependent on the second 'I found a ten pound note'. The first cannot be uttered on its own as a statement (one which is not a reply to a question), whereas the second clause can. The subordinating conjunction 'while' introduces the dependent clause. A subordinate clause need not contain a main verb group. For example, in the example above, we might have written:

> Walking down the street, I found a ten pound note.

Although it is not very likely to occur in any discourse or speech situation, there may be ambiguity as to whether the 'I' or the 'ten pound note' was walking down the street. The clause 'walking down the street' is subordinate with what is known as a *non-finite* verb at its head. The verb 'walking' is not complete; it expresses an action, but we do not know when the action took place, or , in the clause, who was performing that action, hence the ambiguity. In our example:

> Arachne is particularly fond of graveyards; they are her ideal picnic grounds.

there are also two clauses: 'Arachne is particularly fond of graveyards' and 'they are her ideal picnic grounds'. Both are independent (main). A clause-level description of each of these is:

Arachne /is /particularly fond/ of graveyards(;)
S   P C^i A
They/ are /her ideal picnic grounds(.)
S   P C^i

Both clauses contain the copula verb 'to be' as discussed above, and therefore have intensive complements following the predicator. The two clauses together form the highest formal syntactic unit, the sentence. In fact, a single clause can be (and frequently is) a sentence. Formal linguistics, as we have said, stops at the sentence, but there are clearly relationships which exist beyond sentence level. For example, if the two clauses had been separated into two sentences, then such relationships would become apparent. The pronoun 'they' which begins the second 'sentence' refers back to the 'graveyards' of the first. This kind of reference, known as *anaphora*, (to re-fer) is a fundamental feature of language and functions beyond the single sentence.

This is a very basic introduction to sentence grammar, and we have not yet focused on those elements that function beyond that supposed maximal unit of analysis. We have been concerned not with meaning, but with the formal relation between the elements of a sentence. What can this tell us about a text? The analyst must go beyond this formal description to account for the effects of a text. As Jakobson noted, linguistic description with no interpretation is a sterile activity. But interpretation without some basis in the structure and description of that structure must be ultimately impressionistic. How can one say anything meaningful about the language of a text if one has no knowledge *about* that language?

Let us go a little further now and discuss a larger text fragment. The text will still be rather short, but description at all kinds of levels will be possible. The text is the opening few lines from John Fowles' *The Collector*:

> When she was home from her boarding school, I used to see her almost every day sometimes, because their house was right opposite the Town Hall Annexe. She and her younger sister used to go in and out a lot, often with young men, which of course I didn't like.
>
> (Fowles 1963: 1)

The text opens with the subordinate clause 'When she was home from her boarding school'. The pronoun 'she' is a cataphoric reference: a pronoun that anticipates a fuller reference later in the text. At this stage we don't know who the 'she' is. This kind of delaying of names and other full forms of pronominal expressions is typical of prose fiction. The 'I' had, at some time in the past, seen 'her', 'almost every day sometimes'. This suggests that the narrator is observing her in specific chunks of time. The 'their' of the second subordinate clause of the opening sentence ('I used to see her almost everyday sometimes' is the main clause) has no proper antecedent: it is part of the narrator's discourse to use anaphoric reference in a 'lazy' manner. Presumably the pronoun 'their' refers to her parents. The following sentence begins rather clumsily, as if the narrator was attempting some kind of formality or 'proper' English, but was unsure of the construction ('She and her younger sister'). The final subordinate clause, 'which of course I didn't like', assumes more knowledge about the narrator on the part of the reader.

There is an opposition set up between the items 'boarding school' and 'Town Hall Annexe'. The narrator works for local government, but not in the central office. What does this tell us about the narrator? Can we be sure at this stage that he does work in the annexe? A clue to the age of the narrator is given in the nominal group 'young men'. Who would use such a phrase?

It is clear that such a text demands of the reader both linguistic and non-linguistic knowledge. In particular, Fowles' text demands knowledge of the English class system, and linguistic elements interact with this knowledge. Let us look, finally, at another text – the text where the initial fragment is to be found. The following is the surrounding paragraph from *No Fixed Address* cited earlier:

> When she sees the roadside sign slide past her window, Arachne slams on the brakes, backs up and pulls into the parking bay. The old highway is deserted, and up the hill to the southwest she can see the dominoed map of a graveyard. Arachne is particularly fond of graveyards; they are her ideal picnic grounds. She slides down from the car's high seat and stretches her arms. Tracing a finger over the dusty fender, she walks around to inspect the plaque. Chief Crowfoot: his dates and a generalization on his life. Arachne kicks the marker; she hates the way they minimize everything, reduce even enormous people and events. The graveyards should be better.
>
> (Van Herk 1989: 16)

i) Compare and contrast the use of pronouns ('him', 'her', 'she', 'it', etc.) in this text to the opening of Fowles' *The Collector*.

ii) Does the syntax of the piece suggest anything about the narrator in the way it does in the Fowles extract (even though it is a third person narrative)?

iii) What kinds of knowledge are implied in the text? Can you pick out specific linguistic elements which demand such knowledge?

3 Language, literature, education

We have included basic grammatical description in this book for two reasons. First, it enables more precise statements to be made in the close readings of texts; second, it will serve as useful knowledge for the understanding of linguistics-based critical theories explored in Chapter 3. The role of grammar in English teaching is a perennial problem. Some urge a return to the so-called 'traditional' teaching of grammar, which would include such activities as the parsing (formal description) of sentences. Others feel that no formal knowledge of one's own language is needed to communicate effectively (a distinction is again drawn between knowing your language and knowing *about* your language). It is nevertheless interesting to note that while linguistics has been a major influence on literary studies during the past thirty years, the teaching of English Language has radically altered. While exposing students to complex theories such as structuralism (a theory which used linguistics as a model for its enquiry), students at degree level (and beyond) are often unsure about the workings of their own language.

But how important is this 'knowledge about language' and how might it be used in literary studies? There are really two separate issues here. The first relates to the status of such knowledge in society. In Britain at least, if language is 'degenerating', the country's morals must be on the same path (although it is frequently not clear from the proponents of this argument whether the 'fall' of language is a cause or an effect of moral decline). If this sounds too fanciful, a sobering reminder is evident in the newspapers that daily have letters complaining about the general decline in standards of spoken and written English. Prescriptive linguistics remains the domain of the angry few (or many, depending on your point of view); and such people often accuse professional linguistics of hiding behind a mask of 'description' – that is, claiming that the linguist's task is not to *tell* people how to speak or write, but merely to *describe* how they do. The linguist is thus, for good or bad, cast as a 'neutral' observer. Some again would suggest that this is an abnegation of responsibility, and that the role of the linguist is partly to preserve standards.

But can linguists actually affect the way that language is used, either in its written or spoken form? If people start (or continue) to split infinitives ('to boldly go') or end sentences with prepositions ('something I will not put up *with*'); use 'different *than*' rather than 'different *from*' (or 'different *to*') or get 'imply' mixed up with 'infer' – all repeatedly cited as evidence of declining standards of English – would linguists, or anyone else for that matter, be able to do anything about it? Language has a momentum all of its own; even though it is something *used* by people, the individual, as Saussure noted, is in no position to effect change. No matter how much we bewail the loss of the subjunctive ('If I *were* you') and the subtle differences between 'will' and 'shall', or the appearance of the suffix '-ise' to form verbs ('prioritise'), the effect of our protests will be small.

i) Is it possible to be prescriptive about the language of literature in the same way that some wish to be prescriptive about everyday speech and writing?

ii) By analogy, are there 'standards' to preserve in literature?

4 What is stylistics?

So far we have not only been questioning the relationship between linguistics and literature, but also providing a formal linguistic framework, grammatical description, which was then applied to literary texts. This linking of the language of linguistics and the analysis of literary texts is essentially the domain of stylistics. This unfortunate term has connotations of a very genteel, rarefied discipline. However, we can immediately distinguish between two kinds of stylistics: *linguistic stylistics* and *literary stylistics*. Neither of these terms is wholly satisfactory, and we shall return to the problem of naming the discipline shortly. Presumably, both literary and linguistic stylistics have something to say about the relation of language to literature. Linguistic stylistics foregrounds the linguistic over the literary, and does not merely see the application of linguistic practices in terms of their function in an analytical 'tool kit'. Ronald Carter and Paul Simpson state:

> Linguistic stylisticians believe that in the analysis of language there are dangers in compromising the rigour and systematicity of analysis of stylistic effects and that practitioners in related disciplines are unwilling to accept the kind of standards of principled language description necessary to a genuinely mutual integration of interests.
>
> (Carter and Simpson 1989: 4)

Of literary stylistics, they say:

> Although the precision of analysis made available by stylistic methods offers a challenge to established methods of close reading or practical criticism of texts, the procedures of literary stylistics remain traditional in character in spite of developments in literary theory. . . which challenge assumptions about the role of language in depicting literary realities.
>
> (Carter and Simpson 1989: 7)

i) What do you feel constitutes the 'precision of analysis' to which Carter and Simpson refer?

ii) What do the terms 'linguistic stylistics' and 'literary stylistics' imply?

iii) Does the term 'literary' in 'literary stylistics' presuppose a specific kind of discourse?

iv) Is 'linguistic stylistics', therefore, 'non-literary stylistics'?

H.G. Widdowson suggests the following relation between linguistics and literature:

> By 'stylistics' I mean the study of literary discourse from a linguistics orientation and I shall take the view that what distinguishes stylistics from literary criticism on the one hand and linguistics on the other is that it is essentially a means of linking the two and has (as yet at least) no autonomous domain of its own. One can conduct enquiries of a linguistic kind without any references to literary criticism, and one can conduct enquiries in literary criticism without any reference to linguistics. Some linguists have said that the latter is impossible since the literary critic must be involved in a discussion about language. But there are all kinds of ways of talking about language and the linguist's way is only one. The linguist would be the first to complain if everyone who talked about language claimed to be talking linguistics. Stylistics, however, involves both literary criticism and linguistics, as its morphological make-up suggests: the 'style' component relating it to the former and the 'istics' component to the latter.
>
> (Widdowson 1975: 3)

We are moving here to a consideration of what might be meant by the term 'style'. First, however, consider the following quotation from Stanley Fish, a key figure in so-called reader-response criticism (see Chapter 5):

> Stylistics was born of a reaction to the subjectivity and impressionism of literary studies. For the appreciative raptures of the impressionistic critic, stylisticians purport to

substitute precise and rigorous linguistic descriptions and to proceed from these descriptions to interpretations for which they can claim a measure of objectivity. Stylistics, in short, is an attempt to put criticism on a scientific basis. . . . [In] their rush to establish an inventory of fixed significances, they [stylisticians] bypass the activity in the course of which significances are, if only momentarily, fixed . . . The shape of the reader's experience is the constraint they decline to acknowledge.

(Fish 1980: 72)

There are two points to be made here. The first is that stylistics has long realised that 'scientific criticism' is not a tenable concept. It would seem obvious to many people both inside and outside academic circles that any approach to literature is essentially *affective* (to do with our response). What would 'scientific criticism' look like? What function could it serve? However, it is not just in the realm of literature that problems about the scientific approach to language emerge. Linguistics itself has a fairly long history based on a tacit assumption of its 'scientific credentials'. Indeed, it has constantly attempted to prove itself as a science. But as Roy Harris (1980) has shown, only a discipline which is fundamentally unsure of its status would need to constantly find it necessary to broadcast that status. Neither physics nor chemistry, for example, need to reaffirm their positions as sciences.

The second point in relation to Fish's comments is that an emphasis on the reader's response to a text, rather than on what are construed as innate features, need not necessarily lead to subjectivism and impressionism. Rather, the emphasis would be on how readers, or interpreters, *make sense* of texts or utterances. Notice that now we have started to talk about 'utterances' and 'interpreters' as well as 'texts' and 'readers'. This is to show the possible relation between a stylistics which would take account of the reader's construction of meaning, and recent movements in mainstream linguistics. These recent movements can be grouped roughly under the heading of *pragmatics*. Before we look at the role of pragmatics we need to suggest some difficulties involved with stylistic analysis.

5 The trouble with stylistics

In a brief, polemical article, Jean-Jacques Lecercle states:

> The trouble with stylistics is that no-one has ever known exactly what the term meant, and that nowadays hardly anyone seems to care. And yet, paradoxically, the object, *style*, seems to be as fascinating as ever, and the subject, stylistics, like the phoenix, is forever reborn.
>
> The reason for the constitutive paradox of stylistics is not hard to find. As a field of research, stylistics has inherited all the problems caused by the polysemy of the word 'style'. Thus it has always hesitated between the generic (stylistics is the study of registers and styles of writing . . .) and the idiosyncratic (the style is the man, and stylistics is the science that accounts for man's inimitable style).
>
> (Lecercle 1993: 17)

It might seem curious to leave a study of the notion of 'style' in stylistics this late in our analysis and discussion, but the idea of 'style' is really only one aspect of stylistics (thus showing the inappropriateness of the term once more). In 1969 Crystal and Davy produced *Investigating English Style*. In this book they did not analyse any discourses which might be considered 'literary'. Crystal and Davy identify style with genre, and often with *topic*. They assume that legal documents, sermons and other discrete texts will have identifiable 'styles'. If we analyse the linguistic features of an example of the genre in question, then the combination of these features will give rise to the style of that discourse. Before we look at a text, consider the following questions:

i) Do either genre or topic define style?

ii) Will the grammatical constructions used in one genre differ from those used in another?

21

Some texts can be seen as 'topic-dominated' in that the subject or topic that the text is 'about' gives rise to certain definite and recognisable stylistic effects. For instance, a science textbook would be topic-dominated in its lexis, or vocabulary:

> The thermal decomposition of diacyl peroxides provides the most convenient source of aryl radicals for the arylation of aromatic substances.

Similarly, a short, lyric poem, such as a sonnet, would be constrained in terms of appropriate phrasing and lexis. Grammatical constructions may also vary. A legal document, such as an insurance policy, for instance, requires a precision of style (or long-windedness, depending on your point of view) that has come to be associated with certain kinds of phrasing:

> Such insurance as is provided by this policy applies to the use of a non-owned vehicle by the named insured and any person responsible for the use by the named insured provided such use is with the permission of the owner.

In this example the noun group 'the named insured' is repeated where a pronoun would normally be used. The result is a rather unnatural and stuffy style. Consider the following extract from *The English Bible in Five Volumes, vol. V* (1909), a lengthier part of which is analysed by Crystal and Davy:

> The same day went Iesus out of the house, and sate by the sea side.
> And great multitudes were gathered together unto him, so that he went into a ship, and sate, and the whole multitude stood on the shore.
> And he spake many things unto them in parables, saying, Behold, a sower went forth to sow.
> And when he sowed, some seeds fell by the wayes side, and the fouls came, and devoured them up.
> Some fell upon stony places, where they had not much earth: and forthwith they sprung up, because they had no deepenesse of earth.
>
> (Crystal and Davy 1969: 151)

iii) List the features of the above extract which you would consider to be characteristic of the text's language. You should consider grammatical, lexical and graphological elements.
iv) Does this list seem to make up an inventory of the stylistic features of religious discourse?
v) Is it possible to separate what you might have considered 'religious discourse' from merely 'early Modern English language'?
vi) Does the term 'the language of religion' have any meaning? If so, in what way?

Here are Crystal and Davy on the passage:

> First, the language of this text is distinguished at the phonological/graphological level through a number of features: one should note in particular the carefully controlled rhythmical framework of the whole, involving balanced structures . . . and a generally slow rate of progression (through the splitting up of the text into 'verses', and the frequent use of commas) . . .
>
> The main area of grammatical distinctiveness is the verbal group, where the use of the old third person singulars (*hath, saith*), old strong forms of verbs (*spake, sprung*), and the inflected second person singular (*speakest*) is common . . .
>
> The vocabulary provides the third area of distinctiveness. We note the wide range of archaisms, . . . Then there are the relatively technical religious terms, such as *parables, disciples, prophecy*; the formal locutions such as *gathered together, perceive, therefore* . ; and the words which have changed in meaning, such as *foules* . . .
>
> (1969: 152–3)

Crystal and Davy's points can be summarised as follows:
The text is distinguished phonologically (realised graphologically). Graphological aspects of the texts are features of the writing system, including typography.

23

There are balanced structures within the text.
The verbal group is distinctive.
The vocabulary is archaic.
There are formal locutions and technical words.

These elements (according to Crystal and Davy) contribute to the distinctive and recognisable 'language of religion'.

Consider the following discourses and state which of the above features are (or can be) present:

Advertising
Law
The novel
Lyric poetry
Essays

From this exercise it can be seen that it is difficult to pin down the language of a particular genre, topic or discourse through a recognition of distinctive 'formal' features alone. Although, for instance, many scholars in stylistics are interested in the way that literary language might differ from 'ordinary' language, the whole issue is riddled with difficulties. It is generally accepted that there are no features of literary language which do not exist, to a greater or lesser extent, in other kinds of discourse. The concept of 'ordinary' language is also problematic; it is difficult to conceive of some generalised norm by which other discourses can be measured. Features recur in varying degrees in varying discourses. How then are we to analyse them stylistically? What would a valid stylistic analysis do if it cannot rely on the presence of significant (and also 'deviant', from an agreed 'norm') features?

You might at this point feel that some kinds of discourse do have recognisable distinctive features. Lyric poetry would be a case often cited. If an individual is out walking one day and sees a kestrel (a bird of prey), he or she might say 'Look, a kestrel', or later on 'I saw a kestrel today'. Surely it is unlikely that the following sentence would be uttered:

> I caught this morning morning's minion, kingdom of daylight's dauphin, dapple-dawn-drawn Falcon.

This is the opening to Gerard Manley Hopkins' 'The Windhover'.

vii) Do you consider this a reasonable argument in support of the theory of the distinctiveness of literary (or poetic) discourse? List the elements you would cite in support of this theory.

Two elements you are likely to focus on are the alliteration and the phonological density. However, consider the following phrase:

> IT 'ASDA BE ASDA

Here, phonological 'density' makes the text cohesive, projecting this cohesion into grammatical and thematic unities. 'Has to' and 'ASDA' are phonologically equated, made graphologically almost identical (the apostrophe being the exception) and linked in the linear sequencing of the sentence to give the effect of 'ASDA' 'equalling' 'necessity'. Is this not the same as the Hopkins example? You might argue that both texts are in some way 'creative'. Are there other texts which one might not consider 'creative' which exhibit the same degree of phonological density?

6 Pragmatics

Much of the stylistic and linguistic analysis we have been concerned with has been formal, concentrating on observable features of language and effects realised in the text. A tradition of formalist linguistics exists whereby, despite internal arguments, language is treated as a system, and one whose deep structure is the object of linguistic enquiry. The characteristics of this kind of investigation are that it is formal and syntactic, rather than semantic and pragmatic (that is, it is concerned more with form than meaning and more with structure than use), and it tends to deal with

25

'artificial' sentences, rather than 'real' utterances. Language is thus not treated as discourse as Bakhtin insists (see page 8), but as abstract text. This conception of language is mapped on to literary studies with the same kind of formalism – and it is easy to view literary texts as containing these artificial sentences, divorced from any context of use.

Charles Morris (1946) grouped certain aspects of language under three headings which he called 'semiotic categories': *syntax, semantics* and *pragmatics*, and his distinctions are useful for us here. He described *syntax* as the formal relation between signs and other signs ('signs' here can mean 'words', for simplicity). Essentially, then, syntax is the ordering of elements in a text, and the relations which exist between those elements. Syntax is not overtly concerned with meaning, but with relations between meaningful elements. *Semantics*, on the other hand, is concerned with what Morris called the relation between signs and the world. Semantics is concerned with sense and meaning. *Pragmatics*, however, is that branch of linguistics which Morris characterised as the relation between signs and interpreters and users. It is all very well discussing the formal relations within language, and gaining a formal knowledge of how elements combine meaningfully (and non-meaningfully) in texts, but we communicate by implication rather than by a language which has a one-to-one correlation between elements and intentions. Linguistics has come to take the 'non-realised' element of communication into account, and has focused on such phenomena as presupposition, speech acts and implicature: what is presupposed in any utterance; what people do when they utter certain language fragments and what is *implied* by an utterance (and, conversely, what can be *inferred*).

The pragmatic element of an utterance can be fairly easily shown. If, after somebody has entered the room, Jill says:

Were you born in a barn?

she would be performing a linguistic act which is completely at odds with the utterance's 'actual' form and meaning. Thus neither syntax nor semantics will help us understand the utterance. Syntax will not help us because, although the utterance has an interrogative form (or sentence mood), no question is being asked (you would not expect the reply 'No, I was born in a hospital' unless the addressee was being deliberately awkward and misreading the intentions of the first speaker). Rather an imperative is being issued ('Shut the door') – or, at least, this is one possible interpretation and use of the utterance. Semantics will not help us because no analysis of the meanings of 'born' or 'barn', for instance, will tell us what the utterance actually means (or, rather, *might* mean).

Although the above example is an idiomatic expression in English, and therefore 'ready-made' for this kind of analysis, it is clear that we use language for all kinds of purposes on all kinds of different occasions to many different people and groups of people. The form of any utterance simply does not match in any 'natural' way with its *function*.

This can be seen clearly in a brief example from a literary text. The following extract is from Ken Kesey's *One Flew over the Cuckoo's Nest* (1973), and is discussed at length in Leech and Short's *Style in Fiction: A Linguistic Introduction to English Fictional Prose*. Here is an exchange between a patient and nurse in a mental hospital:

> 'Wait just a shake, honey: what are these two little red capsules in here with my vitamin?'
> I know him. He's a big, griping Acute, already getting the reputation of a troublemaker.
> 'It's just medication, Mr Taber, good for you. Down it goes now.'
> 'But what *kind* of medication. Christ, I can see that they're pills—'
> 'Just swallow it all, shall we, Mr Taber – just for me?'
> (Kesey, quoted in Leech and Short 1981: 306)

The patient asks about his 'little red capsules', but what is he really doing? What kind of response from the nurse would be adequate? If he has a reputation for being a troublemaker, he could be asking for information that he knows cannot be supplied, just to be antagonistic. The nurse's reply equally has concealed motives. The information she gives does not really answer the question, if we were to take the question on its surface form alone. The form of the sentence 'Down it goes now' is declarative, yet it has the force of an imperative, a command. Taber repeats his question, but this time it seems more of a genuine enquiry rather than provocation. The nurse responds with a sentence of mixed syntactic form and ambiguous pragmatic function. 'Just swallow it all' is an imperative, but this is swiftly followed by the interrogative 'shall we?', which does not seem to warrant an answer. The use of 'we', to imply empathy with the patient, is coupled with the romantic/motherly discourse of the moodless clause with interrogative intonation 'just for me?' The nurse uses a variety of syntactic forms which conflict with their pragmatic function, and Taber is left without a firm footing in the discourse. He eventually loses control and is dismissed.

We have been moving to a view of language which takes into account not only the formal elements of any text of utterance, but its *implicatures*, function and role. This is essentially to see text as *discourse* – that is, a text with social, interpersonal and communicative functions, not merely a site where language is organised. The linguist who analyses discourse analyses language as a 'living' thing. It does not mean that a written, historical text cannot be subject to discourse analysis – all texts form part of a social matrix and are read in particular ways and have implicatures, features of context, etc., and are therefore amenable to such analysis. Discourse analysis has influenced literary criticism to an extent (for example, Anthony Easthope's book *Poetry as Discourse* [1984] and R.A. York's *The Poem as Utterance* [1987]), but has certainly revitalised stylistics (see Carter and Simpson 1989).

With the discourse analyst's approach, there need not be a great divide conceptualised between literary and non-literary discourse. 'Literature' becomes just another contextual and pragmatic frame which generates texts, in the same way that a courtroom, for instance, will generate certain texts that can be analysed as discourse. Another way of using pragmatics in the analysis of literary texts is to focus on the text as 'quasi-utterance', something that exhibits all the features of language as social phenomenon, but presented in a certain, often denser, form. One can analyse conversation in a novel or in a dramatic text in the same way, then, that one would analyse 'real' conversation. One might also focus on the communicative function of literary texts, and it is this aspect that we will deal with in the following section.

7 Speech acts

One aspect of pragmatics is the phenomenon of speech act theory. Particularly associated with the work of Austin (1962) and Searle (1969), it is a theory which focuses on what speakers do when they use language. Apart from this general focus on the 'action' of language, speech act theorists state that certain verbs actually 'perform' an act when they are uttered. Verbs such as those to do with warning, prohibiting or promising and so on perform the very function encoded in the word. These are the so-called *performative* verbs. For example, when one says 'I promise not to tell anyone', the act of promising is performed. One important point to add here is that such performance is not guaranteed. The verb must be accompanied by the relevant conditions which make such a performance possible. The speaker cannot, therefore, pronounce a couple husband and wife if he or she not empowered to do so. Similarly, if a speaker 'promises' to pay another ten million pounds tomorrow, the act cannot be performed truthfully if there is no possibility of him or her paying such a sum. Notice that the performative verb is invariably accompanied by the first person 'I' and the present tense form of that verb ('I promise' – if It were 'I promised' there would no be performance).

Austin and Searle both proposed that speech act verbs form a limited sub-class of verbs. The 'normal' function of a sentence, that is, one that does not contain a speech act verb, was said to be *constative*. A constative utterance describes a state of affairs, whereas a *performative* utterance enacts a function. However, it became apparent that all utterances mask an implicit performative – even basic statements. Thus if we say 'This table is brown' we are *asserting* that it is so. A performative 'realisation' of this utterance might be 'I assert to you that this table is brown'. The original sentence is embedded in a performative utterance which typically has a present tense verb and first person subject. The implications for language study are profound, for language does not simply happen, nor are sentences uttered without purpose. Language becomes a dynamic activity, as each utterance is associated with an *illocutionary force*. This is essentially its *pragmatic function*.

A basic aspect of speech act theory is the distinction between *locution* and *illocution*. The locution of an utterance is simply the syntactic form with its 'base' meaning. Thus in our earlier example, 'Were you born in a barn?', the *locution* seems to be a question about the addressee's origins. However, the illocution, or pragmatic meaning, is actually a request or command to shut the door. The distinction between locution and illocution is therefore one between form and function.

Let us now have a look at aspects of speech act theory in relation to a short extract of dramatic dialogue. The extract is from Edward Bond's *Saved* (1965):

> The scene is a living room. '*The door opens.* LEN *comes in.*
> He goes straight out again':
> PAM: (off): In there.
> LEN *comes in. He goes down to the sofa. He stares at it.*
>   All right?
> *Pause.* PAM *comes in.*
> LEN: This ain' the bedroom.
> PAM: Bed ain' made.
> LEN: Oo's bothered?
> PAM: It's awful. 'Ere's nice.
> LEN: Suit yourself. Yer don't mind if I take me shoes
>   off?
> (He takes them off) No one 'ome?
> PAM: No.
> LEN: O.
> *Pause. He sits back on the couch.*

Yer all right? Come over 'ere.

PAM: In a minit.

LEN: Wass yer name?

PAM: Yer ain' arf nosey.

LEN: Somethin' up?

PAM: Can't I blow me nose?

She puts her hanky back in her bag and puts it in the table.
Better.

She sits on the couch.

LEN: Wass yer name?

PAM: Wass yourn?

LEN: Len.

PAM: Pam.

(Bond 1965: 14)

This piece of domestic, realistic drama exhibits a number of features relating to speech act theory and pragmatics. First, a relationship is being established, so the characters (particularly Len) are involved in a linguistic negotiation as a prelude to a physical act. Second, the relationship is somewhat conventional in that the 'object' is implicit from the beginning. The discourse thus has two functions working with, and sometimes against, each other. The characters are engaged in a conventional arrangement, which will dictate their actions and to a certain extent their speech acts; and they are attempting interpersonal dialogue in order to keep communication channels between them open.

i) Go through the exchange line by line and pick out utterances which seem to have a dual function: to initiate the physical activity and to maintain a social relationship.

ii) Who is in the position of power here?

iii) What effect does the power balance/imbalance have on the speech acts of the speakers?

iv) Pick two lines where the locution seems distinct from the illocution.

31

8 Gender

Our discussion so far has been concerned with 'language', 'linguistics' and 'stylistics' in such a way as to imply that these categories transcend the particularities of socialisation – that is, gender, class and 'race'. To be sure, linguistics, because it is a metalanguage, is often seen to be unconcerned with those particularities, most significantly under the hegemony of Chomskyan 'idealised' competence. Chomsky, arguably the most influential linguist of the mid and late twentieth century, concentrated his theory and practice on the notion of 'linguistic competence'. This competence was, once more, idealised in that it was not concerned with individuals' use of language (or 'performance') but with the 'universal grammar' which underlies language. This universal grammar is said to transcend boundaries of nation, gender, class and personality; our ability to acquire and then manipulate language is, to a great extent, genetically determined. This universalist, deterministic approach to language seems completely at odds with both a feminist and Marxist linguistics, which would put the *social* nature of language at the core of any theory. Formal linguistics, which has dominated during the century, is seen as essentially masculine, with its scientific pretensions and lack of concern for language as social practice.

'Language', once again, is seen as something that 'people' have and learn: the underlying system, or *la langue* as Saussure termed it, is certainly neutral with respect to gender. But this in itself masks an underlying androcentrism: a belief that *man* is at the centre of things. Both sociolinguistics and pragmatics are fairly recent phenomena in the history of linguistics.

It is beyond the scope of this chapter to look at the relationship between gender and language in any detail. Our point is rather to see what implications there may be for linguistic stylistics and literary stylistics given a focus on gender issues. The term 'gender issues' is itself rather worn and inadequate. Recent studies such as Jennifer Coates' (1986) and Deborah Cameron's (1992) have focused on the differences between men's and women's speech. These hark back to earlier studies by Lakoff (1975), and

Otto Jespersen in 1922 (Jespersen was extremely disparaging about women's language). Although feminist criticism has been enormously influential in literary studies, there are areas of linguistics which remain untouched by the feminist challenge, as Deborah Cameron (1992) comments:

> If we confine ourselves to examining the impact of feminism on the institutionalised discipline of linguistics, we will find relatively little to report: the mainstream, what people refer to as 'core' linguistics, that is, phonology and syntax, has changed very little . . . and while in the sub-disciplines of sociolinguistics, psycholinguistics, discourse analysis, etc. there has been a certain amount of change, with questions of gender being investigated more frequently and more seriously, this is more a matter of extending and modifying existing research methods than it is of thinking of linguistic knowledge generally.
>
> (Cameron 1992: 213)

Note that Cameron cites syntax and phonology as areas which have not been influenced or affected by feminism and gender issues.

i) Why should this be? Is it possible for feminism to contribute to syntactic knowledge in some way? What form would this knowledge take?

A number of problematic and sometimes plainly contradictory views on the language of women (seen as a homogeneous group) have been held since Jespersen's pronouncements in the 1920s. The first common notion of women's speech is that it is essentially 'gossip' or 'prattle'. Jespersen himself considered that women did not think before they spoke and were therefore less competent at complex syntactic structures such as elaborate subordination. Women were thought to speak with a greater degree of *parataxis*; that is, where syntactic elements are juxtaposed and co-ordinated rather than bonded and subordinated (bonding and subordination are known jointly as *hypotaxis*). Subordination is seen as an advanced grammatical structure which requires complex brain functions (which women, for Jespersen, cannot perform). Crudely, the distinction is realised in the following examples:

> a) *parataxis* 'I went down the road and went to the shops. I bought some fruit'
>
> b) *hypotaxis* 'While I was out down the road I went to the shops and bought some fruit'

This notion of the 'paratactic woman' does not fit very easily with that other dominant folk-linguistic idea of women's language; namely that women have a preference for elaborate constructions and a predilection for 'specialised lexis'. On the one hand, women are supposed to only be able to master (*sic*) simple sentence structure, while on the other they lean towards the elaborate in expression. Similarly, men are supposed to speak 'low and infrequently' to prove their manliness, as any elaboration (or, by implication, subordination) is seen as 'flowery' and 'womanly'.

To explore these arguments in relation to literary texts, consider the following extracts from Virginia Woolf's *To the Lighthouse* (1927) and Ernest Hemingway's 'In our time' (1926). One cannot consider these or any other pair of writers to be representatives of their gender. Yet Woolf and Hemingway are frequently cited as exhibiting masculine and feminine characteristics:

> 'Yes, of course, if it's fine tomorrow,' said Mrs Ramsay. 'But you'll have to be up with the lark,' she added. To her son these words conveyed an extraordinary joy, as if it were settled the expedition were bound to take place, and the wonder to which he had looked forward for years and years it seemed, was, after a night's darkness and a day's sail, within touch. Since he belonged, even at the age of six, to that great clan which cannot keep this feeling separate from that, but must let future prospects, with their joys and sorrows, cloud what is actually at hand, since to such people

even in earliest childhood any turn in the wheel of sensation
has the power to crystallise and transfix the moment upon
which its gloom and radiance rest, James Ramsay, sitting on
the floor cutting out pictures from the illustrated catalogues
of the Army and Navy Stores, endowed the picture of a
refrigerator as his mother spoke with heavenly bliss.

(Virginia Woolf [1927] 1980)

At the lake shore there was another rowboat drawn up. The
two Indians stood waiting. Nick and his father got in the
stream of the boat and the Indians shoved it off and one of
them got in to row. Uncle George sat in the stream of the
camp rowboat. The young Indian shoved the camp boat off
and got in to row Uncle George. The two boats started off in
the dark. Nick heard the oar-locks of the other boat quite a
way ahead of them in the mist. The Indians rowed with quick
choppy strokes. Nick lay back with his father's arm around
him. It was cold on the water. The Indian who was rowing
them was working very hard, but the other boat moved
further ahead in the mist all the time.

'Where are we going, Dad?' Nick asked.

'Over to the Indian camp. There is an Indian lady very
sick'.

'Oh,' said Nick.

(Hemingway [1926] 1981)

ii) Comment on the use of hypotaxis and parataxis in each of
the extracts.

iii) What differences do you note in the range of the lexical
items used? Are they purely related to the 'subject' of the
extracts?

iv) What differences do you perceive in the portrayal of male
characters in the extracts?

v) Are the styles of these pieces gendered? Or is gender
incidental to the styles?

vi) Do the pieces conform to or reject the folk-linguistic assumptions discussed above?

Attempts to theorise or describe a 'woman's language' are fraught with difficulties, as the above exercise alone should demonstrate. Katie Wales states:

> Granted that it might be difficult for women to find a stylistic 'space' that is not occupied by men, what emerges is a kind of definition that is still marked by the presence of men, in that they provide the 'norm' for the resulting anti-norm. If men's style is 'rational', women's must therefore be 'emotional', even 'irrational'; if 'logical' then women's must be 'illogical', and so on. And while it may be praiseworthy to turn negative attributions into positive . . . the resulting discourse can still give the impression of reinforcing all the stereotypical images of women's discourse and style . . .
>
> (Wales 1994: xiv)

Although feminist linguists such as Lesley Jeffries have attempted to locate the specific stylistic attributes of women in particular genres, much of the discussion about women's discourse has come from feminist theorists such as Irigaray, Cixous and Kristeva. These figures are discussed in Chapter 6, on feminisms.

9 Cognition, linguistic relativity, literature

One of the ways in which stylistics has dealt with the interface between language and literature is by adopting a perspective based on the Sapir–Whorf hypothesis. This hypothesis, otherwise known as *linguistic relativity* or *linguistic determinism*, is based on the work of the early twentieth century anthropologists Edward Sapir and Benjamin Lee Whorf. The theory is essentially simple, but its proof (or disproof) notoriously difficult: differences in world view are to be accounted for by differences in linguistic structure, or as David Lee (1992) states: 'Coding creates reality'. The idea that language is not merely reflective of our world, but an active creator of it, is extremely useful and attractive: language becomes central to human activity, and the analysis of that language of prime importance and significance. Our world, to a greater or lesser degree (and the degree is rather problematic), is linguistic. An analysis of a stretch of language will tell us something about 'world view', and the literary text, therefore, is no exception. By analogy, the literary text is its own 'text world' which evinces micro-conceptual patterns. Whorf and Sapir suggest that because the Inuit peoples have so many different words for snow it in some way reflects their conceptual system. But as George Lakoff (1987) has said, it is no more surprising that Inuits have many words for snow than it is that Americans have many words for cars. It merely reflects the growth of a specialised lexis; one cannot say that it is reflective of a profoundly different conceptual system.

It would be tempting to think that language in some way imposes a particular world view on its users, and then suggest that each literary text is a 'world' in itself, as we have outlined above. But to what extent can we infer conceptual distinctions from linguistic activity alone? And how might this relate to literary texts? In order to investigate these issues we must first look at the work of George Lakoff. Rather than return to Sapir and Whorf we will look at Lakoff, because he develops the work of the anthropologists as well as that of cognitive linguists. We begin by considering the linguistic 'activity' of a single word.

i) Write down a definition of the word 'bachelor'.

Most of you will have written down something like 'unmarried man', and you might consider this to be evidence that such a word has a reasonably stable meaning — one that we can agree on: providing we know what the word 'means' we know to what elements the term *'bachelor'* refers. A traditional semantic description of this word would be slightly more complex. One might say that the *denotative* meaning of the word 'bachelor' is 'unmarried man', but its *connotative* meaning (that is, what the word seems to suggest) is more slippery. With *'bachelor'* we get connotations of independence, youth and the transition from one life-state (unmarried) to another (married – one state implies the existence of the other). None of these 'meanings' is present in the formal semantic description of the word's denotative meaning. When I utter the word 'bachelor', the denotative, plus the range of connotative meanings, all come into play. Does this seem a sensible semantics? Can we agree, then, on the 'meaning' of the word 'bachelor'? And can we agree on its possible extensions – that is, those elements in the world which fits the category 'bachelor' in accordance with the 'meaning' thus prescribed?

Consider the following discussion of the word 'bachelor' by Lakoff (1987). He first quotes the linguist Charles Fillmore (1982):

> The noun *bachelor* can be defined as an unmarried adult man, but the noun clearly exists as a motivated device for categorizing people only in the context of a human society in which certain expectations about marriage and marriageable age obtain. Male participants in long-term unmarried couplings would not normally be described as bachelors; a boy abandoned in the jungle and grown to maturity away from contact with human society would not be called a bachelor; John Paul II is not properly thought of as a bachelor.

In other words, *bachelor* is defined with respect to an ICM [Idealized Cognitive Model] in which there is a human society with (typically monogamous) marriage, and a typical marriageable age. The idealized model says nothing about the existence of priests, 'long-term unmarried couplings', homosexuality, Moslems who are permitted four wives and only have three, etc. With respect to this idealized cognitive model, a *bachelor* is simply an unmarried adult man.

This idealized model, however, does not fit the world very precisely. It is oversimplified in its background assumptions. There are some segments of society where the idealized model fits reasonably well, and when an unmarried man might well be called a bachelor. But the ICM does not fit the case of the pope (*sic*) or people abandoned in the jungle, like Tarzan. In such cases, unmarried adult males are certainly not representative members of the category of bachelors.

(Lakoff 1987: 70)

Lakoff's suggestion is, then, that meaning is idealised, and some examples fit this idealised meaning more than others. A robin is more representative of the word 'bird' than is a chicken or an ostrich; 'table' is more representative of a noun than is 'democratisation'. The theory, then, even has a metalinguistic aspect: it can be related to the way we think about the structure of language itself (as in the example of the 'representative' noun).

How might this theory of meaning be related to a literary text? To conclude this chapter on language, linguistics and literature we shall look at a text and try to bring a number of issues discussed so far together, particularly pragmatics, gender and cognition. The following extract is from Daphne Marlatt's collection of prose and poetry, *Salvage* (1991):

Territory & co.
It was the way they kept taking his joke and playing with it, making it a familiar part of their exchange, knock, knock. Who's there? and then a word, some ordinary obvious word like banana or tank capitalized, her son would capitalize on the exchange and back again, T'ank you. It was the unacknowledged door all of it got said through that intrigued her. Why can't he or she just open it? for the joke, he said, and mummy rhymed with dummy – you have to talk to each other, right? I mean you can't just see it's not, it's not who? Van. Van? couver the eggs will you. That's not one. Why not? You made it up, he chimed in on her son's behalf.

No I didn't, it's what he does when she's giving birth you know, couvade, they do that in some societies. And they were off on their own, their grown up game now. Well you can't blame him for wanting to keep all his eggs covered. His eggs? Oh you mean he has to know they're his? Of course.

What if there's some stranger knocking? Isn't that the point? There's always some stranger knocking at the family door.

And anyway, she thought, it always feels stranger when it comes to claiming territory. After all they were only playing . . . clearly it's all about naming, he said.

(Marlatt 1991: 71)

This text can be read as a 'metatext', one that reflects upon, either overtly or implicitly, its own textuality. Much of the meta-textuality of the extract is overt, and this throws into relief all sorts of issues relating to cognition and subjectivity. How we understand utterances; how thoughts are 'realised' in texts (and how they are not); how language engages with itself and how perception is gendered – these are all *metatextual* issues.

The first thing we might consider is the graphology of the text. Graphological elements are those elements which are to do with the graphic (written, as opposed to phonic or spoken) form of the text. Punctuation, capitalisation, paragraphing, apostrophes, typefaces and type weights are all graphological features.

ii) How does the graphology of the text contribute to its metatextuality?

In your response to this question you should consider the ways in which the content of the text is 'realised' graphologically. The early part, for instance, discusses the 'exchange of words' in a game. But this exchange is part talked about (is part of the content of the text) and part realised in the text's graphological features.

The function of lexical items is perhaps the most central metatextual issue here. Very often the forms of words are toyed with. This is done in various ways:

Through explicit phonological parallels ('mummy rhymed with dummy')
Through syllabic or morphemic breaks ('Van. couver the eggs will you'.)

Through explicit reference to a lexical item ('like banana or tank capitalized')

Through ellipsis or elision (some element missed out or some sound suppressed: 'T'bank')

iii) Are there any other ways in which word functions are exploited?

The text further exploits language's *syntagmatic* relations, the relations which exist between one unit of meaning and another in sequence. The pragmatic aspect of language is also foregrounded because language items are obviously being 'used' in a deliberate way. But the meaning of a particular item is not stable, as an element may be picked up in a slightly modified form further along the 'chain' of meaning. The following lines demonstrate this:

> . . . and then a word, some ordinary obvious word like banana or tank capitalized, her son would capitalize on the exchange and back again.

Here, one meaning of the lexical item 'capitalize' is first foregounded and then thrown off by addition of the bound morpheme *ed*, introducing another meaning.

iv) Are there further examples of this kind of 'exchange'?

One thematic concern in the text is family relationships. Gendered roles are part of the 'exchange' and this exchange is made largely through language, and particularly through speech:

> . . . you have to talk to each other, right? I mean you can't just see it's not, it's not who?

v) Consider the ways in which gender roles are made part of the issues of the text. Are these part of the metatext?

Finally, consider the sentence:

there's always some stranger knocking at the family door.

vi) Describe possible ICMs for the items 'stranger' and 'family'. Look up the dictionary definitions. How might a knowledge of the ICM elucidate the problems of the text?

Clearly, it's all about naming . . . .

Glossary

anaphora: From the Greek 'to refer' anaphora is the phenomenon where an item is referred to, usually by a pronoun, through a backward relation. The anaphor refers back to an antecedent which usually has a full form: '*Fred* came into the room. *He* sat down.') In rhetoric it refers to the simple repetition of words at the beginning of clauses.

cataphora: 'Forward-looking' anaphora. Pro-forms are given full forms in subsequent reference.

constative: From speech act theory. A constative utterance is one which describes a state of affairs.

declarative: One of the sentence moods. Declaratives form statements (rather than questions or commands).

discourse: Language in use. A text transformed by context or interpretation. Discourse is language in its 'concrete living totality' .

discourse stylistics: Stylistics which incorporates and uses developments in pragmatics, such as implicatures, speech act theory and conversational analysis.

grammar: The formal arrangement of a language. A grammar is a system for accounting for possible meaningful sentences in English.

graphology: The writing and typographic system of a language such as punctuation, line endings, etc.

hypotaxis: The linking of a dependent element in a sentence through subordination.

Idealised Cognitive Model: From Lakoff (1987). In the processing of lexical items, addressees construct ICMs: idealised pictures of the lexicalised element.

illocution: An act performed in the process of uttering e.g. offering, promising. The function of an utterance.

imperative: Another sentence mood. The imperative forms commands, and is typically subjectless ('Get down!').

implicature: Generally, those elements which are *implied* in any utterance. Although this term has a more specialised use, it can refer to all those theories which see human communication as largely an implied act. Much of what we say is not stated directly, but implied.

interrogative: The sentence mood of questions ('What are you doing?') rather than statements or commands.

lexical semantics: A branch of linguistics which studies the meaning of lexical items.

lexis: A technical term for vocabulary.

linguistic stylistics: Stylistics which sees the linguistic description of elements as coming prior to any interpretative function. Linguistic stylistics is more rigorous in its application of linguistic methodologies than is *literary stylistics*.

locution: The form of an utterance. The physical act of uttering.

literary pragmatics: The application of pragmatic theory to literary texts.

metalanguage: Language that is used to talk about language. Linguistics is a metalanguage.

modality: *Epistemic modality* is language's provision for the expression of beliefs, attitudes and capability. *Deontic modality* expresses, among other things, permission and obligation.

parataxis: The linking of clauses through juxtapositon rather than subordination.

pragmatics: Essentially the investigation into language *use* and language as it relates to interpreters and users.

semantics: The study of meaning in language. Areas of semantics include *logical semantics* and *text semantics*, which is the investigation into the semantic relations of whole texts.

speech act theory: Following Austin (1962) and Searle (1969), this branch of linguistics looks at the role of language in the behaviour of the utterer. Speakers are said to perform certain functions through language.

syntax: The formal arrangement of signs; the relation of signs to other signs. 'Syntax' and 'grammar' are sometimes used synonymously.

text: A stretch of language.

Select bibliography

1 Basic relations

The literature on the subject of this chapter is diverse and widespread,. but the Routledge Interface series is designed to bridge the gap between linguistics and literature. For accessible introductions Roger Fowler's *Linguistic Criticism* (1986) and Traugott and Pratt's *Linguistics for Students of Literature* (1980) are worthy, although the latter uses a Chomskyan transformational model of grammar, rather than the systemic model we use in this volume. Norman Blake's *An Introduction to the Language of Literature* (1991) is lucid and traditional. The series 'The Language of . . .' contains accessible literary stylistic readings of authors. A good example is Katie Wales' *The Language of James Joyce* (1992). Katie Wales' *A Dictionary of Stylistics* (1989) is an extremely useful reference work, covering linguistics and literature – and all the bits in between. Geoffrey Leech's *A Linguistic Guide to English Poetry* (1969) is a good starting point, although some may find the inclusion of traditional rhetorical terms (mostly Greek) rather off-putting. Leech and Short's *Style in Fiction* (1981) has good material on style and 'mind'.

There are many collections of essays, not all forming coherent works. Ronald Carter's (ed.) *Language and Literature: An Introduction to Stylistics* (1983) has some 'classic' papers ('The Conditional Presence of Mr Bleaney'). Michael Toolan's (ed.) collection *Language, Text and Context* (1992) takes on race, gender and class issues and reflects the growing interest in context. Other works refered to in this part include Chomsky's *Syntactic Structures* (1957), David Lodge's *The Language of Fiction* (1966) and Sebeok's (ed.) *Style in Language* (1964). Lodge's book is a language-focused book from a non-linguist, and Sebeok's book contains a famous 'closing statement' on linguistics and poetics. The Fowler/Bateson debate can be followed in Fowler's *The Languages of Literature: Some Linguistic Contributions to Criticism* (1971). Bateson has two essays in this volume.

2 Texts, grammars, discourses

M.A.K. Halliday's work on systemic linguistics is fairly abundant, but for a clear introduction see Margaret Berry's *Introduction to Systemic Linguistics* (1977). Halliday's own *Explorations in the Functions of Language* (1973) has a discussion of William Golding's *The Inheritors* from a systemic grammar perspective. Halliday and Hasan's *Cohesion in English* (1976) was among the first systematic discussions of text-level cohesion. Brown and Yule's *Discourse Analysis* (1983) develops some elements of Halliday and Hasan's and is an excellent introduction to the topic, relating usefully to literary texts (although they do not explicitly discuss 'literature'). Malcolm Coulthard's (ed.) *Advances in Written Text Analysis* (1994) has some more advanced papers on clause relations and text features in general.

3 Language, literature, education

Walter Nash's *An Uncommon Tongue: The Uses and Resources of English* (1992) has readable and lively discussions of 'standards' in English, punctuation and dictionary meaning. H.G. Widdowson's *Explorations in Applied Linguistics* (1979) ranges over discourse issues, scientific English and the teaching of English as a foreign language. A useful pamphlet issued by the British Association of Applied Linguistics is 'University Students' Knowledge about Language' by Thomas Bloor (1986). Philip Howard's *The State of the Language* (1984) has material on the perennial issues of grammar and use. Roy Harris' *The Language Myth* (1980) has persuasive material on the pretensions of linguistics. Steven Pinker's *The Language Instinct: The New Science of Language and Mind* (1994) is a 'popular' and very readable account of how language works, from a Chomskyan viewpoint.

4 What is stylistics?

Carter and Simpson's (eds) *Language, Discourse and Literature: An Introductory Reader in Discourse Stylistics* (1989) is usefully read in conjunction with Carter's (ed.) (1983) earlier volume. Crystal and Davy's *Investigating English Style* (1969) has sections on the language of advertising and law. A number of early stylistics volumes include Howard Babb's (ed.) *Essays in Stylistic Analysis* (1972) and Roger Fowler's (ed.) *Essays in the Language of Literature* (1968) reflect the American and British strains of stylistics respectively. H.G. Widdowson's *Stylistics and the Teaching of Literature* (1975) defines the roles of linguistics and literary criticism in stylistics and presents some very clear applications. Leech and Short's *Style in Fiction* (1981) is a good, clear analysis of basic stylistic issues as they relate to fiction.

5 The trouble with stylistics

David Birch's *Language, Literature and Critical Practice* (1989) attempts to set stylistics in a radical strain. Jean-Jacques Lecercle's views on stylistics and his methodologies for analyses of texts can be found in his *The Violence of Language* (1990). For a more theoretical approach to the relation between language and literature see Fabb *et al.* (eds) *The Linguistics of Writing: Arguments between Language and Literature* (1987). Willie Van Peer's (ed.) *The Taming of the Text* (1986) is another good example of what stylistics can and cannot do.

6 Pragmatics

Stephen Levinson's *Pragmatics* (1983) is still the best introduction to the topic and suits the needs of the more advanced student, too. Jacob Mey's *Pragmatics: An Introduction* (1994) is clear and has exercises and questions. For those with a developing interest Steven Davis's (ed.) volume, *Pragmatics: A Reader* (1991), has some of the most important papers on pragmatics, but literature students may find some of it hard-going. Try papers by Donnellan and Sperber and Wilson. Stylistic work with a pragmatic bias can be found in Carter and Simpson's (eds) (1989) volume cited above. Diane Blakemore's *Understanding Utterances* (1992) sets pragmatic analysis in a relevance-theoretical framework, and has good chapters on 'poetic effects' and metaphor. Roger Sell's (ed.) *Literary Pragmatics* (1991) shows the diversity or unfocused nature of the phenomenon, depending on your point of view. Charles Morris's *Signs, Language, Behavior* (1946) has his essential definitions of semantics, syntax and pragmatics.

7 Speech acts

The only full-length treatment of speech act theory in literature is Mary Louise Pratt's excellent *Towards a Speech Act Theory of Literary Discourse* (1977). The classic linguistic discussions of speech acts and speech act theory are J.L. Austin's *How to do Things with Words* (1962) and J.R. Searle's *Speech Acts* (1969). Both Austin and Searle dismiss 'literary' language, but their arguments are relevant and applicable, and feature in much critical theory. The relation of speech act theory to literary critical theory is perceptively analysed in Sandy Petry's *Speech Acts and Literary Theory* (1990).

8 Gender

There is a mass of literature on gender issues generally, and a fair amount on gender and linguistics. Deborah Cameron's *Feminism and Linguistic Theory* (1985) is very accessible and scholarly. Cameron has also edited *The Feminist Critique of Language: A Reader* (1990). Some unusual essays are collected here, and it includes Jespersen on 'The Woman'. Jennifer Coates makes sense of conflicting views in *Women, Men and Language* (1986). Katie Wales' (ed.) *Feminist Linguistics in Literary Criticism* (1994) contains student-friendly essays on such topics as the stylistics of gender, lexical choices in fairy-tales and verb relations in pop lyrics. This volume includes an essay by Lesley Jeffries on apposition in women's poetry.

9 Cognition, linguistic relativity, literature

David Lee's *Competing Discourses* (1992) discusses cognitive theories against a background of the Sapir–Whorf hypothesis. Eve Sweetser's *From Etymology to Pragmatics* (1990) has extremely good and interesting material on the history of semantic change. George Lakoff's enormous *Women, Fire and Dangerous Things* (1987) has a detailed discussion of the issues of this section. It could have been considerably shorter, but you can dip into the book. The Sapir–Whorf hypothesis is articulated in Edward Sapir's *Language* (1963).

Structures of literature

1 Of signification

T HE MAIN BODY of this chapter is concerned with the phenomenon of structuralism, although we shall talk about the 'structures' of texts in more general ways. In the previous chapter we began by drawing a distinction between linguistics used somewhat eclectically and 'practically' for the explication of literary texts, and linguistics used as a metaphor or model, for literary studies. It is this second aspect of linguistics which concerns us here, for structuralist methodologies draw on linguistic theory, and in particular the theories of C.S. Peirce and Ferdinand de Saussure. The first part of this chapter will be a discussion of the methodology of structuralism, as it relates to the linguistic base. To begin with, we need to consider relevant passages from Saussure's *Course in General Linguistics* (*Cours de Linguistique Générale*, 1916), which has been so influential on structuralist thought. In these extracts, Saussure is talking about the fundamental concepts *signifier*, *signified* and *sign*. The terms *word* and *sign* are often used synonymously in structuralist discussions of language, although the sign as such can be larger or smaller than a word (a compound such as 'pickpocket', for example, or a semi-bound morpheme such as 'anti').

> The linguistic sign unites, not a thing and a name, but a concept and a sound-image . . . The two elements are intimately united, and each recalls the other. Whether we try to find the meaning of the Latin word *arbor* or the word that Latin uses to designate the concept 'tree', it is clear that only the associations sanctioned by the language appear to us to conform to reality, and we disregard whatever others might be imagined.
>
> (Saussure 1974: 66–7)
>
> I call the combination of a concept and a sound-image a *sign* . . . I propose to retain the word *sign* [*signe*] and designate

the whole and to replace *concept* and *sound-image* respectively by *signified* [*signifié*] and *signifier* [*signifiant*].

(67)

The bond between the signifier and the signified is arbitrary.
Since I mean by sign the whole that results from the associat-
ing of the signifier with the signified, I can simply say: *the
linguistic sign is arbitrary.*

The idea of 'sister' is not linked by any inner relationship to the succession of sounds *s-o-r* which serves as its
signifier in French; that it could be represented equally by
just any other sequence is proved by differences among
languages and by the very existence of different languages.

(68)

The word *arbitrary* also calls for comment. The term should
not imply that the choice of signifier is left entirely to the
speaker (we shall see below that the individual does not have
the power to change a sign in any way once it has become
established in the linguistic community); I mean that it is
unmotivated, i.e. arbitrary in that it actually has no natural
connection with the signified.

(68, 69)

the only real object of linguistics is the normal, regular life of
an existing idiom.

(72)

Language is radically powerless to defend itself against the
forces which from one moment to the next are shifting the
relationship between the signified and the signifier. This is
one of the consequences of the arbitrary nature of the sign.

(75)

These quotations from Saussure form much of the basis of
structuralist and semiotic thought. You may notice that in terms
of *signification*, (or word meaning, if you prefer) a tripartite
system exists, even though Saussure only mentions the crucial
binarism *signifier/signified,* united in the *sign.* The word, whether

in graphic or phonic form (written or spoken) is the *signifier*; the concept attached to the word is the *signified*. The *sign* unites the two. We must add a third term to avoid confusion at this stage: *referent*. The *referent* is the 'item' to which the sign (unifying the signifier and the signified) refers. Thus there is not simply a 'word' and a 'thing', there is a 'word', a 'concept' and a 'referent'. This is important to remember, as many literary critics have mistakenly taken the *signified* to be the referent. This is partly because Saussure himself does not use the term 'referent'. This term comes from the German philosopher Gottlob Frege, but we include it here to avoid confusion. Not all words have 'concepts' or even 'referents' associated with them. Words whose function is largely grammatical, such as '*and*', '*if*', '*or*' and '*but*' cannot be said to 'name' or 'refer' to something. However, much of the discussion of *signification* centres on the words which appear to perform those functions. The signified is a concept, and as such functions within a *system of signification*. Meaning, in other words, is possible only by virtue of its *systemic* function. Meaning does not exist in isolation. A linguistic element 'means' because it is part of a system wherein meaning is generated. This is an important point, particularly in relation to our discussion of literary structuralism.

i) What is the significance of having the concept of a word (signified) functioning between the form (sound-image) and the referent?

The inclusion of the concept within the triad of signification suggests that there is no natural or immediate relation between the words and the 'thing'. The graphic or phonic form of an utterance, combined with some notion of 'concept', produce a dominantly internal or cognitive language function. The referent is only one-third of the 'meaning'.

ii) Saussure calls the relationship between signifier and signified arbitrary. What precisely does he mean by this? Are

there any instances of language you can think of where the relationship is not completely arbitrary?

Saussure states that there is no natural relation between the signifier as acoustic sound-image and the signified as 'concept'. Neither phonic nor graphic form in any manifestation is naturally linked to any particular concept. There is nothing, for instance, in the collection of phonemes (meaningful sounds) which constitute the word 'woman' that encodes, by virtue of its graphic or phonic form, any 'womanness'. The phenomenon of onomatopoeia is sometimes cited as an example of non-arbitrariness in language, where the link between the sound and the sense is very close (e.g. 'bang'). But onomatopoeic sounds are culturally and linguistically specific – that is, loud noises do not go 'bang' in China, so the relation cannot be entirely necessary.

iii) What concept of 'meaning' is implied by Saussure's focus on the 'normal, regular life of an existing idiom'?

To a great extent, meaning is 'now'. The history of a word will not tell you anything about its current meaning. The fact that the word 'oblivious' once meant 'forgetful' has no bearing on its current meaning. However, the fact that 'gay' has a historical meaning – 'light-hearted and happy' – does have bearing on its current meaning.

iv) Does a linguistic sign ever unite 'a thing and a name'?

Certainly, some linguistic signs unite an *action* and a name. The *performative* verb reflects this possibility:

I *hereby grant* that . . . (see page 29)

Is there a similar kind of nominal unity; where a name and a thing appear to 'coincide'?

2 Systems

The structuralist, perhaps rather tautologously, analyses structures; but what kind of structures, and how do they themselves and the methodologies relate to the discipline of literary studies? Structuralism is characterised by two perspectives: the belief that the social universe is, in its nature, both arbitrary (see above, on Saussure), and conventional, like language itself; and the reversal of the traditional view of the relationship between humans and their social environment. Structuralists aim to show that what we might consider to be 'natural' in some way is actually social, 'man-made' ('*man*' is used deliberately here) and arbitrary. A structure is something created by human beings, or rather *through* human beings, and comprises smaller, linked units. This again is exemplified by the linguistic model, where the language system is made up of units descending from the 'text' through to word and finally to the smallest meaningful unit, the phoneme (see page 9).

The structuralist methodology uses the analogy of the phoneme as the 'smallest meaningful unit'. A phoneme cannot be said to have any 'intrinsic' meaning (whether it is a bound or a free morpheme does not really matter): it is only meaningful by virtue of its place in a complex system. It is distinguished precisely because it is *not* something else. We can demonstrate this with an analysis of the phonemes /b/ and /p/. This is important for the concept of binary oppositions which will be picked up later in this chapter. The two phonemes are very close in terms of articulation. That is, in order to produce the sounds /b/ and /p/, similar movements of the mouth and of the expulsion of air are made. They are both *bilabial*, made with both lips, and *plosive*, incorporating a sudden expulsion of air where formerly the air channel had been blocked. The difference in the two phonemes is that the /b/ is 'voiced' and the /p/ is 'voiceless'; the vocal cords 'hum' with /b/, but they do not do so with /p/. The sounds, therefore, are said to be related in some way, and distinguished by the voiced/voiceless binarism. The phoneme /p/, therefore, has meaning by virtue of the fact that it is not /b/ (its close relation). Other phonemes exhibit similar traits, and all have meaning by virtue of their place in the linguistic system. What is more, the forty-five phonemes in English are capable of generating, through combination, an infinite number of signs. Thus, a *complex, interdependent and finite system* underwrites language. Saussure has said:

> Language is a system of interdependent terms in which the value of each term results solely from the simultaneous presence of the others . . .
>
> (1974: 114)

> in language there are only *differences without positive terms.* Whether we take the signified or the signifier, language has neither ideas nor sounds that existed before the linguistic system, but only conceptual and phonic differences that have issued from the system.
>
> (120)

The concept of the phoneme can be used analogously for the smallest unit of meaning in a system. The arbitrary and conventional nature of language makes the linguistic sign the sign *par excellence*; but other systems can be interpreted in the same way. Before we look at more formal definitions of the concepts 'system' and 'structure' we can summarise some essential points about structuralist concepts of language:

Language is a group, or social, institution.
The syntax and semantics of a language yield a set of rules to which the speaker must submit or conform.
Language is independent of the decisions and use of the individual.
The history of a word may give inadequate account of its meaning.

Consider the following quotation from Piaget. His book *Structuralism* is a critical document in the history and philosophy of the discipline. Here he discusses structures and 'transformations':

> As a first approximation, we may say that a structure is a

system of transformations. Inasmuch as it is a system and not a mere collection of elements and their properties, these transformations involve laws: the structure is preserved or enriched by the interplay of its transformation laws, which never yield results external to the system nor employ elements that are external to it. In short, the notion of structure is comprised of [*sic*] three key ideas: the idea of wholeness, the idea of transformation, and the idea of self-regulation.

(Piaget 1971: 5)

Piaget densely summarises structuralist methodology here. Notice the expressions 'laws', 'transformations' and 'properties'. What kind of language is this? Notice further the 'internal' quality of the methodology: nothing 'external' is possible, because nothing external is conceived. A transformation is the realisation of one element into a base element: the system is thus complete in itself (whole); it transforms elements into structural properties, and regulates itself so as to admit no other influence.

i) What are the consequences for literary criticism if its methodology of analysis is based on the ideas outlined above?

ii) What does it mean that nothing external can influence the system?

A theory of literary criticism using Piaget's ideas would focus on the internal workings and structures of texts, both individually and as part of a larger framework of 'literature'. Structures are seen to be complete in themselves, and to a great extent evident in the texts. If we treat 'literature' as a system, then it is a system that works and responds to its own internal laws rather than admits influences from outside the system. Literature can be sealed off from other systems, for there are no external influences able to intrude upon its own structures. Structuralism in this respect is an extreme formalism: 'history' and 'context' can be thought of as things 'external' to the system and therefore of no influence on its workings.

3 The macro-level: grammars

One of Saussure's most troublesome, yet influential, distinctions is between *la langue* and *la parole* – a particular language and the speech of that language respectively. As David Holdcroft (1991) points out, Saussure in fact made a distinction between three terms: *langage*, *langue* and *parole*, the *langage* being 'language' in general. Now there are all sorts of problems associated with attempts to define what precisely belongs to *langue* and what to *parole*, but we can initially describe these as an underlying system and an individual speech act or utterance respectively. Any individual 'act' of language *(parole)* is underwritten by the language 'system' *(langue)*. The distinction between system and individual realisation has been extremely influential in both linguistics and literary criticism, because it enables the analyst to posit a theoretical base for the elucidation of individual utterances. Language is systemic, use of language is individual and creative; yet no creation or use is possible without the underlying system, which has its own rules and forms.

One of the early enterprises of structuralists was the attempt to describe the 'grammar' of literature. Taking the linguistic model, the question remains as to whether the individual text or literature *per se* was structured like a language. In its highest and most self-defeating aspect, structuralism saw literature as a whole structured like a language; but this was an extremely optimistic project, and of little use when attempting to account for individual texts. Structuralism at its most optimistic macro-level wished to find the 'grammar' of literature. What might this mean?

i) What is a 'grammar' of a language?

ii) By analogy, what then would be the grammar of the text?

iii) How would you differentiate between 'syntax' and 'semantics'?

A 'grammar' of a given language is, on one level, a description of the rules which enable sentences to be generated. The terms 'grammar' and 'syntax' are sometimes used synonymously in that they relate to the *formal arrangement* of the signs of any text (theoretical or otherwise). A *semantic* analysis of a text (or sentence) would be an analysis of meaning; a *grammatical* or *syntactic* analysis would be analysis of *form* and *structure*. The structuralist analysis of texts is analogous to the role of grammar in discourse: syntax does not tell us *what* a sentence means; it tells *how* it might mean. Some linguistic theories, such as Chomsky's transformational grammar, bracket off the 'meaning' of a sentence from its grammatical form and suggest that semantic functions have little bearing on form. To a certain extent this is mirrored in structuralist analyses of texts (although Chomsky was not a structuralist as such). However, it is ultimately difficult to separate form from meaning, and semantic functions affect grammatical functions and vice versa. A familiar illustration of the problem is seen in this example from Chomsky's *Syntactic Structures* (1957):

Colourless green ideas sleep furiously.

Chomsky considered this sentence to be both meaningless and grammatical, in other words, semantically anomalous but syntactically or grammatically well-formed. The separation of grammar from meaning in this respect is only possible, however, when the sentence is decontextualised (as most of the examples from *Syntactic Structures* are). If we simply create a meaningful context for the sentence (that is, transform it into an *utterance*) it becomes both meaningful and grammatical. We would have little trouble interpreting the sentence (or at least trying to interpret it) if it were from a poem, for example. It would be possible, in that case, to gloss it as 'Bland, naive considerations about the environment seem dormant but mask an underlying anger'. Granted this is not the most likely utterance or 'translation' of the sentence, but its possibility troubles Chomsky's and any other theory which seeks to divorce meaning from form.

Consider the following quotations relating to structure, form and structuralist practice:

> The critic is not to take as a moral goal the decipherment of
> a work's meaning, but the reconstruction of the rules and
> constraints upon that meaning's elaboration.
>
> (Barthes, quoted in Culler 1980: 21)

Again, the rejection of the search for meaning is evident here. The
grammar might be said to be 'rules and constraints', the semantics, the 'meaning'. In a literature, what *kind* of text it is might
stand analogous to the grammatical system, in that it both
constrains and generates certain possibilities.

> I thus do not aim to show how men think in myths, but how
> myths think in men, without their knowing [*comment les
> mythes se pensent dans les hommes, et à leur insu*]
>
> (Lévi-Strauss, 1970: 51)

Men do not simply create structures for their own purposes.
Structures are innate and govern cognitive processes.

> We may therefore understand the Structuralist enterprise as a
> study of superstructures, or, in a more limited way, of
> ideology. Its privileged object is thus seen as the uncon-
> scious value system or system of representations which
> orders social life at any of its levels, and against which the
> individual, conscious social acts and events take place and
> become comprehensible. Alternately, we may say that as a
> method, Structuralism may be considered one of the first
> consistent and self-conscious attempts to work out a philo-
> sophy of models (constructed on the analogy with language):
> the presupposition here is that all conscious thought takes
> place within the limits of a given model and is in that sense
> determined by it.
>
> (Jameson 1972: 101)

For the structuralist, form *is* content; meaning is the structure
which generates it.

> If a working hypothesis is needed for an analysis whose task
> is immense and whose materials infinite, then the most
> reasonable thing is to posit a homological relation between

sentence and discourse insofar as it is likely that a similar formal organisation orders all semiotic systems, whatever their substances and dimensions. A discourse is a long 'sentence' (the units of which are not necessarily sentences), just as a sentence, allowing for certain specifications, is a short 'discourse'.

(Barthes 1977: 83)

Formal linguistic analysis traditionally stops at the sentence. Barthes does not reject this tradition, but draws a homological relation between sentence and discourse.

In a way the 'literature' of mankind as a whole (that is to say, the way in which written works are organised in men's minds) can be regarded as being constituted in accordance with a similar process – bearing in mind the crude simplification that is involved here: literary production is a *parole*, in the Saussurean sense, a series of partially autonomous and unpredictable individual acts; but the consumption of this literature by society is a *langue*, that is to say, a whole the parts of which, whatever their number and nature, tend to be ordered into a coherent system.

(Genette 1982: 18–19):

Genette here adapts the Saussurean ideas of *langue* and *parole* to a theory of literary meaning.

iv) Make a list of the possibilities which would constitute the 'rules and constraints upon [that] meanings elaboration'.

v) Before we look at the issue in greater detail, try to suggest what might be meant by a transformation of form into content.

vi) What other similarities between sentence and discourse can you note?

4 The micro-level: syntax of texts

So far we have considered the possibilities for a 'grammar' of the literary text. This grammar is idealised in that it does not take into account 'material' elements such as context and history, and class, race and gender differences. The grammar is, in a sense, 'universal'. In the same way that a grammar accounts for the generation of sentences in a given language, a grammar of the text will account (theoretically) for the generation of texts in a given genre ('language' and 'genre' here are used analogously). However, the micro-level of analysis is far more workable than the macro-level. On the micro-level the relation is drawn between sentence and text; on the macro-level, between grammar and texts. The macro-level analysis seeks to find underlying principles in a vast range of possible and actual texts. The micro-level analysis sees the individual text as analogous to the sentence. Here we shall look at the possibilities of this relation.

In order to do this we need to adopt a functional view of syntax and at a simple level transform grammatical relations into functional properties. Consider the following simple declarative sentence (the grammatical relations of such a sentence are discussed in Chapter 1):

She kicked the football

Here we have a grammatical subject: the pronoun 'she'; a predicator comprising the simple verb 'kick' with the morpheme indicating past activity 'ed'; and the complement (in traditional grammars the *object*) comprising the nominal referring expression 'the football'. Grammatical subjects are not always the thematic or topic subjects of the sentence. In the sentence:

She kicked me

the first person has the topic pull which gives it thematic prominence. Alternatively, the initial example can be passivised:

The football was kicked by her

Notice here that the agent is still the same; the action is predicated by 'her'/'she' but the grammatical subject has changed (it is now 'the football'). The same event is realised, then, in two different ways, each with its different focus. For the structuralist, however, that variation in form is always transformed, as Genette says, into a proposition about content. The manner of telling only super-ficially masks the underlying similarity (or identical relation) of the events predicated.

Within the structures of the simple grammatical roles there are many possibilities for substitution. A finite grammar, in other words, generates an infinite number of realised sentences. In the simple syntagm above any number of nominals could replace the 'she' for the subject ('Jane', 'Fred', 'my hamster', 'two large red fire-engines', 'the Prime Minister', etc.). This is also true in relation to the verb 'kicked' and the other nominal 'the foot-ball'. What remains the same in any of these substitutions, however, is the functional relation of element A performing a process on element B. A basic function is expressed.

If we expand this to text level we can see that certain elements in a story, for instance, take on the analogous roles of sentence nominals or sentence subjects. Similarly, an event itself can be seen as a verbal process. Adjuncts of time and place have analogous structures in setting and point of view and syntactic transformations of the kind ACTIVE $\rightarrow$ PASSIVE are realised textually in a variety of formal choices. Again, the form of the story is transformed into content, while paradoxically the content itself is ignored.

5 Structural analysis of narratives

As we know, linguistics stops at the sentence, the last unit which it considers to fall within its scope. If the sentence, being an order and not a series, cannot be reduced to the sum of the words which compose it and constitutes thereby a specific unit, a piece of discourse, on the contrary, is no more than the succession of the sentences composing it. From the point of view of linguistics, there is nothing in discourse that is not to be found in the sentence . . . Hence there can be no question of linguistics setting itself an object superior to the sentence, since beyond the sentence are only more sentences – having described the flower, the botanist is not to get involved in describing the bouquet.

And yet it is evident that discourse itself (as a set of sentences) is organised and that, through this organisation, it can be seen as the message of another language, one operating at a higher level than the language of the linguists. Discourse has its units, its rules, its 'grammar': beyond the sentence, and though consisting solely of sentences, it must naturally form the object of a second linguistics.

(Barthes 1977: 82–3)

There are two aspects to Barthes' pronouncements here. First is the attempt to see the text as a kind of expanded sentence and to seek a critical approach that will stand in relation to the text as linguistics stands to the sentence. Second, there is the recognition that discourse has its own rules, which operate 'beyond the sentence'.

i) What features of a discourse are constituted 'beyond the sentence'?

ii) What features might characterise elements of the 'grammar' of a text?

iii) What might the 'rules' of a discourse be? Are the rules the same for every kind of discourse?

One of the successes of structuralism has been narratology, or the study of narratives. Narratives are no longer seen as restricted to certain aspects of culture and, as such, reasonably 'transparent', but as fundamental aspects of human life. Figures like the structural semanticist A.J. Greimas and the narratologist Tzvetan Todorov are concerned with the way in which the social being is constructed through narratives; and they attempt to describe their constitutive elements. Greimas is concerned not with individual texts, but with the 'grammar' that underwrites and generates narratives. A narrative sequence thus mobilises binary oppositions through two 'actants', the relation of which generates essential actions. Greimas further argues that, like language, the grammar of narratives is finite. The attempt to describe the grammar of narratives lies at the heart of the structuralist enterprise.

We should first consider the question 'What is a narrative?', and further ask 'What are its constituent features?'. E.M. Forster in *Aspects of the Novel* (1926) draws a distinction between 'plot' and 'story'. He states that 'The King died and then the Queen died' is a story and 'The King died and then the Queen died of grief' is a plot. They are both features of narrative, but the plot transfroms the events by combining temporal succession with *cause*. Variations upon this binarism are central to narrative theory, notably Genette's (1982) distinction between 'histoire' and 'récit'; Tomashevsky's (1925) 'fabula' and 'syuzhet', Chatman's (1972) 'story' and 'discourse' and Rimmon-Kenan's (1987) 'story' and 'text'. The essential distinction is between the events that can be said to happen in 'real' time and their transformation and realisation in a text. Thus 'real' time may be said to be linear, while the textual realisation of an event may occur out if its linear sequence, as in a flashback. In the Forster example, the statement of the *cause* of the Queen's death transforms the story into a plot, or story into discourse: it embellishes the simple temporality of 'x then y', transforming it into 'x then y because a': Rimmon-Kenan states:

> Whereas 'story' is a succession of events , 'text' is a spoken or written discourse which undertakes their telling. Put more simply, the text is what we read. In it, the events do not necessarily appear in chronological order, the characteristics of the participants are dispersed throughout, and all the items of the narrative content are filtered through some prism or perspective ('focaliser').
>
> (Rimmon-Kenan 1983: 3)

To the two fundamental aspects of narrative we can add a third: narratives do not simply happen; they are told by someone, and that someone tells from a particular point of view. Rimmon-Kenan calls this aspect 'narration'. Crucially, the text, plot, or discourse is what the narratologist deals with. The story behind the narrative is already transformed when we read it as text, and the narration can only be inferred.

Texts, or discourses (these uses must not be confused with the more linguistics-based uses of the term), are said to transform only a limited number of stories, and these can be said to be essential narrative structures. In the Forster example cited above, we have a simple temporality of 'x then y' In this sequence there is a move from one state to another. One basic narrative form can be described as:

[state] x . . . [event] y . . . [state] z where z inverts x

Thus the plot of *Cinderella* can be reduced to something along the lines of:

Cinderella poor and unhappy   [state x]
Cinderella goes to the Ball   [event y]
Cinderella wealthy and happy   [state z]

We could substitute the states 'poor and unhappy' and 'wealthy and happy' with others, such as 'unmarried' and 'married', but the final state is always an inversion of the first (x). Further, characters can be reduced to 'functions'; it is not necessary for 'Cinderella' to be part of the narrative. 'Cinderella' is only one name in the realization of the narrative sequence. Structuralists and narratologists have variously attempted to reduce and describe the essential character functions of narratives. Barthes, in 'Structural Analysis of Narratives', states:

> Structural analysis, much concerned not to define characters in terms of psychological essences, has so far striven, using various hypotheses, to define a character not as a 'being' but as a 'participant' . . . Greimas has proposed to describe and

classify the characters of narrative not according to what they are but what they do (whence the name *actants*), inasmuch as they participate in three main semantic axes (also to be found in the sentence: subject, object, indirect object, adjunct) which are communication, desire (quest) and ordeal. Since this participation is ordered in couples, the infinite world of characters is bound by paradigmatic structure (*Subject/Object, Donor/Receiver, Helper/Opponent*) which is projected along the narrative. These . . . conceptions have many points in common. The most important . . . is the definition of the character according to participation in a sphere of actions, these spheres being few in number, typical and classifiable.

(Barthes 1977: 106–7)

There are well-known narratologies in the work of Vladimir Propp, Roland Barthes and Greimas (also in Todorov and Genette). Propp outlines seven spheres of action found in his Russian folktales:

Villain
Donor
Helper
Sought-for person (and her father)
Dispatcher
Hero
False hero

Greimas locates types of narrative syntagm (sequence):

Les syntagmes performanciels (relating to performance of tasks, etc.)
Les syntagmes contractuels (action towards an end)
Les syntagmes disjonctionnels (movement or displacement)

Barthes notes five narrative codes:

Proairetic code (code of actions, which are sequential; the
   construction of the plot)
Hermeneutic code (code of puzzles, mystery suspense, questions)
Cultural code (system of values and knowledge evoked)
Semic code (of person and character)
Symbolic code (themes of action; extrapolation of symbols from
   the text)

It should be stressed that none of these narratologies is exhaustive,
and we aim by the above just to give an idea of their essential
features. They remain basic ways of looking at the structure of
narratives. It would be a good idea, however, to work through
some of these theories in the analysis of a particular narrative. For
our purposes, the narrative must be reasonably short.

The Stolen Farthings
A father was one day sitting at dinner with his wife and his
children, and a good friend who had come on a visit ate with
them. As they thus sat, and it was striking twelve o'clock,
the stranger saw the door open, and a very pale child dressed
in snow-white clothes came in. It did not look around, and it
did not speak; but went straight into the next room. Soon
afterwards it came back, and went out of the door again in
the same quiet manner. On the second and on the third day,
it came also in exactly the same way. At last the stranger
asked the father to whom the beautiful child that went into
the room every day at noon belonged. 'I have never seen it,'
said he, neither did he know to whom it could belong. The
next day when it again came, the stranger pointed it out to
the father, who however did not see it, and the mother and
the children also saw nothing. At this the stranger got up,
went to the room door, opened it a little, and peeped in.
Then he saw the child sitting on the ground, and busily
digging and seeking about between the boards of the floor,
but when it saw the stranger, it disappeared. He now told
what he had seen and described the child exactly, and the
mother recognised it , and said: 'Ah, it is my dear child who

died a month ago.' They took up the boards and found two farthings which the child had once received from its mother that it might give them to a poor man; it, however, had thought: 'You can buy yourself a biscuit for that,' and had kept the farthings, and hidden them in the openings between the boards; and therefore it had no rest in its grave, and had come every day at noon to seek for these farthings. The parents gave the money at once to a poor man, and after that the child was never seen again.

(Grimm and Grimm 1983: 652)

The questions we want to ask in the application of narrative theories will inevitably point to certain inadequacies in them. But just as they may be shown to contain errors and gaps, they may also show us the character of structuralism and a potentially enlightening way of looking at texts. A key figure in the kind of narratology we are beginning is Vladimir Propp. Propp's list of characters (actants) noted above is based on the analysis of Russian folk-tales. Propp further proposed that different sequences of a narrative can be understood as essentially *the same events* expressed differently. All stories (at least, the folk-tales he looks at) mobilise a finite number of event-sequences (31), but they do not all mobilise all these sequences.

But can we perform the same kind of analysis on a single example of a Grimm's fairy-tale, or do we need a larger corpus? In theory we should be able to transform content into stable forms, with a single text. Rather than seeing the text as one element in a complex system, we are isolating it: in a sense we are looking, by analogy, at one sentence. We could do two things in respect of this sentence (in terms of structuralism): we could infer and then reconstruct the grammar which enabled the sentence (text) to be generated in the first place; or we could break the sentence (text) down into its essential, formal structures. Both are aspects of the structuralist enterprise, although the second is the more grand and less successful venture.

In answering the following questions and performing the following tasks, remember that individual elements are not important: setting and character, for instance, must be transformed into general elements. Not all of the characters, syntagms and codes listed above need be present, of course.

> iv) Is it possible that such a story with limited characters can conform in any way to Propp's narratology?
>
> v) Assess the two characters' roles according to Propp's classifications.
>
> vi) Do they take other roles? If, so, which?
>
> vii) What is the role of the stranger?
>
> viii) What roles are left over?
>
> ix) Does classification of this sort tell us anything about the story?
>
> x) What are we meant to do with the detail of the story?

As a coda to this exercise you could try chopping up the text into binary oppositions. You may remember that the phonemes /b/ and /p/ are in binary relation. The same relations are said to exist in elementary concepts of thought. Humans have a cognitive faculty which is fundamentally binary. In the following examples, some oppositions might be considered 'cultural', some 'biological', some 'thematic', etc. The binary relation is not realised on one simple level:

Dark	:	Light
Male	:	Female
Left	:	Right
Straight	:	Gay
Active	:	Passive
Nature	:	Culture

> xi) Look at the story in terms of binary oppositions. What are the similarities between this activity and the activity of locating character functions?

xii) Is there a difference in the description of binary oppositions between prose and poetry?

Barthes was always aware of the limitations of his work, and
of theory in general, and he often takes a self-conscious stand in
his works. One of his most well-known books *S/Z* (1974) – in
which he developed his idea of narrative codes, first displayed in
the essay 'The Structural Analysis of Narratives' (Barthes 1977) –
has been called both a structuralist and post-structuralist work.
Barthes himself would not have claimed that his narrative codes
are exhaustive – indeed, many Anglo-American critics seem to
have misread the playful nature of some of his work – but the
codes are nevertheless useful to an extent and provide a variation
of the structuralist methodology. First, we can expand the descriptions of the codes, before we look at how they might apply to the
text.

Proairetic code: every action in a story, from the smallest to the
   greatest, is considered here. Actions are syntagmatic, but are
   often meant to overlap. Syntactically, of course, there can be
   no 'overlapping'.
Hermeneutic code: this also works along the syntagm. Puzzles,
   questions and other enigmas are either resolved or left
   unresolved in a story.
Cultural code: all elements that appeal to a system of shared
   knowledge, such as proverbs and other cultural 'assumptions', are located here.
Semic code: this is a rather more nebulous code, but is to do with
   thematic elements embedded in character.
Symbolic code: the location and extrapolation of symbols from
   textual features.

A simple way to begin is to try to locate these codes in the text and
then see what is 'left over'.

xiii) Which codes are you able to locate linguistically (that is, part of the 'words on the page')?

xiv) Which codes call for some other kind of perspective? What kind?

xv) List all the elements functioning under the proairetic and hermeneutic codes. Can you relate these in any way to Propp's functions and spheres of action?

Before we look at Greimas' syntagms, here is an extract from Barthes *S/Z*. The whole of the book is an analysis of a short story by Balzac, 'Sarrasine':

> La Zambinella and Sarrasine exchange lines of dialogue. Each line is a snare, a misuse, and each misuse is justified by a code. Honor of Women corresponds to Typology of Women: codes are hurtled back and forth, and this volley of codes is the 'scene'. Thereby appears the nature of meaning: it is a force which attempts to subjugate other forces, other meanings, other languages. The force of meaning depends on its degree of systematization: the strongest meaning is the one whose systematization includes a large number of elements, to the point where it appears to include everything noteworthy in the world: thus great ideological systems which battle each other with strokes of meaning. The model for this is always the 'scene', the endless confrontation of two different codes communicating solely through their interlockings, the adjustment of their limits (dual replication, stichomythia).
> (377) *'But today is Friday,' she replied*, SEM Superstition (pusillanimity, timorousness).
> (378) *frightened at the Frenchman's violence*, ACT. 'Danger'. 3 the victim's repeated fright.
> (379) *Sarrasine, who was not devout, broke into laughter.* SEM. Impiety, Sarrasine's impiety paradigmatically corresponds to La Zambinella's superstition; this paradigm is (will be) actually tragic: the pusillanimous being will draw

the virile being into its deficiency, the symbolic figure will contaminate the strong mind.

(Barthes 1974: 154)

This rather dense extract is typical of Barthes' style and approach in *S/Z*. One can see that variations on the content of the story are transformed into formal elements. For instance, the characters 'Sarrasine' and 'La Zambinella' are not seen as individuals but are transformed into 'pusillanimous' and 'virile' beings in a paradigm of binary relation (impiety/superstition).

xvi) How different is this approach to other kinds of criticism you are familiar with?

xvii) Is the structuralist impulse part of a general critical impulse to reduce individual elements to thematic constants?

Greimas is a semanticist, and therefore has an interesting methodology to contribute to structuralism, which generally is not concerned with what texts may mean, but rather with *how* they mean. One aspect of Greimas' work which appealed to certain Anglo-American critics is the concept of *thematic homology*. This is easily explained, and hence quickly assimilated into an interpretative tradition. The structure of any text can supposedly be reduced to fundamental binarisms, which then form a homology. David Lodge used this idea to some effect in *Working with Structuralism* (1980). Analysing a short story by Hemingway ('Cat in the Rain'), he uses a variety of structuralist ideas, but eventually plumps for Greimas and the following homology:

> loving is to quarrelling as stroking a cat is to reading a book, a narrative transformation of the opposition between joy and ennui, thus:
>
> Loving (joy): Quarrelling (ennui): Stroking a cat (non-joy, a giving but not receiving of pleasure): Reading a book (non-ennui)

(Lodge 1980: 32)

This kind of reading is based on Greimas' notion of the 'semantic rectangle'. Based on logic we have an overarching category, let's say A, which is further represented by non-A, anti-A and negative anti-A. Sometimes the fourth term is not evident. Let us take an example based on simple relations. Let A stand for 'natural' and non-A 'non-natural'. Anti-A is then 'artificial' and negative anti-A 'not non-natural'. An example of the possible missing fourth term is given by Jameson in *The Prison-House of Language*. Here, he discusses Greimas' theory in relation to Dickens' novel *Hard Times*:

> In *Hard Times* we witness the confrontation of what amounts to two antagonistic intellectual systems: Mr. Gradgrind's utilitarianism ('Facts! Facts!') and that world of anti-facts symbolized by Sissy Jupe and the circus, or in other words, imagination. The novel is primarily the education of the educator, the conversion of Mr. Gradgrind from his inhuman system to the opposing one. It is thus a series of lessons administered to Mr. Gradgrind, and we may sort these lessons into two groups and see them as the symbolic answers to two kinds of questions. It is as though the plot of the novel . . . were little more than a series of attempts to visualize the solutions to these riddles: What happens when you negate or deny imagination? What would happen if, on the contrary, you negated facts? Little by little the products of Mr. Gradgrind's system show us the various forms which the negation of the negation, which the denial of the Imagination, may take: his son Tom (theft), his daughter Louisa (adultery, or at least projected adultery), his model pupil Blitzer (delation, and in general the death of the spirit). Thus the absent fourth term comes to the center of the stage; the plot is nothing but an attempt to give it imagina tive hypotheses until an adequate embodiment has been realized in terms of the narrative material.
>
> (Jameson 1972: 167)

Look again at 'The Stolen Farthings'. Try to see if this short story is amenable to analysis based on Greimas' four-term structure.

xviii) Locate a thematic binary opposition.

xix) Where in the story are these oppositions located? Are they to be found in action, character, imagery?

xx) Set the terms in homologous relation, as in the Lodge example. What kind of reading of the text is this?

Consider the following quotations:

> It is not the literary work itself that is the object of poetics; what poetics questions are the properties of that particular discourse that is literary discourse. Each work is therefore regarded only as the manifestation of an abstract and general structure, of which it is but one of the possible realisation. Whereby this science is no longer concerned with actual literature, but with a possible literature, in other words with that abstract property that constitutes the singularity of the literary phenomenon: *literariness*. The goal of this study is no longer to articulate a paraphrase, a descriptive resumé of the concrete work, but to propose a theory of the structure and functioning of literary discourse, a theory that affords a list of works appear as achieved particular cases. The work will then be projected upon something other than itself, as in the case of psychological or sociological criticism; this something other will no longer be a heterogeneous structure, however, but the structure of literary discourse itself.
>
> (Todorov 1981: 6–7)

xxi) What elements would characterise the 'abstract and general structure' of which Todorov talks?

Apparently, structuralism ought to be on its own ground whenever criticism abandons the search for the conditions of existence or the external determinations – psychological, social, or other – of the literary work, in order to concentrate its attention on that work itself, regarded no longer as an effect, but as an absolute being. In this sense, structuralism is bound up with the general movement away from positivism, 'historicising history' and the 'biographical illusion', a movement represented in various ways by the critical writings of Proust, an Eliot, a Valery, Russian Formalism, French 'thematic criticism' or Anglo-American 'New Criticism'.

(Genette 1982: 11)

xxii) To what extent can any discipline 'concentrate its attention on the work itself'? What exactly is 'the work itself'?

The question then becomes: what sort of knowledge is possible? Instead of taking the proliferation of interpretations as an obstacle to knowledge, can one attempt to make it an object of knowledge, asking how it is that literary works have the meanings they do? The institution of literature involves interpretive practices, techniques for making sense of literary works, which it ought to be possible to describe. Instead of attempting to legislate solutions to interpretive disagreements, one might attempt to analyse the interpretive operations that produce these disagreements – discord which is part of the literary activity of our culture.

(Culler 1981: 48)

xxiii) How might a structuralist approach be co-opted for the analysis of 'interpretive operations'?

If much of human activity is seen in terms of systems, then the activities of reading and interpreting, being basic human activities, would be subject to the same kinds of rules and constraints as other systems. Interpretive operations may be finite and systemic: the shift in focus away from the text itself enables the structuralist to conceive of literature as a finite system of reading responses, rather than an infinitely varied textual phenomenon.

6 Structures and intention

In this part we want to look more generally at the kinds of 'rules and constraints' upon text meaning that Barthes noted. To do this you need to perform a simple exercise. We shall deliver this with minimum of instruction:

WRITE YOUR LIFE STORY IN ONE PARAGRAPH

Perform this exercise before continuing.

Now consider and answer the following questions and tasks:

i) Did you begin 'I was born . . .'?

ii) Did you include material on school, housing, marriage etc.?

iii) What was your final point?

iv) Consider the number of words spent on one topic. Does this seem an accurate reflection (in terms of overall percentage of your life) of the importance of that topic?

v) Look through the paragraph again. Are there important points missed out?

vi) Try to assess why you included certain bits of material and left others out.

It should be clear that there is at least a little disparity between what you tried to do and what actually 'came out'. This is not to say that you have no control over the text; it is acknowledged, however, that you were (mostly unconsciously) responding to a number of forces and constraints. First, there is the restriction to one paragraph. This formal constraint must have implications for the kind of content included. Second, there are the problems of vagueness and an undefined audience (we have deliberately left the 'instructions' brief). We suspect that many began with the opening 'I was born . . .'. You may argue that this is actually the beginning of your life, but you are responding to a generic and linguistic convention. Of course, writers aren't often instructed to write in this way, and so to a certain extent the choice of material is widened. However, every author is responding to a number of constraints and forces. Here are some of these variables:

Language itself (it imposes its own rules)
Tradition and genre
Unspoken assumptions of society
Unconscious desires
Class
Race
Gender
The process of publication

7 Semiotics

Semiotic analysis is often the most common form in which structuralist criticism is encountered. It is a practice that has taken the firmest hold in approaches to popular culture, when the 'texts' considered are less likely to be canonical literary works than advertisements, Hollywood movies, television programmes, women's magazines and so on. In fact, semioticians were in the forefront of attempts to break down the divisions between serious critical consideration of 'high art' and passive consumption of popular culture, arguing that the latter has so much influence on contemporary imaginations that it cannot be allowed to go unscrutinised.

There are difficulties with treating sign systems that are not primarily linguistic – such as cinema, photography and so on – in the same way as we treat language. For instance, the visual image of a chocolate bar can convey the idea of a chocolate bar to a group of people, none of whom speak the same language. However, the word 'chocolate' addressed by one English speaker to another only communicates effectively if both can draw on some kind of mental concept of chocolate. That is, there seems to be *more* than a merely conventional relationship between photographic signifiers and their signifieds, in contrast to the arbitrary relationship between linguistic signifiers and *their* signifieds.

However, the arbitrary and conventional nature of the relationship between signifier and signified *is* drawn upon in certain cultural fields other than literature, especially that of advertising. In fact, advertising frequently relies on the way in which an audience of consumers can make meaningful connections between apparently disparate signifiers and signifieds.

For instance, instead of the example of a generic chocolate bar, let's look at a specific one: a Cadbury's 'Flake'. The advertisements for this product have, for many years, represented young, beautiful women, alone in fantasy environments, enjoying a sensual experience with a crumbly chocolate stick. During the 1970s, the advertisement featured a long-haired blonde woman in a floaty dress and floppy hat, wrapping her lipsticked mouth around her 'Flake' in a poppy-strewn field of wheat. Recently, this romantic dreamscape has been replaced by a post-modern bathroom where a short-haired brunette languishes in a Victorian-style tub overflowing with perfect bubbles as her overglossed lips caress the 'Flake'.

These images of solitary women in fantasy worlds appeal to the consumer to make many connections. The beautiful women are apparently content in their independence, yet these little scenes are curiously eroticised. The women appear to have sexualised relationships with their phallic chocolate bars instead of with beautifully muscled male models, as one might more conventionally imagine. Their surroundings suggest luxury and self-indulgence; the heedlessly overflowing bathtub indicates even a certain excessiveness. Alone in their private worlds these women have space to dream, but they seem to require substitutes for the absent men, in the form of the consoling chocolate bars.

Judith Williamson, in her thorough discussion of ways of 'decoding' advertisements explains:

> Advertisements must take into account not only the inherent
> qualities and attributes of the products they are trying to

sell, but also the way in which they can make those properties *mean something* to us . . . The components of advertisements are variable and *not* necessarily part of one 'language' or social discourse. Advertisements rather provide a structure which is capable of transforming the language of objects into that of people, and vice versa.

(1978: 12)

So, in the 'Flake' example, the attributes of the chocolate, its distinctive shape and texture, are harnessed and made to mean sexual desire and satisfaction. The luxurious bathroom and the woman's emotional response to the product become associated with that product: they become part of its identity. Thus, the 'Flake' is transformed into a sign for luxury, self-indulgence and erotic pleasure (rather than an inconveniently messy construction of chocolate in a twisted yellow wrapper). This is not the only recent advertisement to insist on these meanings for chocolate. A series of 'Galaxy' advertisements connect the confectionery with silk, and again with the solitary indulgence of women and the capacity for the sweets to function as substitute sexual partners.

The meanings we have suggested for the 'Flake' are not explicitly stated in the advertisement, of course. It requires the participation of the consumer to make the appropriate connection. A system must already exist in which chocolate is seen as luxurious and sensual, and in some way associated with sexuality, for the advertisement to operate successfully. This is only one of several systems in which chocolate can circulate. Other kinds of chocolate, implausibly as it may seem, place emphasis on their lightness: for instance, 'Milky Way' bars are supposed not to fill you up between meals; 'Maltesers' can be eaten even by sylph-like ballerinas before a performance; 'Aero' is full of bubbles and so on. Such advertisements contradict the assumption that chocolate is calorific and fattening, which might be off-putting to some consumers (especially women).

In a marketplace where there is apparently a wide variety of chocolate bars, all with only slight variations, the purpose of the advertisement is to create a difference between products, when in fact there is very little to choose between them. 'Flake' is crumbly whereas 'Galaxy' is silky; we are encouraged to think this, rather than that they are both bars of chocolate that are shaped differently; Flake is to be consumed slowly and luxuriatingly, whereas 'Maltesers' can be eaten whilst dancing in a classical ballet(!).

Such advertisements do not work successfully if we begin to think that it is ridiculous for a woman with such perfect hair and make-up to eat chocolate in a bath that is flooding the staircase. Judith Williamson explains that advertisements involve:

> a false assumption which is the root of all ideology, namely that because things are as they are (in this case, because certain things are *shown* as connected in ads, placed together, etc.), this state of affairs is somehow natural, and must 'make sense' simply because it exists. So when advertisements put two things side by side so that they co-exist, we do not question the sense of it. The form of advertisements, and their processes of meaning through our acceptance of implications in that form, constitute an important part of ideology. Non-senses [the illogical juxtaposition of, say, a bath and a chocolate bar] become invisible – which is why it is important to state what may seem very basic, once seen, very obvious, in this field; and sense is assumed simply on the basis of *facts*, that magical word whose original meaning is merely 'things already done' . . . Images, ideas or feelings, then, become attached to certain products, by being transferred from signs out of other systems . . . *to* the products, rather than originating in them. This intermediary object or person is bypassed in our perception; although it is what gives the product its meaning, we are supposed to see that meaning as already there, and we rarely notice that the correlating object and the product have no inherent similarity, but are only placed together . . . So a product and an image/emotion become linked in our minds, while the process of this linking is unconscious.
>
> (1978: 29–30)

There is no good reason why chocolate should seem more

luxurious or self-indulgent than any other food, except that we have been sold the myth. It is unlikely that, for instance, we would see anyone in the same setting as the 'Flake' advertisement eating mashed potato as a substitute for sexual satisfaction, yet it is just as 'unnatural' as seeing chocolate in this way.

Although there are difficulties, the kind of structuralist analyses of narratives outlined in the preceding sections of this chapter *can* be used to look at advertisements and other kinds of visual texts, especially those that clearly have a narrative sequence: for example, the notorious 'Gold Blend' coffee series which developed a traditional romantic relationship between two protagonists, and adhered to all the familiar devices of popular romance.

Advertisements without such a clearly defined narrative operate through a modified discursive system. Instead of character functions interacting and creating meaning by differentiation, as in the hero/villain binary in a narrative, particular relationships are suggested instead by a variety of visual signs. For example:

Colour: systems of relationships can be produced by having a product placed in the same frame as a similarly coloured item or a person in similarly coloured clothes, or by making a contrast (or affiliation) between product and surroundings.

Size and position: relationships between products and other items can be produced simply by putting the two items next to one another, or by making one larger than the other, or by standing in one form or the other.

Texture: the invocation of our knowledge of the senses to produce an association or transferral of meaning. For example, our experience tells us that silk is a smooth fabric, and its prohibitive cost means that we tend to associate it with luxury. The wrapping of a woman (eating a 'Galaxy' bar) in brown silk transfers the quality of the cloth to the chocolate.

Celebrity endorsement: all the meanings associated with a particular celebrity (beautiful actors and athletes are popular choices) become transferred on to the product. There are numerous other ways in which an otherwise meaningless or undifferentiated product can come to take on, apparently naturally, a variety of qualities by association.

i) Find an advertisement such as those in the examples above and try to 'decode' it for yourself. Try to work out what systems of meaning, which are already in place, the advertisement relies upon.
ii) Does the advertisement rely on a narrative of some kind? If so, how does this work on the consumer?
iii) Does the product operate as a signifier or a signified? That is, do the other objects in the advertisement point towards the concept of the product, or does the product signify those qualities?

8 The failures of semiotics

Advertisements and other semiotic systems rely on the consumer to make the relevant connections between signifier and signified. The consumer 'invents' the signified through the suggestions of the signifiers utilised by the campaigners. Semiotic systems cannot operate without this involvement of the human subject, the viewer or reader, and it is the failure of semiotic analysis to consider this fully that has resulted in severe criticism of its methodologies:

> Semiotics involves the study of signification, but signification cannot be isolated from the human subject who uses it and then is defined by means of it, or from the cultural system which generates it. The theoretical intimacy of the terms 'signification', 'subject', and 'symbolic order' has long been apparent to readers of Freud and Lacan, but it has perhaps remained less obvious to those semioticians who trace their lineage to Saussure.
>
> (Silverman 1983: 3)

One of the principles of structuralist analysis is that it artificially fixes a 'slice' of language on which to work: it works synchronically, without attention to aspects outside the system, such as historical context and change, and the differences between users of the sign system. As we have seen, the interest of traditional structuralists is in *langue* and not in *parole*: in the functions of elements as indicative of the workings of the language *system*, not the individual utterances in their own, quirky right. Sign systems are seen as operating as a closed set.

The problem with this is not the operation of a closed set in itself but the fact that we often forget that this is the way in which semiotic systems operate: 'signs do not give access to things but we forget this' (Blonsky 1985: 509). We tend to think that language and other semiotic systems, particularly visual ones such as advertisements, connect us to referents: 'As a result of great advertising, food tastes better, clothes feel snugger, cars ride smoother. The stuff of semiotics becomes the magic of advertising' (509). In other words, we tend to treat the signifieds in advertisements as though they were truths rather than our own constructions enabled by sophisticated publicity teams.

The tendency to accept sign systems such as advertisements without scepticism has changed since semiotic practice became part of popular culture, but that scepticism has been incorporated into the very practices it was once turned against. To continue using the advertising sign system as a source of examples, it has become commonplace for one advertisement to use the signs of another in a witty parody that nonetheless sells its own product. There are many of these parodic ads to choose from, but you might think of the extremely well-known 'Cornetto' ice-cream promotion which has a woman being punted through Venice with a catch-song that names the product. This scene, in itself sending up certain aspects of the romantic myth of Venice, has been recreated by comedians numerous times, and most recently reappears in pastiche form, as in an advertisement for Boddington's bitter. An elegant, immaculately made-up woman, familiar from an earlier ad for the beer, takes a pint from a fellow traveller, gulps it down, and wipes the froth from her crimson mouth with the back of her hand, smearing lipstick across her face, and expressing her appreciation with a broad Lancashire accent. The slapstick humour of this promotion is part of its appeal: it sends up the sophisticated women of the advertising trade by smudging this woman's make-up, giving her a regional accent which does not belong in the codes of sophistication, and giving her a pint of beer to drink rather than something sweet out of a small and delicate glass.

We are being invited to share in this exposure of the signs of advertising. This ad is telling us that it does not buy into the system that invites the consumer to identify with the product via the model on the screen. However, although we do not identify with the beer-drinking lass from Manchester as she is portrayed, we identify instead with the *humour* of the advertisement. It is this, rather than the woman, that gives us a cultural location for Boddington's bitter. The ad gives the illusion that it is mocking the system, and invites us knowingly to share the joke, but it has to be remembered that this ad is still part of exactly the same process, and shares in the same operations, as the original. The problem that this raises for us as critics can be asked as follows:

i) Is there a critical position that we can take that leaves us outside the semiotic system that we are analysing?

Milton Glaser, a designer, gives an account of semiotics working in the design of a supermarket and of product packaging. He explains clearly how consumers will buy something when they think that they have seen through the mythologies created by semiotic systems, when they think that they have positioned themselves critically outside the system of meaning:

A very funny story is that we were doing this market and the client decided that it was essential to have a concrete floor. Why? Because one of the signals that it is not a fancy place is that you have a concrete floor. And at a cost of $50,000 they tore up that perfectly good tile floor so that they could reveal the rather crummy-looking concrete underneath! Semiotics!

(Glaser 1985: 470)

Glaser goes on to explain how poorer-grade products, which had always been sold in supermarkets, were given recognisable signifiers to identify them as 'good value for money':

> We are so used to colours that when we see black and white it is like a kick in the stomach, yet it is a clear signal. And the satisfaction comes out of the reassurance that it is a plain operation. You are really getting good value because 'look how skimpy and lousy the package looks. They really went out of their way to cut corners' . . . There is, of course, a difference, one of quality, to generically packaged food. It is nutritious but certainly of lesser quality than brand-name food. Now the funny thing is that they had this category in the market for years not moving, and now it has become the hottest part of the supermarket. Why?
>
> People are much more serious. The truth is that people probably realise, with or without the packaging, that they can use broken mushrooms to make their stew and it will taste the same, and it will be nutritionally the same, and they do not have to get a national brand for the purpose . . . Generic marketing is a response to a kind of calculating consumer able to read through the myth of ads and know that he or she does not require the fancier food.
>
> (Glaser 1985: 470–1)

The point that we have emphasised is that a subject must participate *in* a semiotic system to create meaning, and thus critics are put in the awkward position of maintaining the system of meaning which they are attempting to criticise.

The consideration of the position of the subject in relation to systems of meaning begins to take us into areas that are covered by developments relating to structuralism and semiotics. These issues are discussed in Chapters 4 and 5.

Glossary

actant: Particularly associated with Greimas, the actant is a function of a text which is a participant of actions. Propp and other formalists and structuralists see character roles as essential and universal.

arbitrary: Linguistic forms, according to Saussure, lack physical correspondence with the world of 'things'.

code: A systematic set of rules which assigns meanings to signs. A code is a symbolic system. For Barthes, it is part of our competence in drawing on certain frames of reference.

conventional: Again, according to Saussure, language is not only arbitrary but 'conventional'. Meaning is tacitly agreed upon by members of the linguistic community.

diachronic: Diachronic linguistics is a historical perspective on language activity. Whereas *synchronic* linguistics is the study of language as it functions at a particular time, diachronic linguistics traces the history and development of elements.

grammar: In terms of structuralist methodology, a grammar is a systematic classification of linguistic structure. It is theoretical and descriptive.

hermeneutic: The theory of the interpretation of texts.

homology: Correspondence between two or more structures.

index: According to Peirce an index is a natural sign. For example one might say that heavy nimbus clouds are an index of rain. This relation is opposed to the arbitrary relation which exists in language between words and 'things'.

langue: Languages in particular. The *langue* is the underlying system which makes meaning possible.

mytheme: Analogous to the *phoneme*, the mytheme, according to Lévi-Strauss, is the smallest unit of signification in myths.

paradigmatic: Paradigmatic, or associative relations are those relations functioning on the vertical axis of language. Words (or signs) combine in sequences (syntagmatic relations), but each can be substituted for other items of the same paradigm.

parole: A linguistic element realised. An utterance or token of language.

phoneme: The minimal unit in the sound system of a language.

referent: The question of reference is that of the relation between words and the world. The referent is the 'last' element in the process of signification. The word cat signifies a concept and ultimately can refer to a specific 'cat'.

sign: The linguistic sign unites the signifier and the signified in the triad of signification.

structure: A structure is a self-contained system in which individual elements are transformed into essential elements.

subject: The subject of a sentence can be grammatical ('Jane broke the window') or thematic ('He hit me'). Here we refer only to these aspects of the term 'subject'. In other chapters the term's complexities are discussed.

symbol: Peirce distinguished between icon, index and symbol. The symbol is an arbitrary element of signification, such as traffic lights and, of course, language itself.

synchronic: A synchronic description of language, according to Saussure, is a description of the language as it functions at a particular time. Synchronic descriptions of elements do not take into account historical change, but rather concentrate on the meaning they have for speakers at a particular moment.

syntagm: A syntagm is a string of constituents (often in linear order). A sentence, being a string of grammatical elements, is a syntagm. A text can also be thought of as a syntagm, as can different narrative or thematic strands within it.

transformation: In structuralist methodologies, a transformation results when one element is realised into a more essential element. For example, in Propp's analysis of folk-tales, the individual characters are transformed into actants and spheres of action within the folk-tale 'system'.

Select bibliography

1 Of signification

There are many introductions to structuralism as it relates to literary criticism, including Terence Hawkes' *Structuralism and Semiotics* (1977) and Jonathan Culler's *Structuralist Poetics* (1975). The chapter on the linguistic base of structuralism in Culler's book is particularly good. Robert Scholes' *Structuralism in Literature: An Introduction* (1974) has the advantage of containing practical application of the theories. We urge students to read Saussure where possible – even though that source is not reliable, in that it is a reconstruction of his lectures by his students. Culler (1974) has introduced the text in translation, but most of his comments appear in greater detail in *Structuralist Poetics* (1975). A small book by Culler, *Saussure* (1976), is readable, and Roy Harris's *Reading Saussure* (1987) corrects many misreadings. David Holdcroft's *Saussure: Sign, Systems, Arbitrariness* (1991) builds on Harris's work. Raymond Tallis's vitriolic *Not Saussure* (1988) attacks literary critics for failing to read Saussure correctly.

2 Systems

Piaget's *Structuralism* (1971) has good, if often difficult, material on the theory of structuralism as it relates to a number of different disciplines, including mathematics. Michael Lane's (ed.) (1970) *Structuralism: A Reader* contains essential theory not only relating to literature, but to history, physics and mathematics. You can certainly get an idea of the scope of structuralism from this book. On the structuralist methodology and literature Leonard Jackson's *The Poverty of Structuralism* (1991) is a sustained reassessment of both structuralism and deconstruction.

3 The macro level: grammars

Though not a structuralist text in the fashion discussed in this chapter, Chomsky's *Syntactic Structures* (1957) posits the important and influential theoretical distinction between deep and surface structure. Seminal texts from which the quotations are drawn include Barthes' *Critical Essays* (1972a); Lévi-Strauss' *The Raw and the Cooked* (1970). Genette's essay 'Structuralism and Literary Criticism' is reprinted in *Figures of Literary Discourse* (1982). Jameson's *The Prison-House of Language* (1972) explores the relation between structuralism and Russian formalism.

4 The micro level: syntax of texts

This section has focused on the grammar which can be seen as analogous to the actions in a text. On this micro-level, Halliday's *An Introduction to Functional Grammar* (1987) fully develops the idea of roles in grammar. Hodge and Kress's *Language as Ideology* (1979) explores the theory of 'transformations' as formulated by Chomsky (1957) and develops radical readings of texts. On a more 'stylistic' level, Paul Simpson's *Language, Ideology and Point of View* (1993) discusses grammatical functions as they relate to world view. Richard Harland's *Beyond Superstructuralism* (1993) is an essential account of syntagmatic and paradigmatic relations.

5 Structural analysis of narratives

Barthes' essay 'The Structural Analysis of Narratives' (1966) is a classic example of overblown 'high' structuralism (see Barthes 1977). Theories here were later modified and developed in *S/Z* (1974). A useful collection of Barthes' early work (containing the 1966 essay) is *Image/Music/Text* (1977). Lodge's *Working with Structuralism* (1980) is a good example of British and American critics' attempts to enlist structuralist theory for the simple interpretation of texts. Jonathan Culler's *The Pursuit of Signs: Semiotics, Literature, Deconstruction* (1981) is rather diffuse, but is worthwhile for its discussion of the borders of structuralist analysis – its relation to semiotics and the later phenomenon of deconstruction, for instance. Todorov's *The Poetics of Prose* (1971) is a genuine attempt to balance structuralist methodologies with expositions of texts. Barthes' *S/Z* (1974) remains the classic structuralist document; yet this book contains much thinking and exposition which is closer to deconstruction. Rimmon-Kenan's *Narrative Fiction: Contemporary Poetics* (1983) covers much ground and has clear expositions of the essential theory. Wallace Martin's *Recent Theories of Narrative* (1986) contains some excellent surveys, as well as detailed discussions of point of view, realism and genre. Mieke Bal's *Narratology* (1985) is an extremely stimulating distillation of theories.

6 Structures and intention

Northrop Frye's *Anatomy of Criticism* (1957) has been frequently misread as a classic text of 'New Critical' thinking. In fact, there is much structuralist thought here also, and his 'Polemical Introduction' is still a thought-provoking attack on the intentionalist readings, while the main body of the book is the presentation of a protostructuralist (yet clearly *historical*) theory of literary production. E.D. Hirsch Jr's *The Aims of Interpretation* (1976) is a lucid pro-intentionalist tract. The debate about intention is put in a modern critical framework in Belsey's iconoclastic *Critical Practice* (1980).

7 Semiotics

8 The failures of semiotics

Roland Barthes' *Mythologies* (1972b) is the classic work of semiotic analysis; it is made up of short essays on everyday 'myths' with a lengthy, complex theoretical argument at the end, titled 'Myth Today'. Judith Williamson's *Decoding Advertisements* (1978) gives a full discussion of semiotic analysis; her approach is informed by Marx, Freud and Althusser. Although some of the examples are out of date by now, her clear discussion of complex theory remains useful. Guy Cook's *The Discourse of Advertising* (1992) is a similar project to Williamson's, but it has more of a linguistic focus, and it has the virtue of using advertising campaigns that are more likely to be familiar. *On Signs* (1985), edited by Marshall Blonsky, contains over forty essays by a wide range of critics on sign systems such as *Casablanca*, Prince Charles and Lady Diana's wedding, supermarkets and heart attacks. The approaches range from the clear and entertaining to the punishingly abstract, and many of the contributions have more to say about post-structuralism than semiotics. Kaja Silverman's *The Subject of Semiotics* (1983) has particularly good examples relating to cinema and offers an informed, approachable account of the role of the viewer or reader in interpreting signs. Finally, Umberto Eco's novel, *The Name of the Rose* (1985), is made up of strings of semiotic systems and positions the reader as decoder. It was remarkably popular and drew attention to the practice of semiotic analysis.

Chapter 3

Literature and history

1 What is history?

I N THIS CHAPTER we shall look at the relationship between literature and history and consider how historical and literary-critical methodologies differ. We shall also consider the notion of 'literary history' and its relation to genre and historicism. We begin with a discussion of the concept of history, a term often paired with literature in a relation suggestive of weak dependency on literature's part. 'Literature and history' go together in a non-essential relation: literature can be discussed without 'taking history into account', and this history is therefore seen as something other than literature which can be used on relevant occasions. This relation is similar to the one suggested by 'text' and 'context': the text can be discussed either 'on its own terms', or embedded in something other than itself, the con-text.

History may be seen, somewhat naively, as a collection of 'facts'. Crude representations of history suggest that it is objective and therefore opposed to literature, which is ultimately subjective. It can also be seen as a legitimising discipline by which other subjects or disciplines can function. In other words, 'history' is a bedrock of objective facts and data which give credence to any empirical discipline. A 'discipline' here is conceived of as a set of principles and concepts related to a particular field of enquiry. A 'subject' is that field of enquiry. The facts and data of history must also have an internal consistency and coherence which reflects *external* coherence. In other words, the coherence of the *representation* of history reflects the coherence of historical events themselves. Literature is sometimes seen as approximating history if it is 'realistic'. But as Hayden White argues:

> The usual tactic is to set the 'historical' against the 'mythi-cal' as if the former were genuinely *empirical* and the latter were nothing but *conceptual*, and then to locate the realm of

the 'fictive' between the two poles. Literature is then viewed as being more or less *realistic*, depending on the ratio of empirical to conceptual elements contained within it.

(White 1973: 3)

To write a history in the traditional sense is to construct a coherent narrative by weaving together parts of a culture with the thread of values which must necessarily inform the whole. The historical interpretative process is therefore cyclical: parts inform the whole which in turn must inform those parts. But how do we 'know' history, and can it be said to be objective in any way? These are important questions relating to our discussion of literature and history.

> i) Consider the various sites, textual or otherwise, where we might know history. You may have the following, as examples: Political records, personal diaries, archaeological artefacts, ancient or historical scripts, history books, literary texts, cultural artefacts
>
> ii) Can you add to these? What is remarkable about these 'sites'?

In the first place, they are, in the majority, textual. They are, like literature, texts themselves. Texts are human-made, and therefore 'subjective'. These texts are further ordered and shaped into narratives, and that which fits the coherent world view is fore-grounded, that which does not is suppressed. Now it might be argued that the assassination of the Archduke Franz Ferdinand in Sarajevo on 28 June 1914 is an objective fact, but how that fact will be ordered and foregrounded in a narrative will be significant in a subjective, rather than objective, way. By 'subjective' we do not suggest the pejorative use of the term: we mean it to refer to that which is constructed by and through human beings. Even those events which might appear to be evident 'facts' are con-tested, however, as the recent denial of the Holocaust (mass murder of Jews in World War Two) by some historians shows.

Historical interpretation is necessarily political. The following is
an extract from a typical historical narrative:

> The Germans had been, even before the war, the most readily
> inclined of the leading nations to question the norms and
> values of nineteenth-century liberal bourgeois society, to
> elevate the moment beyond the grasp of the law, and to
> look to the dynamics of immediate experience, as opposed
> to those of tradition and history, for inspiration. In the war
> they concentrated from the start on the idea of 'victory', on a
> Dionysian vitalism, which meant that the moment of con-
> quest would proffer, of and by itself, an exciting range of
> opportunities, primarily spiritual and life-enhancing and
> only secondarily territorial and material.
>
> (Eksteins 1990: 216)

Here we have the familiar discourse of the 'history book': The
generalisations about a country's inhabitants, the speculations
about their thinking, are linked to a 'real' event. The German
nation is seen as a homogeneous whole which acts according to the
prescriptions of a particular historical world view. The past tense
of the narrative enables the text to declare itself as authoritative in
some way: the events described are already completed and the
narrative reflects this. Note, however, that the simple past is also
the tense traditionally used for story-telling.

We can, at this stage, make a distinction between the arbitrary elements of history and the narrative selection and organisation of those elements. E.H. Carr in *What is History?* makes the
distinction between facts about 'history' and facts about 'the
past':

> Let us assume for present purposes that the fact that Caesar
> crossed the rubicon and the fact that there is a table in the
> middle of the room are facts of the same or of a comparable
> order, that both these facts enter our consciousness in the
> same or in a comparable manner, and that both have the
> same objective character in relation to the person who
> knows them. But, even on this bold and not very plausible

assumption, our argument at once runs into the difficulty that not all facts about the past are historical facts, or are treated as such by the historian. What is the criterion which distinguishes the facts of history from other facts about the past?

What is a historical fact? This is a crucial question into which we must look a little more closely. According to the commonsense view, there are certain basic facts which are the same for all historians and which form, so to speak, the backbone of history – the fact, for example, that the Battle of Hastings was fought in 1066. But this view calls for two observations. In the first place, it is not with facts like these that the historian is primarily concerned. It is no doubt important to know that the great battle was fought in 1066 and not in 1065 or 1067, and that it was fought at Hastings and not at Eastbourne or Brighton. The historian must not get these things wrong. But when points of this kind are raised, I am reminded of Housman's remark that 'accuracy is a duty, not a virtue'. To praise a historian for his accuracy is like praising an architect for using well-seasoned timber . . . It is a necessary condition, but not his essential function . . .

The second observation is that the necessity to establish these basic facts rests not on any quality in the facts themselves, but on an *a priori* decision of the historian.

(Carr 1961: 10–11)

iii) What is the relationship between 'facts' and 'history' as suggested by the above passage?

Carr's view is still essentially a common-sense one. He does not deny the existence of stable, objective facts, but he sees the selection and arrangement of these facts as the very nature of the historian's task. However, many recent scholars have suggested that history itself is largely a textual phenomenon, or at least that its realisations are largely textual. It is not merely an arbitrary collection of objective facts, but something which has been organised, shaped and made significant by human endeavour. When held to be objective, however, one of its functions has been to 'authorise' literary texts. The objective ground of history is precisely that which enables the subjective elements which constitute literary texts to function beyond the aesthetic. In terms of significance for literary studies, to locate a literary text in its historical context is to say something 'other' about the text which is beyond its immediate aesthetic significance. The Russian formalists, particularly Victor Shklovsky, Boris Eichenbaum and, later, Roman Jakobson, were largely responsible for setting up an aesthetic objectivity for literature and jettisoning the validating adjunct, history. Eichenbaum states:

> The chief strength of the Formalists . . . was neither the direction of their study of so-called 'forms' nor the construction of a special 'method'; their strength was founded securely on the fact that the specific features of the verbal arts had to be studied and that to do so it was first necessary to sort out the differing uses of poetic and practical language.
>
> (Eichenbaum 1965: 114–15)

For the formalists, literary writing is special and suppresses the referential functions of language. It foregrounds the 'poetic', in Jakobson's terms.

History and literature, if we accept both formalist theories and traditional views of history, seem to be governed by very different and distinct analytic procedures. Historical discourse can be seen as discourse which hooks on to the world through its referentiality; literary discourse, on the other hand, is discourse which turns back on itself, proclaiming itself as literary through its metaphors and other dominant self-reflexive tropes. To deny literature historical significance is to give it aesthetic significance. The poet, as Sidney said in *The Defense of Poesie*, 'nothing affirms and therefore never lieth'.

But if we see 'literature' and 'history' as functionally rather than ontologically (relating to 'essence') distinguishable, a rather different picture emerges. History and literature are labels which we choose to assign to certain texts, in this view; they are not separate by virtue of any intrinsic linguistic property. One might complain that despite superficial similarities literature does not rest upon that bedrock of fact which is the essence of historical discourse. However, much historical discourse is a questioning of such fact, and much literary discourse makes reference to a 'real', historical world.

For a final consideration of the discourse of history books and historians, we shall look at the following extract from Geoffrey Best's *Mid-Victorian Britain 1851–1875*:

> The least disputable ground for regarding the period of years covered in this book as in some sense a unity is an economic one. These were years of unchallenged British ascendancy over the family of nations in commerce and manufacturing: a sort of ascendancy upon which the peace-loving British optimists were inclined to congratulate the world. If this ascendancy in fact involved a kind of sterling imperialism and an economically enforced Pax Britannica – and most historians believe that it did – it was arguably a beneficent one; everyone got richer, while some got richer quicker than others. If Britain got richest quickest of all, who should complain of that? The world's eagerness for British goods, skills and services, was matched only by British eagerness to sell them. There were no inducements or pressures but those of the market. For twenty rare years, something like free trade nearly prevailed; and idealistic free-traders' dreams of international prosperity and concord seemed sometimes to be coming true.
>
> (Best 1979: 19)

iv) How is the notion of period construed in this passage?

In this extract Best overtly states his ground for considering the period in question. From the very beginning there is a declared interest, and a striving for, 'unity'. That the period in question can be seen as a whole is sanctioned by the most objective criterion,

97

the 'economic'. Once this search for unity and objective criteria have been set up, the author is free to speculate, paradoxically, on the history of the isolated years. We find that the years are characterised by an 'unchallenged British ascendancy'; This is evidenced by the fact that in Britain 'everyone got richer'. This is not a history of individuals, nor is it a history of flux and chance: an economic climate prevailed such that 'Britain' was a homogeneous element in a 'world' which was functioning according to its own economic principles.

This kind of view of history can readily be seen in approaches to literature, where a totality which reflects a national spirit is drawn out of textual phenomena. The totalising impulse of historicist criticism, of the traditional variety, is most keenly discernible in E.M. Tillyard's *The Elizabethan World Picture* (1943). Tillyard is something of a straw dog for the latter-day historicist; attacked for his naive interpretation of history and equally naive assumptions about the objective nature of history itself. For Tillyard the Elizabethan 'world' was characterised by an unalterable belief in the chain of being – a belief that is evident in all kinds of discourses, including Shakespeare. Tillyard's Elizabethan world is ordered and coherent. Ultimately, we shall see the extent to which Tillyard's historicism differs from more recent accounts. First, here is an extract from Tillyard's text, which was standard undergraduate 'background' reading on literature courses in the 1960s and 1970s:

> One of the clearest expositions of order (and close to Shakespeare's though a good deal earlier in date) is Elyot's in the first chapter of the *Governor*. It has this prominent place because order is the condition of all that follows; for of what use to educate the magistrate without the assurance of a coherent universe in which he can do his proper work?
>
> > Take away order from all things, what should then remain? Certes nothing finally, except some man would imagine eftsoons chaos. Also when there is any lack of order needs must be perpetual conflict. And in things subject to nature nothing of himself only may be

nourished; but, when he hath destroyed that where-
with he doth participate by the order of his creation,
he himself of necessity must then perish; whereof
ensueth universal dissolution. . .

This is all very explicit and prosaic. It is what everyone
believed in Elizabeth's days and it is *all* there behind such
poetic statements of order as the following from Spenser's
Hymn of Love describing creation.

The earth the air the water and the fire
Then gan to range themselves in huge array
And with contrary forces to conspire
Each against other by all means they may,
Threat'ning their own confusion and decay:
Air hated earth and water hated fire,
Till love relented their rebellious fire . . .

The conception of order described above must have
been common to all Elizabethans of even modest intelli-
gence. Hooker's elaborated account must have stated pretty
fairly the preponderating conception among the educated.
Hooker is not easy reading to a modern but would have been
much less difficult to a contemporary used to this kind of
prose . . . Hooker's version is of course avowedly theological
. . . but the order it describes is Elyot's and Shakespeare's.
His name for it is law, law in its general sense. Above all
cosmic or earthly orders or laws there is Law in general, 'that
law which giveth life unto all the rest which are commend-
able just and good, namely the Law whereby the Eternal
himself doth work'.

(Tillyard 1972: 19–21)

v) What is the relationship between literary and non-literary
writing as implied by Tillyard?
vi) How do the knowledge and beliefs of 'ordinary people'
relate to those beliefs expounded by writers such as Shakespeare and Elyot?

In conjuction with the historical texts so far presented, consider the following extract from Hayden White's *Metahistory: The Historical Imagination in Nineteenth Century Europe*:

the elements in the historical field are organized into a chronicle by the arrangement of the events to be dealt with in the temporal order of their occurrence; then the chronicle is organized into a story by the further arrangement of events into the components of a 'spectacle' or process of happening, which is thought to possess a discernible beginning, middle, and end. This *transformation of chronicle into story* is effected by the characterization of some events in the chronicle in terms of inaugural motifs, of others in terms of terminating motifs, and of yet others in terms of transitional motifs. An event which is simply reported as having happened at a certain time and place is transformed into an inaugurating event by its characterization as such: 'The king went to Westminster on June 3, 1321. There the fateful meeting occurred between the king and the man who was ultimately to challenge him for this throne, though at the time the two men appeared destined to become the best of friends . . .' A transitional motif, on the other hand, signals to the reader to hold his expectations about the significance of the events contained in it until some terminating motif has been provided: 'While the king was journeying to Westminster, he was informed by his advisers that his enemies awaited him there, and that the prospects of a settlement advantageous to the crown were meager'. A terminating motif indicates the apparent end or resolution of a process or situation of tension: 'On April 6, 1333, the Battle of Balybourne was fought. The forces of the king were victorious, the rebels routed. The resulting Treaty of Howth Castle, June 7, 1333, brought peace to the realm – though it was to be an uneasy peace, consumed in the flames of religious strife seven years later.' When a given set of events has been motifically encoded, the reader has been provided with a story; the chronicle of events has been transformed into a *completed* diachronic process, about which one can then ask questions as if he were dealing with a *synchronic structure* of relationships.

(White 1973: 6)

vii) Look again at the Best, Ekstein and Tillyard texts. Can you find any examples of the kinds of transformations that White details?

Finally, in the light of White's points, consider the following extracts. The first is from Christopher Hill's *The Century of Revolution 1603–1714* (1961). Hill claims in his introductory chapter that 'History is not a narrative of events. The historian's difficult task is to explain what happened' (1):

> Queen Elizabeth died on 24th March 1603, and James VI of Scotland succeeded without opposition. An alleged plot to put Arabella Stuart on the throne, for which Lord Cobham was executed and Sir Walter Raleigh imprisoned, was widely suspected to have been manufactured, or at least grossly exaggerated, by Sir Robert Cecil to strengthen his own position. Cecil, later Earl of Salisbury, son of Elizabeth's great minister, Burghley, had been largely responsible for James' peaceful succession, and the King retained him as Secretary, advancing him to the office of Lord Treasurer in 1608.
>
> (Hill 1961: 9)

The second extract is from George Eliot's novel *Middlemarch* (1872):

> When George the Fourth was still reigning over the privacies of Windsor, when the Duke of Wellington was Prime Minister, and Mr Vincey was mayor of the old corporation in Middlemarch, Mrs Casaubon, born Dorothea Brooke, had taken her wedding journey to Rome. In those days the world in general was more ignorant of good and evil by forty years

than it is at present. Travellers did not often carry full information on Christian art either in their heads or in their pockets; and even the most brilliant English critic of the day mistook the flower-flushed tomb of the ascended Virgin for an ornamental vase due to the printer's fancy. Romanticism, which has helped to fill some dullblanks with love and knowledge, had not yet penetrated the times with its leaven and entered into everybody's food; it was fermenting still as a distinguishable vigorous enthusiasm in certain long-haired German artists at Rome, and the youth of other nations who worked or idled near them were sometimes caught in the spreading movement.

(Eliot 1965: 219)

viii) Find examples of inaugural, terminating and transitional motifs. What are the fundamental differences between the text when looked at in this way?

ix) Is irony possible in historical discourse (irony = 'simulated ignorance')?

2 Literary history

Traditionally, literary works have been arranged chronologically on literature courses. A typical course might begin with, say Anglo-Saxon literature (roughly AD 650–1100), or Chaucer (fourteenth century) and end with something 'modern', such as T.S. Eliot. Literature is then seen as not merely an indiscriminate collection of texts in arbitrary relation with each other, but a series of moments, or sequences, which together form a narrative which is coherent and plausible. Nineteenth-century literary histories were grand narratives with major characters, plots, minor figures, progression, linearity, action and reaction. Literary history was a teleological genre (that is, had a final course).

Although the increasingly modular character of many Literature, English, or Cultural Studies courses today has offset the dominance of the chronological and historical model, such a model is still both influential and difficult to escape. The consequences of the discipline's fierce debates about its own *raison d'être* during the past twenty years have ensured a mistrust of any simple model of literary history or related pedagogical practice. But the selection and organisation of texts into coherent groups which unfold in time and have internal cohesion is a basic, motivating force. To label something as 'Romantic' is to give it identity, even if that identity is erroneous and based on the suppression of other identities. To see that Romantic period in terms of its relation to the 'Augustan' is to posit an historical, causal and often generic relation. The similarity of texts and writers can be seen as the result of heterogeneous literary forces provoking action and reaction. Although we may posit literary periods which have a multi-generic character ('the literature of the 1790s'), the focus is often narrower, and we see Romantic poetry in relation to Augustan poetry, rather than to Augustan prose (although Augustan prose might be used for other literary-historical purposes). Literary history is an immanent or intrinsic history: although it sometimes does acknowledge the 'other' history, it need not do so, and its borrowings are eclectic. As literary studies carved out its own distinctive space in the 1930s and 1940s, it came to be seen, particularly according to the Russian formalists, as working according to its own internal laws. It was not simply an adjunct to social studies, or history, but had its own rules. These rules were internal and formal, and they were added to the narrative rules of the nineteenth-century literary history-makers. An example is given in the contents page dicussed below. The formalists denied that literary laws and literary developments could be explained only by reference to things external to literature itself. We tend now to think of 'literature' and 'history' as a binarism; the move to see one in terms of the other is a secondary impulse. The term 'literary history' makes history, in the sense of external events, subservient to literature: the *extrinsic* is subsumed within the *intrinsic*.

CONTENTS

104

Consider this contents page from Legouis and Cazamian's *A History of English Literature* (1964). The authors begin, as we suggested earlier, with Anglo-Saxon literature, and they conclude with 'Years of Strain 1914–58'. You will notice that the chronology is organised around two or three supposedly distinct literary periods, in particular the 'Renascence' and the Romantic period. Years immediately before or after are still seen in relation to the dominant period. The Renascence is therefore prefigured by 'The Preparation for the Renascence' and followed by 'The End of the Renascence'. Similarly, the Romantic period is prefigured by the 'Pre-Romantic Period'. As major periods become increasingly difficult for the authors to locate in the nineteenth and twentieth centuries, a thematic approach is preferred, with the period 1832–75 characterised as 'The Search for Balance', and the period 1875–1914 as 'Years of Strain'. Sometimes in chronological studies of literature, or period-based analyses, a single literary figure dominates. Boris Ford's well-known guides to English Literature are characterised largely in terms of dominant, exemplifying writers: *From Donne to Marvell*; *The Age of Shakespeare*; *From Dickens to Hardy*. The age itself is given over to Shakespeare: all other writers, of whatever genre, are seen as subservient. But whether the approach to chronology and literary history is thematic, author-centred, genre-centred or period-centred, the dominant impulse remains the same: to homogenise the past. This notion of the homogenising impulse is central to our discussion not only of literary history, but of the whole area of literary-historical relations.

Literary histories perform a number of functions. We will consider the organisation of literary texts in the light of these possible functions:

To focus on the literature of the past.
To select the texts and authors which can be discussed.
To arrange authors and texts into groups based on varied criteria.
To construct a narrative of literature.
To bring points in the past to bear on other points in the past and
    on the present.

To evaluate texts through the construction of a coherent narrative.
To account for the development and character of literary texts by
relating them to their historical context.

In the light of the points set out above, consider the following extract from G.H. Mair's *English Literature 1450–1900* (1911).
The author is discussing Spenser's *The Fairie Queene:*

Its reception in England and at the Court was enthusiastic.
Men and women read it eagerly and longed for the next
section as a later generation longed for the next section of
Pickwick. They really liked it, really loved the intricacy and
luxuriousness of it, the heavy exotic language, the thickly
painted descriptions, the languorous melody of the verse.
Mainly, perhaps, that was so because they were all either
in wish or in deed poets themselves. Spenser had always been
'the poets' poet'. Milton loved him; so did Dryden, who said
that Milton confessed to him that Spenser was 'his original',
a statement which has been pronounced incredible, but is, in
truth, perfectly comprehensible, and most likely true. Pope
admired him; Keats learned from him the best part of his
music. We can trace the echoes of him in W.B. Yeats. What is
it that gives him this hold on his peers? Well, in the first place
his defects do not detract from his purely poetic qualities.
The story is impossibly told, but that will only worry those
who are looking for a story. The allegory is hopelessly
difficult; but as Hazlitt said 'the allegory will not bite
you'; you can let it alone. The crudeness and bigotry of
Spenser's dealings with Catholicism, which are ridiculous
when he pictures the monster Error vomiting books and
pamphlets, and disgusting when he draws Mary Queen of
Scots, do not hinder the pleasure for those who read him for
his language and his art. He is great for other reasons than
these. First because of the extraordinary smoothness and
melody of his verse and the richness of his language – a
golden diction which he drew from every source . . . Second
because of the profusion of his imagery and the extraordi-

narily keen sense for beauty and sweetness that went into its making. In an age of golden language and gallant imagery his was the most golden and the most gallant. And the language of poetry in England is richer and more varied than that in any other country in Europe today, because of what he did.

(Mair 1969: 26–7)

In this extract we see the subordination of the historical to the aesthetic, the primacy of form over content. There are speculations on the layman's reception of *The Faerie Queene* as well as its courtly reception, and a lineage is constructed whereby Spenser is seen to be reborn in poets through to W.B. Yeats. Spenser's defects are both historical and related to the content of his work, and these are set in opposition to his 'purely poetic qualities'. Thus 'crudeness and bigotry' are not as relevant to an appreciation of Spenser as are his 'keen sense for beauty and sweetness'. Spenser's linguistic innovation is the most important aspect of this literary moment.

i) What, implicitly, is Mair's view of the function of literature?
ii) Is it possible to reconcile the appreciation of Spenser's 'purely poetic qualities' with a political reading of *The Faerie Queene*?

Mair's primary view of the function of literature seems to be that it should present fundamentally an aesthetic, formal experience. The content of the experience – the content of the literary texts themselves – is not so important. Literature and linguistic innovation are natural, intimate relatives. It might be argued that the 'appreciation of poetic qualities' and the reading of a text in terms of its ideology and politics are fundamentally differerent activities, and are therefore representations of different disciplines. To focus on the aesthetic, however, is not necessarily to 'appreciate'. Consideration of a text's formal features can also lead to the bypassing of explicit evaluation. For example, other cultural artefacts which display a high degree of cohesion and semantic ingenuity, such as certain advertisements, can be treated formally without explicit references to the texts' aesthetic value. A literary history, however, necessarily is the expression of evaluation, even if the criteria for such evaluation are not stated explicitly. The 'poetic qualities' of a text constitute only one possible aspect of that text.

3 Literary classifications

When we attempt to classify literary texts we put into motion a process that is not only naturally inclusive and homogeneous, but also exclusive and heterogeneous. From the multiplicity of writings we must first designate to the selected the title *literary*. These texts, authors, styles and periods must then be grouped in manageable sets which can be characterised, named, compared and labelled. Of course the process is not so easy or so cynically done, but the fundamental impulses remain: to group what is perceived similar, to exclude what does not fit the chosen paradigm, to neutralise the deviant. Classifications are themselves organising principles with culturally determined, often hidden, agendas. As we shall see, the classifier is not a neutral commentator, but someone entangled in the politics of literary reception.

The notion of a literary period, or indeed historical period, is a necessary fiction. Unless we can envisage or construct discrete events we cannot, paradoxically, imagine a narrative. A narrative is not an indiscriminate and unmarked flow of time: it is a selection of discrete elements juxtaposed to form a whole. But if we join single elements to form that whole, we must be able to isolate those elements, and if we can isolate them, we can only do so by virtue of seeing their part in the whole narrative. A fundamental narrative paradox is exposed. If we isolate we not only include, we exclude what is, by implication, also isolated. Before we consider the criteria by which literary classifications are made, look at the following:

Jacobean drama
Writing in the age of Shakespeare

Georgian poetry
Romantic poetry
Augustan poetry
Novels of World War Two
Feminist poetry
War poetry
Early Victorian realists
Modernist novels
The Age of Reason

i) Separate the headings into varieties of texts.

ii) Can you suggest alternatives to traditional classifications?

iii) Consider whether they are anything other than convenient ways of homogenising heterogeneous material. Do they suggest a particular point of view?

iv) Are some more generic, others more historical?

The perception of material in terms of decades is a simple way of homogenising the past. History rarely fits neatly into these spans. An essentially inchoate history is shaped into acceptable patterns. For example, the popular image of the 1960s is more relevant to the years 1963–73, particularly in Britain. The 1980s have come to be seen as a homogeneous decade with Margaret Thatcher's premiership spanning the years 1979–91 (Ronald Reagan's time at the White House overlapping for a large part), but the question remains as to whether Thatcher's terms as premier have any relevance to literary studies, or indeed to any other aspect of culture and society. Because they were years of radical policy-making, one would be justified in thinking that they stand out in some way, but their relation to literary studies is not clear. If we were to propose a course entitled 'Novels of the Thatcher Era', what kinds of novels do you think would be included, and what kinds of philosophy might the course presuppose? Would any novel written in the period (or published?) June 1979–November 1991 be relevant? Or would novels which typify Thatcherism be more apposite (novels such as Martin Amis' *Money*). Or perhaps those which stand against it? Even if we were to merely characterise the course as 'literature from 1979 to 1991', we would presuppose first that the years themselves were significant in some way, and second that we know what 'literature' is.

When we classify texts we not only indicate the assumed similarities between them, but also suppress any differences, for a group of texts cannot be similar at every level and point. When we posit a particular period we implicitly stipulate two analogical axes. First, to name a period is to see it in terms of some development from another period, otherwise that period itself would not be discrete. Second, we imply that that diachronic movement and development has actually ceased during the period in question, so the span becomes a synchronic, discrete event. The before and after give rise to the period in question, but those very spans must be suppressed in order for the period to function.

David Perkins makes the following points about classifications:

> We might argue . . . that we can classify texts anyway we like, since the label will not change our actual experience of reading. In this last point I am sure he [Croce, a critic discussed earlier by Perkins] is wrong, for a classification brings with it a context of other works. If we change the context, we activate a different system of expectations, of hermeneutic fore meanings . . . If 'Lycidas' and 'Adonais' are interconnected as pastoral elegies, this genre classification calls attention to certain formal features of the poems and not to their very unlike *Weltanschauungen* [philosophical survey of the world as a whole]. Thus a classification is also an orientation, an act of criticism.
>
> (Perkins 1992: 62)

In order to classify according to genre, we must be able to locate and describe aspects of similarity. It is convenient to see this similarity as based on four possible distinctions:

Similarity between the attitudes of authors – producing similarity of texts
Similar effects on the reader
Similarity as verbal constructs
Similarity of imaginative worlds expressed or evoked by the constructs

These criteria are based on the work of M.H. Abrams, particularly *The Mirror and the Lamp* (1952), and Paul Hernadi's *Beyond Genre* (1972). They are characterised, respectively, as:

Expressive
Pragmatic
Structural
Mimetic

v) Take any 'period' that you have studied. Try to break up the texts concerned into different genres and sub-genres. For example, the lyric poem functions as a genre, but the confessional poem might be considered a sub-genre of lyric, provided it expresses one of the relationships of similarity shown above.

vi) Now try to gather the texts of a genre or sub-genre, but this time move across historical boundaries (for example, the 'novel of manners').

4 New Historicism

We have already seen the kind of relationship between history and literature as shown by critics and historians such as Tillyard and Best. But the formalisms which dominated the middle part of the century marginalised the problem of history, and it was not until the publication of Stephen Greenblatt's *Renaissance Self-Fashioning* (1980) that a full-blown return to some kind of historicism was acknowledged. This later manifestation is quite different from its homogenising ancestor, although the differences between the two methodologies are far from clear. Influenced by the ideas of Michel Foucault (although we should not conflate the two), the 'New Historicists', so-called by Greenblatt himself, see history not in terms of discrete episodes forming an homogeneous whole, but as fractured, subjective, and above all *textual*. Where Tillyard proposed a cohesive and coherent world view as a context for literary histories, Foucault sees literature as just another discourse manipulated through and by a culture's power struggles. Foucault's historicist perspective is one based on a *suspicion* of truth rather than a *presumption* of truth. Thus any historical representation is not unified, truthful and coherent, but contingent, unstable and partial. That they are also textual brings them closer to another group of texts: those traditionally labelled 'literary'. Literature and history are therefore no longer in binary opposition.

Healy (1992) suggests that formalist approaches to the Renaissance have traditionally dominated partly because of the importance attached to the lyric poem. We should consider why such a focus on the lyric should necessarily lead to a formalism. Before we demonstrate and discuss the language and methodologies of New Historicism we shall consider some functions of lyric poetry. Here is Shakespeare's sonnet 29:

> When in disgrace with Fortune and mens eyes,
> I all alone beweepe my outcast state,
> And trouble deafe heaven with my bootlesse cries,
> And looke upon my selfe and curse my fate.
> Wishing me like to one more rich in hope,
> Featured like him, like him with friends possest,
> Desiring this mans art, and that mans scope,
> With what I most injoy contented least,
> Yet in these thoughts my selfe almost despising,
> Haplye I thinke on thee, and then my state,
> (Like to the Larke at breake of day arising)
> From sullen earth sings himns at Heavens gate,

Fot thy sweet love remembred such welth brings,
That then I skorne to change my state with Kings.
(Shakespeare, quoted in Barrell 1988: 20–1)

This is a version of the sonnet which is in the 1609 quarto (some typographical modernising has been made) and is discussed at length in John Barrell's *Poetry, Language and Politics* (1988). We shall return to Barrell's reading, but first we should consider how we might read such a poem. The poem is, for us, largely decontextualised, although the appendage of the author's name, 'Shakespeare', does provide some contextual framework. The poem is highly formal, it is a sonnet, and the genre also provides some framework for interpretation. As in many lyric poems, names and the antecedents or full forms of pronouns are not given. The 'I' is never formally identified, the 'him' is pointed to but never made explicit, the 'thee' is also not identified. This pronominal, deictic activity is typical of much lyric poetry (see Chapter 1) and enables readers to interpret the protagonists as non-specific. That is, although they clearly refer to definite individuals, those individuals can never be pinned down from evidence within the poem itself. If we are to attach names to the pronouns, for instance, we need a context whereby they can be realised into their full forms. The difficulties and ambiguities concerning the precise addressee in the sonnets substantiates this. It is much easier to read the pronouns, and hence the poem as a whole as specific, but also at the same time *generalised*, experience. The critic need not, therefore, look outside the poem in order to interpret it. Paradoxically, the genre which most evidently points beyond itself gives rise to the most formalistic and decontextualised literary theory. Barrell convincingly demonstrates how critics have consistently edited Shakespeare's texts, for instance, on the basis of the implicit insistence on formalist methodologies. A tradition of Shakespearean scholarship is based on the elevation of Shakespeare beyond the historical and merely contingent (his works are 'timeless'). Sonnet 29, therefore, can very simply be read as a poem addressed to an anonymous loved one. It is, therefore, 'about' the transcending and transmogrifying power of love. 'Love'

113

is its timeless concern. However, if we let, for instance, the pronouns 'I' and 'you' refer not to an unspecified poetic persona and a loved one respectively, but to historically determined, material beings who lived and operated in a world with specific economic and social conditions, a rather different picture may be seen to emerge.

Here is Barrell's reading of the sonnet. At this point he is first discussing Steven Booth's 1977 edition of the sonnets. In that edition, lines 10–12 are rendered as:

> . . . and then my state,
> Like to the Lark at break of day arising
> From sullen earth, sings hymns at heaven's gate.

Barrell's preferred quarto version is:

> . . . and then my state
> (Like to the Larke at breake of daye arising)
> From sullen earth sings himns at Heavens gate.

The difference here is syntactic. In Booth's version both 'Lark' and 'my state' sing hymns at Heaven's gate. In the quarto version only 'my state' sings, having arisen 'from sullen earth'. 'My state' is subject, 'from sullen earth' is an adjunct, 'sings' is the main verb, and 'at Heavens gate' in another adjunct (preposition-headed). Barrell explains:

> I have claimed that much of the pathos of the poem derives from the narrator's simultaneous desire and inability to escape from the limiting conditions of earth and perhaps of discourse; and if the narrator's state can do all that the lark can do, that source of meaning and pathos is abolished. But that argument has no status, as we shall see, in relation to a text in which the meanings it presupposes have been at best concealed, at worst erased.
>
> And it is by this change of punctuation that they are concealed. For if both lark and state arise from sullen earth to heaven's gate, we have to find a meaning for 'state' which is compatible with the notion that it can be successfully

elevated above the earth – that it can change its position as
the narrator's mood, or the content of his mind, changes.
And there is of course such a meaning available, by which
'state' would mean not social condition, which must be
changed by social action; not economic condition, which
must be changed by material means – not in short something
akin to 'estate', but 'state of mind'.

(Barrell 1988: 34–5)

Barrell's thesis is that Shakespeare has been continually read and
edited according to formalist and humanistic principles. In the
case of sonnet 29, the very punctuation has been rendered to
support this reading. All material concerns are 'overread' as being
about the rather more abstract element, the mind.

Barrell's reading of the sonnet is historicist because it seeks
to locate the text in its contingent discursive context and to undo
traditional, humanist readings. The transient, the particular and
the marginal are favoured over the timeless, the general and the
central, and again this reversal of traditional thinking typifies
historicism. However, we do not wish to suggest that historicism
is programmatic or that all historicists agree on methodologies.
There is disagreement, for instance, on the extent to which
historicism is overtly political; and there is dispute as to whether
the use of marginal material, such as the anecdote, favoured by
some historicist followers of Greenblatt, is central to the practice
of historicism.

Despite such disagreements, H. Aram Veeser (1989) finds five
key assumptions which 'bind together the avowed practitioners of
historicism':

1. that every expressive act is embedded in a network of
material practices;
2. that every act of unmasking, critique, and opposition uses
the tools it condemns and risks falling prey to the practice it
exposes;
3. that literary and non-literary texts circulate inseparably;
4. that no discourse, imaginative or archival, gives access to
unchanging truths nor expresses inalterable human nature;

115

> 5. finally, . . . that a critical method and language adequate to describe culture under capitalism participate in the economy they describe.
>
> (Veeser 1989: xi)

The first point is close to Marxist thinking in that literature, as an 'expressive act', is seen as part of the material base, rather than a transcendent, aesthetic superstructure. The second point moves us closer to deconstructive practice and theory (Chapter 5). To criticise, and to historicise, is to use the same language (one example of the historian's 'tools') as that which is being criticised. An example of this might be the historian's or critic's attempt to see history or literature as fractured and discontinuous. To express this discontinuity and fragmentation in a coherent, homogenising text is to produce a narrative the content of which is completely at odds with its form. The barrier between the literary and the non-literary is broken down in Veeser's third point. Further, the focus is on the 'circulation' of texts in, presumably, socio-cultural and socio-economic contexts. Contrary to traditional views of both literature and philosophy, no writing transcends the contingent. By implication all texts are caught in the here-and-now of their production. The final point has a similar self-reflexive twist to Veeser's second point. The historian/critic cannot escape the determinants of his or her own history under capitalism.

5 Foucault and history

Foucault attempts to discover the 'rules' of a particular discourse period, and then relate them to the study of knowledge and power. His enterprise is essentially to historicise discourse and to textualise history. Foucault refuses to see history in terms of linearity and development. Rather, he sees it in terms of a kind of synchronic power struggle. Power for Foucault is not necessarily a repressive, tyrannical thing; it is a generative, productive force. Power is that which binds together the disparate forces of a society (even though that binding is illusory). No event stems from a single, coherent cause, but is the product of a vast network of signification and 'power'. This is evident in his volume *Discipline and Punish* (1979).

Here are two extracts from 'Nietzsche, Genealogy, History'. In the first he discusses, approvingly, Nietzsche's vision of historical processes:

> The final trait of effective history is its affirmation of knowledge as perspective. Historians take unusual pains to erase the elements in their work which reveal their grounding in a particular time and place, their preferences in a controversy – the unavoidable obstacles of their passion. Nietzsche's version of historical sense is explicit in its perspective and acknowledges its system of injustice. Its perception is slanted, being a deliberate appraisal, affirmation, or negation; it reaches the lingering and poisonous traces in order to prescribe the best antidote. It is not given to a discreet effacement before the objects it observes and does not submit itself to their processes; nor does it seek laws, since it gives equal weight to its own sight and to its objects.
>
> (Foucault 1986: 90)

We believe that feelings are immutable, but every sentiment, particularly the noblest and most disinterested, has a history. We believe in the dull constance of instinctual life and imagine that it continues to exert its force indiscriminately in the present as it did in the past. But knowledge of history easily disintegrates this unity, depicts its wavering course, locates its moments of strength and weakness, and defines its oscillating reign. It easily seizes the slow elaboration of instincts and those movements where, in turning upon themselves, they relentlessly set about their self-destruction. We believe, in any event, that the body obeys the exclusive laws of physiology and that it escapes the influence of history, but this too is false. The body is moulded by a great many distinct regimes; it is broken down by the rhythms of work, rest, and holidays; it is poisoned by food or values,

117

through eating habits or moral laws; it constructs resistances. 'Effective' history differs from traditional history in being without constants. Nothing in man – not even his body – is sufficiently stable to serve as the basis for self-recognition or for understanding other men. The traditional devices for constructing a comprehensive view of history and for retracing the past as a patient and continuous development must be systematically dismantled. Necessarily, we must dismiss those tendencies that encourage the consoling play of recognitions. Knowledge, even under the banner of history, does not depend on 'rediscovery', and it emphatically excludes the 'rediscovery of ourselves'. History becomes 'effective' to the degree that it introduces discontinuity into our very being – as it divides our emotions, dramatises our instincts, multiplies our body and sets it against itself. 'Effective' history deprives the self of the reassuring stability of life and nature, and it will not permit itself to be transported by a voiceless obstinacy toward a millennial ending. It will uproot its traditional foundations and relentlessly disrupt its pretended continuity. This is because knowledge is not made for understanding: it is made for cutting.

(Foucault 1986: 87–8)

These are complex extracts, and you may wonder about their precise relation to literary criticism. But as we have seen, history and the history of ideas are crucially linked to the reading and the production of the literary text, a text which is the expression of discursive practices which are historically and materially determined.

> i) What is Foucault's view of historical continuity?
>
> ii) What is 'knowledge' for Foucault?
>
> iii) What is the relationship between the individual self, 'society' and history?
>
> iv) How might the above ideas be related to the study of literature?

v) How might Foucault's work be used in the discussion and analysis of an individual text?

Historical continuity is for Foucault paradoxically an historical discontinuity. It celebrates the fragmentation of the self, and this self is replicated through historical processes. There is no move *towards* the fact, or event, but only a play of historical *cuts* and misrecognitions. Knowledge is not a knowledge of self, or of historical processes, or of facts: it is a tool which cuts through the unifying and instinctual urges of human behaviour. The individual is subject to various bodily, social and psychic oppressions, which seem to suggest a freedom from determinate history but are in fact symptoms of it.

6 Historicism, anthropology, thick description

We have seen that the New Historicists eschew the so-called objectivity of historical and scientific discourses. They see 'facts' as being interpretative and largely textual, and aim to show that society is discontinuous and arbitrary. Some of these ideas are close to the kind of anthropological methodology put forward by Clifford Geertz. Geertz believes that man is 'an animal suspended in webs of significance he himself has spun'. The activity of the anthropologist is ultimately like that of the literary critic: to describe and participate in that significance. In order to understand this link between anthropology and literary criticism we need to look at Geertz's *The Interpretation of Cultures* (1973). In the following quotation he is summarising Ryle's discussion of 'thick description'. The point of analysis and thick description, as Geertz notes, is 'sorting out the structures of signification' and determining their social ground and import.

> Doing ethnography [the description of races] is therefore like trying to read (in the sense of 'construct a reading of') a manuscript – foreign, faded, full of ellipses, incoherencies, suspicious emendations, and tendentious commentaries, but

written not in conventionalised graphs of sound but in transient examples of shaped behaviour.

(Geertz 1973: 10)

We have already seen examples of 'suspicious emendations' and 'tendentious commentar[y]' in the readings of Shakespeare's sonnet (see page 113). The technique of 'thick description' has affinities with deconstructive rhetorical practice inasmuch as it implicitly contains an admission of the complicity of language (and partly the failure of language) in any notion of 'truth'. It also privileges the marginal over the supposedly 'central' (see Chapter 5). Historical anecdotes are privileged over traditional 'facts' and read in such a way as to reveal the ideologies, motivations and behaviours of a culture or society. In the following extract from Geertz, the author is summarising his methodology, having concluded a lengthy discussion on Balinese cockfights. He draws parallels with textual and literary study:

> If one takes the cockfight, or any other collectively sustained symbolic structure, as a means of 'saying something of something' . . . , then one is faced with a problem not in social mechanics but social semantics. For the anthropologist, whose concern is with formulating sociological principles, not with promoting or appreciating cockfights, the question is, what does one learn about such principles from examining culture as an assemblage of texts?
>
> . . . to treat the cockfight as a text is to bring out a feature of it (in my opinion, the central feature of it) that treating it as a rite or pastime, the two most obvious alternatives, would tend to obscure: its use of emotion for cognitive ends. What the cockfight says it says in a vocabulary of sentiment – the thrill of risk, the despair of loss, the pleasure of triumph . . . Attending cockfights and participating in them is, for the Balinese, a kind of sentimental education. What he learns there is what his culture's ethos and his private sensibility (or, anyway, certain aspects of them) look like when spelled out externally in a collective text; that the two are near enough alike to be articulated in

the symbolics of a single such text; and – the disquieting part – that the text in which this revelation is accomplished consists of a chicken hacking another mindlessly to bits.

. . . If . . . we go to see *Macbeth* to learn what a man feels like after he has gained a kingdom and lost his soul, Balinese go to cockfights to find out what a man, usually composed, aloof, almost obsessively self-absorbed, a kind of moral autocosm, feels like when, attacked, tormented, challenged, insulted, and driven in result to the extremes of fury, he has totally triumphed or been brought totally low.

Enacted and re-enacted, so far without end, the cockfight enables the Balinese, as, read and re-read, *Macbeth* enables us, to see a dimension of his own subjectivity. As he watches fight after fight, with the active watching of an owner and a bettor (for cockfighting has no more interest as a pure spectator sport than does croquet or dog racing), he grows familiar with it and what it has to say to him, much as the attentive listener to string quartets or the absorbed viewer of still life grows slowly more familiar with them in a way which opens his subjectivity to himself.

The culture of a people is an ensemble of texts, themselves ensembles, which the anthropologist strains to read over the shoulders of those to whom they properly belong.

(Geertz 1973: 448–52)

Geertz states that his methodology is to treat the cockfight, and other social phenomena, as text because it is uses 'emotion for cognitive ends'. That is to say, the emotion expressed or engendered by the cockfight has direct links with the way the world is perceived by the protagonists. The methodology has explicit linguistic analogues, for the anthropologist is dealing with 'social semantics', the meanings that occur and proliferate in a given society. The meanings occur through actions and gestures, such as the cockfight, but these are similar to the reception of a literary or dramatic text such as *Macbeth*. The play and the cockfight are the particular culture's ways of seeing itself and are cathartic in that they open the subjectivity of that culture. The anthropologist reads the society, which is fundamentally textual, as an intimate observer. Just as lyric poetry is poetry not heard but *overheard*, the significance of the cockfight, or of *Macbeth*, is 'overread'. Thus the anthropologist is at once an outsider but seemingly privvy to gestures of significance.

> i) Consider the material on structuralist methodologies in Chapter 2. What similarities do you find? What essential differences are there between Geertz' 'social semantics' and, say, Barthes' 'grammar of the text'?
> ii) Make a list of the similarities, potential or otherwise, between the methodology of Geertz's 'social semantics' and the practice of literary criticism.

In an essay in Veeser's *The New Historicism* (1989), Stephen Greenblatt discusses the role of what might traditionally be considered peripheral material in literary and historical studies:

> Literary criticism has a familiar set of terms for the relationship between a work of art and the historical events to which it refers: we speak of allusion, symbolization, allegorization, representation, and above all mimesis. Each of all these terms has a rich history and is virtually indispensable, and yet they all seem curiously inadequate . . . And their inadequacy extends to aspects not only of contemporary culture but of the culture of the past. We need to develop terms to describe the ways in which material – here official documents, private papers, newspaper clippings, and so forth – is transferred from one discursive sphere to another and becomes aesthetic property. It would, I think, be a mistake to regard this process as uni-directional – from social discourse to aesthetic discourse – not only because the aesthetic discourse . . . is so entirely bound up with capitalist ventures

but because social discourse is already charged with aesthetic energies.

(Greenblatt 1989: 11)

Here we see the familiar historicist breaking down of the barriers between literary and non-literary discourse and between the social and the aesthetic. If the social and the aesthetic circulate together, then that which might be considered peripheral to one discourse may be foregrounded to show a particular relation or undo a text's discursive logic. If the social and the aesthetic are continually separated, their own internal logics are less likely to be questioned. That which is the 'aesthetic', however, can be read against the significance of that which would be considered the 'social'. An anecdote, a peripheral discourse element (somehow not 'serious'), can be read against the body of the aesthetic. Stephen Greenblatt in an essay entitled 'Fiction and Friction' recounts an anecdote about a servant in Rouen, Marie le Marcis, who in 1601 revealed that she was a man. A doctor is eventually called upon to decide Marie's sex and in the course of an examination by the 'friction' of his touch, causes the servant to ejaculate. He thus pronounces Marie a man. Greenblatt seizes upon this piece of medical orthodoxy and reads it 'against' Shakespeare's *Twelfth Night*. For Greenblatt, the doctor's erotic 'friction' is represented by Shakespeare in the dialogue between Viola and the Clown (Act Three):

CLOWN: You have said, sir. To see this age! A sentence is but a chev'ril glove to a good wit. How quickly the wrong side may be turned outward!
VIOLA: Nay, that's certain. They that dally nicely with words may quickly make them wanton.
CLOWN: I would therefore my sister had no name, sir.
VIOLA: Why, man?
CLOWN: Why sir, her name's a word, and to dally with that word might make my sister wanton.

(3.1.11–20)

Greenblatt states:

at moments the plays seem to imply that erotic friction

> *originates* in the wantonness of language, and thus that the body itself is a tissue of metaphors or, conversely, that language is perfectly 'embodied'.
>
> (Greenblatt 1988: 89)

An anecdote is enlisted to reveal the interrelation of discursive practices and the relation of language to the body that is the site of human subjectivity, power and ambiguity.

7 The ideologies of texts

Although there is much of his work devoted to the arts in general, Marx had no developed theory of literature to offer. Yet Marxist literary criticism and theory are the most coherent, substantial and cogent developments of the twentieth century. Marxism offers a coherent, adaptive theoretical base for critical analysis; yet it has never been part of mainstream criticism in Britain or the United States. Marxism is itself part of the history it seeks to understand and act in: the collapse of the Eastern Bloc can be readily seen in Marxist terms. All Marxist literary theory assumes that texts are products of a particular society and a particular context. With these apparently simple, yet very often neglected, aspects of literary criticism, it is easy to become a 'vulgar' Marxist – crudely reading a text according to certain pre-ordained strategies. The fundamental Marxist postulate is that the economic base of a society determines just about everything with political meaning; that is to say, ideology, institutions and everything that goes to make up the 'superstructure'. Certainly for the Marxist critic, terms like 'the aesthetic' and 'literature' are not absolutes but historically specific concepts and materials. With Marxism we never forget that 'literature' and texts are the products of a specific class and are materially produced at points in history, being determined by factors other than divine or poetic grace.

The kinds of things likely to be discussed under the headings of 'base' or 'infrastructure' offer a corrective to the view that art comes from and is determined by only aesthetic considerations.

Here are some aspects of the 'base', which is fundamentally economic:

What is produced, made or manufactured
Who controls the production
Where things are produced, made or manufactured
How products are circulated and distributed
What results from the circulation and production

An attempt to describe a history of Marxism and Marxist criticism is beyond the scope of this book. Rather, we shall look at the work of selected Marxist critics, beginning with Georg Lukàcs. Lukàcs is the first major Marxist critic, although vilified in some Marxist circles now for his supposedly conservative views. But Lukàcs is Marxist because he stresses the material structure of society and the historical nature of the aesthetic. First, however, consider the following extract from Flaubert's *Madame Bovary* (1857):

> The famous show did indeed arrive. From early morning on the great day the village folk had been standing at their doors discussing the preparations. The façade of the Town Hall was festooned with ivy, a marquee had been erected in one of the meadows, and in the middle of the market-place, opposite the church, stood a cannon that was to announce the arrival of the Prefect and salute the successful competitors. The militia from Buchy – there was none at Yonville – had come to augment the fire-brigade, captained by Binet. He wore an even higher collar than usual today; and, buttoned tight into his uniform, the upper part of his body was so stiff and motionless that it seemed as if all the life in him had descended to his legs, which rose and fell with wooden exactitude as he marked time. A certain rivalry existed between the tax-collector and the colonel of the militia, and to display their talents they drilled their men separately. Red epaulettes and black breastplates crossed and recrossed alternately, staring off again and again, never

ending. Never has there been such a parade! A number of citizens had washed their houses overnight; tricolours hung from open windows; all the inns were full. In the fine weather, starched bonnets, gold crosses and coloured neckerchiefs stood out dazzling as snow, glittering in the bright sunshine, relieving with their scattered motley the sombre monotony of the frock-coats and blue smocks. The farmers' wives from the surrounding district had tucked their dresses up, to avoid getting them splashed, with thick pins which they removed on dismounting. Their menfolk were concerned rather with their hats, covering them with their pocket-handkerchiefs, one corner of which they held between their teeth.

(Flaubert 1982: 144–5)

Although this is an abstracted piece, Lukàcs' comments are easy to pick up. Before we look at Lukàcs' response, however:

i) Would you consider the above extract to be 'realistic' writing?

ii) Whatever you answer to i), what criteria were implicit in your assessment? What, for you, constitutes 'realism' in fiction?

Here is Lukàcs on the passage and on *Madame Bovary* in general:

The description of the agricultural fair and of the awarding of prizes to the famers in Flaubert's *Madame Bovary* is among the most celebrated achievements of description in modern realism. But Flaubert presents only a 'setting'. For him the fair is merely background for the decisive love scene between Rudolphe and Emma Bovary. The setting is incidental, merely 'setting'. Flaubert underscores its incidental character; by interweaving and counterposing official speeches with fragments of love dialogue, he offers an ironic juxtaposition of the public and private banality of the petty bourgeoisie, accomplishing this parallel with consistency and artistry.

. . . But there remains an unresolved contradiction; this incidental setting, this accidental occasion for a love scene, is simultaneously an important event in the world of the novel; the minute description of this setting is absolutely essential to Flaubert's purpose, that is, to the comprehensive exposition of the social milieu. The ironic juxtaposition does not exhaust the significance of the description. The 'setting' has an independent existence as an element in the representation of the environment Flaubert is describing. They become dabs of colour in a painting which rises above a lifeless level only insofar as it is elevated to an ironic symbol of philistinism. The painting assumes an importance which does not arise out of the subjective importance of the events, to which it is scarcely related, but from the artifice in the formal stylization.

(Lukàcs 1978: 114–15)

iii) If Flaubert offers an 'ironic juxtaposition of the public and private banality of the petty bourgeoisie', how does the work still disappoint Lukàcs, from a Marxist point of view?

iv) What does Lukàcs mean by a) the subjective importance of events and b) the artifice of formal stylisation?

v) At first reading, Lukàcs' criticisms may seem to be purely aesthetic or formal, but can you think of a way in which they might be socio-historical? What possible link could there be between this seeming formalism and Marxist analysis?

vi) Is Lukàcs attacking realism, modernism or any other literary mode?

A familiar key term in Marxist analysis is *ideology*. This term is so much used and misused that it is worthwhile at this point providing some definitions. The following come from Raymond Williams' *Keywords* (1972):

Ideology is . . . abstract and false thought, in a sense directly related to the original conservative use, but with alternative knowledge of real material conditions and relationships – differently stated.

Thus there is now a 'proletarian ideology' or 'bourgeois ideology' and so on, and *ideology* in each case is the system of ideas appropriate to that class.

But the neutral sense of ideology, which usually needs to be qualified by an adjective describing the class or social group which it represents or serves has, in fact, become common in many kinds of argument.

Meanwhile, in popular argument, ideology is still mainly used in the sense given by Napoleon. Sensible people rely on *experience* or have a *philosophy*, silly people rely on ideology. In this sense ideology. . . is mainly a term of abuse.

(Williams 1972: 128–30)

Terry Eagleton (1976a) defines ideology in the following manner:

The literary text is not the 'expression' of ideology, nor is ideology the 'expression' of social class. The text, rather, is a certain production of ideology, for which the analogy of dramatic production is in some ways appropriate. A dramatic production does not 'express', 'reflect' or 'reproduce' the dramatic text on which it is based; it 'produces' the text, transforming it into a unique and irreducible entity.

(Eagleton 1976a: 64)

The literary text . . . produces ideology (itself a production) in a way analogous to the operations of dramatic productions on a dramatic text. And just as the dramatic production's relation to its text reveals the text's internal relations to its 'world' under the form of its own constitution of them, so the literary text's relation to ideology so constitutes that ideology so as to reveal something of its relations to history.

(Eagleton 1976a: 67)

The literary text, then, does not merely relect some obvious and open ideology and betray its historical context. Indeed, contemporary Marxist thinkers do not consider history and ideology to be 'background' against which a text must be read. Francis Mulhern states:

> To explore the historicity of the text is, then, not simply to relate a frail singularity to the broad design of a period; it is also to investigate its direct social relations . . . the formations of writing and reading – and these not as 'context' or 'background' but as substantive elements of the practice itself.
>
> (Mulhern 1992: 19)

Contemporary Marxist theory is greatly influenced by the work of Louis Althusser. For Althusser, ideology is a 'system of representations' relating to material practices. This system enables individuals to realise their place in the social network. Ideology therefore is a system which offers the individual a framework of assumptions through which the self (drawing on psychoanalytic theory) is realised. Althusser's theory is applicable to the individual's appropriation of a text. The writer's ideology is expressed through gaps and omissions. As David Forgas explains:

> When we write we do not just record what we see and fail to record what lies outside our field of vision; rather, we see all the elements of reality about which we write, but our written text cannot always make the right connections between them. A text thus tends to present reality partially or incoherently, leaving gaps.
>
> (Forgas 1986: 180–81)

This idea of a structure or system of representations is fundamental in contemporary Marxism. It appears in various guises in the work of two other influential Marxist critics, Lucien Goldmann and Pierre Macherey. For Goldmann, for instance, the text:

> constitutes a collective achievement through which the individual consciousness of its creator, and achievement which

will afterwards reveal to the group what it was moving towards without knowing it.

(Goldmann 1975: 115)

Pierre Macherey is best known for his book *A Theory of Literary Production* (1978). He sees the text as a 'production' where the materials of literature and society blend, clash and are reworked. These materials are naturally beyond the author's control. 'Ideology' becomes part of the text and in the process 'undoes' it by exposing its inadequacies and contradictions. The critic looks for what the text does not say and cannot say (see Chapter 5):

> the work exists above all by its determinate absences, by what it does not say, in its relation to what it is not. Not that it can conceal anything: this meaning is not buried in its depths, masked or disguised; it is not a question of hunting it down with interpretations. It is not in the work but by its side: on its margins, at that limit where it ceases to be what it claims to be because it has reached back to the very conditions of its possibility. It is then no longer constituted by a factitious necessity, the product of a conscious or unconscious intention.
>
> To take up a vocabulary well-known to novices of philosophy, structural criticism or metaphysical criticism is only a variant of theological aesthetics. In both cases the aim is a causal explanation: a personal intention in the case of the aesthetics of creation; an abstract intention, presented in the form of an entity, in the case of structural analysis. Perhaps the time has come to elaborate a positive criticism which would deal with laws rather than causes. The critical question would then be: *In what relation to that which is other than itself is the work produced?* Positive is, as we know, also opposed to negative . . . We also know that metaphysical ideologies and positive science are not just different answers to the same question: positive science requires a different question. Indeed, the structural method is content to give a new answer to the old question

of aesthetics, just as the writers themselves have asked it. The real question is not: What is literature? . . . The question is: What kind of necessity determines the work? What is it really made from? The critical question should concern the material being used and the implements so employed.

From without, then, structure is that which dispossesses the work of its false interiority, its secret cause, revealing that basic defect without which it would not exist. At this point the treaty with linguistics and psychoanalysis takes on its full significance. The literary work is also doubly articulated: at the initial level of sequences (the fable) the themes (the forms) which establish an illusory order; this is the level of organicist aesthetic theories. At another level, the work is articulated in relation to the reality from the ground of which it emerges: not a 'natural' empirical reality, but that intricate reality in which men – both writers and readers – live, that reality which is *their ideology*. The work is made on the ground of this ideology, that tacit and original language: not to speak, reveal, translate or make explicit this language, but to make possible that absence of words without which there would be nothing to say.

(Macherey 1978: 154–5)

There are some discernible similarities to structuralism here. The text is not a product of either the conscious or unconscious intention of an author; nor is its centrality and autonomy evident. The text is always produced in relation to something other. There are, in fact, raw materials of literature which form the necessary base from which it is produced. Structure, for Macherey, reveals not unity, homogeneity and autonomy, but defect, falsity and secrecy. This in part constitutes ideology, and this ideology is in essence 'reality'.

A rather different conception of ideology is formulated by Louis Althusser. Althusser's 'ideology' is not a version of reality, but a representation of the individual's relation to society. Reality, truth and falsehood are not aspects of this ideology; rather it is an

organisation of signifying practices that make up the social subject. There is an analogy with literary texts here, or at least one
conception of literary texts. As Eagleton explains:

> One might say that ideology. . . is less a matter of proposi-
> tions than of 'pseudo-propositions'. It appears often enough
> on its grammatical surface to be referential (descriptive of
> states of affairs) while being secretly 'emotive' (expressive of
> the lived reality of human subjects) or 'conative' (directed
> towards the achievement of certain effects). If this is so, then
> it would seem that there is a kind of slipperiness or duplicity
> built into ideological language, rather of the kind that
> Immanuel Kant thought he had discovered in the nature of
> aesthetic judgements. Ideology, Althusser claims, 'expresses
> a will, a hope or nostalgia, rather than describing a reality',
> it is fundamentally a matter of fearing and denouncing,
> reverencing and reviling, all of which then sometimes gets
> coded into a discourse which looks as though it is describing
> the way things actually are.
>
> (Eagleton 1991: 19)

Ideology here is something subjective that slips into discourse and
pretends to describe reality. On a macro-level, literature itself can
be seen as an example of 'ideology'; on a micro-level, literary texts
can be seen to contain ideology in the same way that all discourse
does. Ideologies, then, may be embedded in broader ideologies: the
particular ideology of a particular text, for instance, is embedded
in the macro-ideology of 'literature'. Althusser himself does not
make this distinction between ideologies, preferring to set up the
term 'ideology' in global opposition to 'science'; but it may be
useful in the characterisation and analysis of literary texts.

Consider the relation between text and ideology in the
following extract from Elizabeth Gaskell's *North and South*
(1854–5):

> Nicholas Higgins was sitting by the fire smoking, as she went
> in. Bessy was rocking herself on the other side.
>   Nicholas took the pipe out of his mouth, and standing

up, pushed his chair towards Margaret; he leant against the chimney-piece in a lounging attitude, while she asked Bessy how she was.

'Hoo's rather down i' th' mouth in regard to spirits, but hoo's better in health. Hoo doesn't like this strike. Hoo's a deal too much set on peace and quietness at any price.'

'This is th' third strike I've seen,' said she, sighing, as if that was answer and explanation enough.

'Well, third time pays for all. See if we don't dang th' masters this time. See if they don't come, and beg us to come back at our own price. That's all. We've missed it afore time, I grant yo'; but this time we'n laid our plans desperate deep.'

'Why do you strike?' asked Margaret. 'Striking is leaving off work till you get your own rate of wages, is it not? You must not wonder at my ignorance; where I come from I never heard of a strike.'

'I wish I were there,' said Bessy, wearily. 'But it's not for me to get sick and tired o' strikes. This is the last I'll see. Before it's ended I shall be in the Great City – the Holy Jerusalem.'

'Hoo's so full of th' life to come, hoo cannot think of th' present. Now I, yo' see, am bound to do the best I can here. I think a bird i' th' hand is worth two i' th' bush. So thems the different views we take on the strike question.'

'But,' said Margaret, 'if the people struck, as you call it, where I come from, as they are mostly all field labourers, the seed would not be sown, the hay got in, the corn reaped.'

'Well?' said he. He had resumed his pipe, and put his 'well' in the form of an interrogation.

'Why,' she went on, 'what would become of the farmers?'

He puffed away. 'I reckon, they'd have either to give up their farms, or to give fair rate of wage.'

(Gaskell [1854–5] 1981: 181)

Here we have a text which explicitly deals with the plight of the proletariat and bourgeois notions of labour. The principal character, Margaret, speaks in what is presumably Received Pronunciation, for the graphology of her speech is not altered in the way that both Bessy's and Nicholas's is. The views of Margaret are implicitly sanctioned by the author, who must necessarily also present graphologically non-deviant 'speech'. Typically the rise of the organised proletariat is dramatised in what is fundamentally a bourgeois art form, the novel. The extract is a dialogue between two characters, one marked by a certain kind of speech, the other not. But it can also be seen, as can the novel as a whole, as a dialogue between the bourgeoisie and the proletariat in the nineteenth century. However, it must not be forgotten that it is not 'actual' dialogue: the ideology it portrays is a dramatisation, and that dramatisation is itself rendered through the ideology of the bourgeois art form, the novel. In the literary text, then, ideology is a multiple element, containing representations and dramatisations of further ideologies.

Glossary

aesthetic: Originating in the nineteenth century, it came to mean 'to do with taste and perception' and is closely linked with the visual arts. *Aesthetics* is now held to be the investigation into the nature of beauty.

anecdote: A short narrative of a minor or private incident.

a priori: Latin – 'from what comes before'. Now tends to be used to suggest knowledge independent of experience.

a posteriori: Latin – 'from what comes after'. The move to ascertain causes from unknown effects.

base: Essentially the economic base which underwrites cultural and social institutions.

chronology: A chronicle is a bare recording of events. A chronology is the sequencing of events.

circulation: A term used particularly in New Historicism describing the interrelationship between, for instance, literary and non-literary discourses.

context: Historical context is traditionally seen as a background of events. *Con*-text (*con* = 'with') suggests something that accompanies a text. Modern historicists have tried to break down the barrier between historical context and text.

contingent: Dependent upon something else; not certain to happen.

determinism: A word with a number of different meanings, but most often used in connexion with the pre-existence or pre-determination of events and things. Determinism is sometimes opposed to free will.

dialectical: *dialectic* is the art of formal reasoning. Dialectical is the Marxist interpretation of the interplay and relationship between opposing forces.

ethnography: The scientific description of races.

fact (of history): An historical fact not seen in terms of a larger narrative (see Carr 1961).

formalism: A critical theory and practice where form and structure are seen as the fundamental elements for aesthetic consideration. Content is subordinated to form.

hermeneutics: Essentially, the theory of interpretation. The hermeneutic circle can be seen in relation to historical discourse: we cannot understand the parts of history without an idea of the whole, and we cannot understand the whole without a knowledge of the parts. This can be applied to the reading process.

heterogeneous: Composed of parts of different kinds.

history: 'A systematic account of the origin and progress of the world'. (*Chambers Twentieth Century Dictionary*)

homogeneous: Of one and the same kind.

humanism: A system which puts human interests above all else. Sometimes used synonymously for atheism.

ideology: 'Abstract speculation' (*Chambers Twentieth Century Dictionary*). See the definitions by Raymond Williams on pages 127–8 and in *Keywords* (Williams 1976).

materialism: Often opposed to the aesthetic materialism relates to the economic base. Economic activity is primary activity. Philosophical materialism views all that exists as material or dependent upon matter for existence. Marx's dialectical materialism is opposed to monologic idealisms such as formal religions. These systems have 'one voice' (a monologic God) and are idealist in that they are ostensibly only concerned with spiritual experience.

mimetic: That which attempts to describe external reality.

objective: Belonging to that which is presented to the conscious mind. Also that which is observably verifiable.

ontology: The science and study of the essence of things.

proletarian: [Marx] The wage-earning class, without capital.

realism: David Lodge defines realism in the following manner: 'the representation of experience in a manner which approximates closely to descriptions of similar experience in non-literary texts of the same culture' (1977: 325).

superstructure: The prefix *super* means 'above'. This term is generally used with reference to cultural institutions and artefacts as well as all kinds of social phenomena, which are seen as 'above' the economic base but dependent upon it.

teleology: From the Greek *telos*, 'end or purpose', and *logos*, 'discourse'. Doctrine of final causes or interpretation of ends and purposes.

thick description: A method of historical description employed by certain New Historicists whereby an anecdote is 'read against' the orthodox history to reveal the codes of a given culture.

Select bibliography

1 What is history?

E.H. Carr's *What is History* (1961), originally published in 1943, was standard undergraduate fare in the 1960s and 1970s. The essay by Eichenbaum on formalism is to be found in Lemon and Reis (eds) *Russian Formalist Criticism: Four Essays* (1965). This also contains the classic essay by Victor Shklovsky, 'Art as Technique'. E.M. Tillyard's *The Elizabethan World Picture* (1943) was also a staple undergraduate text in the 1950s and 1960s. Hayden White's *Metahistory: The Historical Imagination in Nineteenth Century Europe* (1973) is a clear analysis and discussion of the discourse of history. A relevant part is reprinted in Denis Walder's (ed.) collection of critical essays and documents, *Literature and the Modern World* (1991). This also contains extracts from essays by George Steiner on history and Nazism, and Walter Benjamin on the philosophy of history.

2 Literary history

David Perkins' *Is Literary History Possible?* (1992) is both scholarly and accessible, and contains pertinent chapters on literary classifications and genre. Legouis and Cazamian's *History of English Literature* (1964) is an excellent example of the homogenising impulse in literary classifications. E.M. Forster's *Aspects of the Novel* (1927) contains still relevant material of historical versus ahistorical readings of works.

3 *Literary classifications*

Again, Perkins' book has valuable material. M.H. Abrams's *The Mirror and the Lamp* (1952) is a genre-based theory of Romantic poetry. Northrop Frye's *Anatomy of Criticism* (1957) is a monumental attempt at classification over a great time span. The chapters 'Theory of Modes' and 'Theory of Genres' are most relevant. Paul Hernadi's *Beyond Genre* (1972) explores the theories and limitations of those theories relating to genre and classification, and can be usefully read in conjunction with Abrams (1952). The journal *Genre* regularly contains theoretical discussions of classificatory procedures and generic properties of texts.

4 *New Historicism*

Stephen Greenblatt's now classic *Renaissance Self-Fashioning* (1980) has clear discussions of Spenser and, in particular, of Wyatt. John Barrell's *Poetry, Language and Politics* (1988) contains further historicist-based essays on Milton and Wordsworth. Tom Healy's *New Latitudes* (1992) is a good account and summary of the methodologies of historicism. H. Aram Veeser's collection *The New Historicism* (1989) contains essays by many of the 'big names' in historicism, including Greenblatt, Louis Montrose, Gayatri Chakravorty Spivak, Hayden White and Jonathan Arac. Greenblatt's essay 'The Poetics of Culture' is especially relevant, as is Kinney and Collins's collection, *Renaissance Historicism* (1987).

5 *Foucault and history*

Foucault's only sustained work with a literary focus is a book on the novelist Raymond Roussell, *Death and the Labryinth.* (1987). *The Foucault Reader* (1986) ed. Paul Rabinow contains many of the major essays. Simon During's *Foucault and Literature: Towards a Genealogy of Writing* (1992) addresses Foucault's relation to literature and literary theory.

6 Historicism, anthropology, thick description

Clifford Geertz's *The Interpretation of Cultures* (1973) is the precursor to much New Historicism. Stephen Greenblatt's essay 'Fiction and Friction' is reprinted in *Shakespearean Negotiations: The Circulation of Social Energy in Renaissance England* (1988).

7 The ideologies of texts

There is a massive amount of material on Marxism. Of Lukàcs' works, *Writer and Critic* (1978) and *The Historical Novel* (1962) are particularly interesting. Terry Eagleton's slight but useful *Marxism and Literary Criticism* (1976b) and Raymond Williams's *Keywords* (1976) contain much useful information. Eagleton's *Ideology* (1991) contains interpretations of the key Marxists on ideology. Francis Mulhern's (ed.) *Contemporary Marxist Theory* (1992) includes surveys of recent work and illuminating discussions of the major theorists. David Forgas also provides a readable survey in Jefferson and Robey's (eds) *Modern Literary Theory* (1986). Pierre Macherey's *A Theory of Literary Production* (1978) is an accessible and stimulating bridge between Marxism and structuralism. Goldmann's *Towards a Sociology of the Novel* (1975) and Althusser's *Essays on Ideology* (1976) contain important theories of ideology and textual production.

Chapter 4

Subjectivity, psychoanalysis and criticism

1 Defining subjectivity

W HAT IS MEANT by the term 'subjectivity'? Finding a satisfactory definition of the human self, as it is positioned in the world and as it experiences itself and its world, has been one of the most pressing philosophical problems; predictably, there is no *obvious* route that we can offer through the maze of theories that wrestle with the question of 'Who am I?' We can only offer highly selective versions of the way this question has been considered in relation to literature. Below we list a range of definitions of the human subject for consideration.

Paul Smith, in his introduction to *Discerning the Subject* (1988), suggests the term 'subject' can be used to indicate a variety of things:

> Over the last ten or twenty years [discourses of the human sciences] have adopted this term, the 'subject', to do multifarious theoretical jobs. In some instances the 'subject' will appear to be synonymous with the 'individual', the 'personal'. In others – for example, in psychoanalytical discourse – it will take on a more specialized meaning and refer to the unconsciously structured illusion of plenitude which we usually call 'the self'. Or elsewhere, the 'subject' might be understood as the specifically subjected *object* of social and historical forces and determinations.
>
> (Smith 1988: xxvii)

Other definitions of the subject are based on the linguistic issue of the first person pronoun and what space this 'I' demarcates. Linguists Mühlhäusler and Harre begin their discussion with a brief outline of traditional humanist beliefs about the subject:

> Central amongst the conditions for personhood is the possession of a sense of identity, of being one self and continuously one self. The Cartesian tradition treats this sense of

identity as the intuition of, perhaps even the direct experience of 'an inner core' of being, and ego, which is *the self*,
that to which all other mental and moral attributes belong.

(Mühlhäusler and Harre 1990: 87)

However, they find this intuitive belief in a coherent and stable
identity problematic and they offer an alternative way of understanding what we might call a subject:

a person is an embodied being located in a spatio-temporal
structure of things and events, so having a point of view; and
is also an active being located in a structure of rights and
obligations, so having a sense of moral responsibility.

(Mühlhäusler and Harre 1990: 88)

This location of a person, as a biological organism with a solid,
flesh-and-blood existence who also must acquire certain practices, such as languages and other social skills, is referred to by
Mühlhäusler and Harre as the 'Double Location' of the subject.
They continue:

To be a person in the fullest sense in this or that society is to
have a mastery of [linguistic and social] practices . . . We
believe that mastery is equivalent to believing and using a
theory about what it is to be a person in one's native culture.
Theories are built around basic concepts. Looked at this way,
the 'self' is not an object, but the leading concept of a theory
about what it is to be a person in one's native culture.

(Mühlhäusler and Harre 1990: 89)

In other words, people are whatever fits into a theoretical framework of what it is to be a person.

Kaja Silverman similarly defines the term 'subject' as a
location shared between several theoretical discourses, but she
also brings into consideration the issue of the unconscious in
the constitution of subjectivity. The unconscious always exceeds
our ability to conceptualise it – if we can conceptualise it, it
immediately becomes conscious:

The term 'subject' designates a quite different semantic and ideological space from that indicated by the more familiar term 'individual' . . . The term 'subject' foregrounds the relationship between ethnology, psychoanalysis, and semiotics. It helps us to conceive of human reality as a construction, as the product of signifying activities which are both culturally specific and generally unconscious. The category of the subject thus calls into question the notions of both the private, of a self synonymous with consciousness. It suggests that even desire is culturally instigated, and hence collective; and it de-centers consciousness, relegating it . . . to a purely receptive capacity. Finally, by drawing attention to the divisions which separate one area of psychic activity from another, the term 'subject' challenges the value of stability attributed to the individual.

(Silverman 1983: 126–30)

Like Silverman, feminist theorist Chris Weedon accepts that the subject is not necessarily stable, and she emphasises the role of language in the construction of identity:

The position of subject from which language is articulated, from which speech acts, thoughts or writing appear to originate, is integral to the structure of language and, by extension, to the structure of conscious subjectivity which it constitutes. Language and the range of subject positions which it offers always exists in historically specific discourse which inhere in social institutions and practices and can be organized analytically in discursive fields.

(Weedon 1987: 34–5)

These quotations show perhaps some of the less extreme versions of what might be meant by the term 'subject' in recent critical theory. Our task in this chapter is to look at different ways of describing how the subject comes into being, and the difference that makes to our reading of literature. Psychoanalysis is the main consideration, as this discipline transformed any belief in the subject as a coherent, rational and conscious being. We look here at the work of Sigmund Freud and Jacques Lacan, because it is the work of these clinicians that has been most widely used in relation to literary studies, but these are by no means the only schools of psychoanalytic thought.

2 Literature and psychoanalysis

Psychoanalysis is not primarily a *literary* practice, unlike many of the other theories discussed in this volume: it is a clinical and therapeutic methodology. However, it has a long and complex relationship to practices of reading and writing and to the assumptions that we make about why people write and how texts affect their readers.

The relationship between psychoanalysis and literature can be looked at in different ways, but we can reduce it to a question of what is being subjected to the analytic process, and what repressed meaning we thereby hope to uncover. Shoshana Felman explains that we normally tend to see psychoanalysis as the active practice performed upon the passive text:

> While literature is considered as a body of *language* – to *be interpreted* – psychoanalysis is considered as a body of *knowledge*, whose competence is called upon *to interpret*. Psychoanalysis, in other words, occupies the place of a *subject*, literature that of an *object*; . . .
>
> (Felman 1982: 5)

However, Felman explains that psychoanalysis can be interrogated by literature and by literary critics, as well as the other way round:

> it could be argued that people who choose to analyse literature as a profession do so because they are unwilling or unable to choose between the role of the psychoanalyst (he or she who analyzes) and the role of the patient (that which is being analyzed). Literature enables them not to choose because of the following paradox:
> 1) the work of literary analysis resembles the work of the psychoanalyst; 2) the status of what is analyzed – the text –

143

> is, however, not that of a patient, but rather that of a master:
> we say of the author that he is a master; the text has for us
> authority . . . Like the psychoanalyst viewed by the patient,
> the text is viewed by us as 'a subject presumed to know' – as
> the very place where meaning and *knowledge* of meaning,
> reside. With respect to the text, the literary critic occupies
> thus at once the place of the psychoanalyst (in the relation of
> interpretation) *and* the place of the patient (in the relation
> of transference). Therefore, submitting psychoanalysis to
> the *literary* perspective would necessarily have a subversive
> effect in the clear-cut polarity through which psychoanaly-
> sis handles literature as its other, as the mere object of
> interpretation.
>
> (Felman 1985: 7–8)

Thus, Felman suggests that psychoanalysis of literature creates a
power struggle. She suggests that the structure of the relationships
between the critic, the text and the writer can be discussed in
relation to the structure of relationships between the analyst and
patient. This uses psychoanalysis as a determining model, but also
challenges that model, by suggesting that there are things that the
analyst/critic can find out about himself or herself through questioning the patient/text. It is not only the patient/text that is
subject to scrutiny. This way in which readers and critics are
themselves caught up is a very important concept to remember
when using psychoanalytic theories, especially when trying to
avoid creating overly prescriptive commentaries.

These structural relationships between psychoanalysis and
literature are not the only connections between the two discourses.
Some of the most important concepts in psychoanalysis are
defined by their reference to classical myths and historical writers:

> The key concepts of psychoanalysis are references to litera-
> ture, using literary '*proper*' names – names of fictional
> characters (Oedipus complex, narcissism) or of historical
> authors (masochism, sadism). Literature, in other words, is
> the language which psychoanalysis uses in order to *speak of*
> *itself*, in order to *name* itself. Literature is therefore not

simply *outside* psychoanalysis, since it motivates and *inhabits* the very names of its concepts, since it is the *inherent reference* by which psychoanalysis names its findings.

(Felman 1982: 9)

Felman is claiming here a necessary connection between psychoanalysis and literature, with literature providing a practice ground for the analyst as well as informing the theoretical principles on which the analytical methodology is based. However, there are some key differences to remember when working with psychoanalysis as a mode of approaching literary texts. In clinical practice there is only the analyst and the patient to consider, but in literature there are a variety areas which one might analyse – what is the 'patient' might not always be clear. The areas that a critic might be analysing are listed below, and they will be explored in the rest of this chapter. It's unlikely that you'll be able to give firm answers to the following questions. They are speculative rather than practical at this stage, but you might want to reconsider them as you read.

i) Does psychoanalysis give us access to the unconscious of the writer? Do we assume that literature is produced almost without the writer's volition?

ii) Does psychoanalysis give us access to the unconscious world of the text? Is there anything that can be revealed by this approach (about the text, its context or its ideological structure) that might otherwise not be available to us?

iii) Are we able to make meaningful judgements about a text by looking at the unconscious motives and wishes of characters? Is it appropriate to apply the same analytical techniques to the narrator or implied author as we would to a character?

iv) Do psychoanalytic methods give us an insight into our own relationship with a text, as readers or as critics? Can understanding something about our own unconscious help us recognise why we read something in a particular way? Does our critique of a text have an unconscious aspect (that is, we reveal something that we ourselves do not recognise)?

3 Freudian psychoanalysis

Freud does not have a coherent body of work, and there is not a single definitive version of his approaches that can be adopted in a straightforward manner, either for literary purposes or for therapeutic ones. There *are* certain standardised practices within Freudian therapeutic practice as a profession, although even here there are frequent controversies (see Masson 1992). In critical approaches to literature, the ground is even more uncertain, and just as much analytical energy is employed in examining Freud's texts themselves as it is in looking at literary works. Adam Phillips, a family therapist and clinical practitioner, puts it this way:

> Psychoanalysis, at its inception, had no texts, no institutions, and no rhetoric; all it had to see itself with were analogies with other forms of practice. The first practitioners of psychoanalysis were making it up as they went along, Freud being the prototype of the 'wild analyst'. Psychoanalysis, that is to say, was improvised, despite the medical training of the early analysts, out of a peculiarly indefinable set of conventions. Freud had to improvise between the available analogies, and he took them, sometimes in spite of himself, from the sciences and the arts. Something new, after all, can be compared only with something from the past, something already established.
>
> (Phillips 1993: xv)

As Phillips also points out, however, there is little attention given by Freud to the places where these analogies fail to work effectively, to the point at which it becomes inappropriate to treat a patient as a text, or a text as a patient.

Freud's theoretical positions changed radically from his early writings in the 1890s to those which he developed towards the end of his career in the early 1930s. He constantly revised his ideas, re-footnoted them in the light of later discoveries, reinterpreted his clinical data and even suppressed elements of his work that were controversial. Freud's works have come to be received as canonical literary texts in their own right, and there are, as with any literary work, numerous ways of reading him. We can only outline some of the most well-known concepts associated with his name as they have been used for the analysis of literature. A clinician's approach to the work would be quite different.

The idea that there are unconscious processes, operations in the mind that cannot be represented, is the key concept of psychoanalysis. Repression is the action that produces the unconscious by rendering experiences, thoughts, desires and memories irretrievable. Psychoanalysis is the process whereby clues to repression are recognised and represented in a way that can be understood by the conscious mind. Freud lists what he calls the 'corner-stones of psychoanalytic theory' as follows:

> The assumption that there are unconscious mental processes, the recognition of the theory of resistance and repression, the appreciation of the importance of sexuality and the Oedipus complex – these constitute the principal subject-matter of psychoanalysis and the foundations of its theory.
>
> (Freud 1957: 122)

It is therefore these basic principles that we will investigate further in this chapter.

Freud discusses the function of repression through a number of different models. Fundamentally he describes a conflict at work in the operation of the subject, whose physical and emotional demands and desires often come into conflict with forces of reality, including social customs and taboos as well as physical safety and material possibility. The 'reality principle' struggles against the 'pleasure principle' in the mind, and through this struggle the subject has to learn to postpone pleasure and accept a degree of discomfort or 'unpleasure' in order to comply with social demands or in order to attain its desires in the future.

The most well-known of Freud's accounts of the structure and operation of the mind is the model of the id, the ego and the super-ego. In this model, the id applies to the instinctual drives that relate to the needs of the body: the id is primitive and needy, incapable of denying itself. The ego develops out of the id and it pacifies the drives, by offering itself as a substitute for what must be denied the id (a kind of psychic equivalent of a baby's soother). The super-ego is representative of external, social influences upon the drives, and is formed in the image of the earliest identifications of the ego with the father. Thus, the id wants its desires and needs satisfied; this places pressure upon the ego which bears on itself the imprint of what is unacceptable via the operations of the super-ego. There is not just an instinctual force trying to penetrate the ego, but there is another force – the super-ego – working to prevent it: a kind of ego sandwich. Memories of this conflict – the conflict of the wishes of the id with the requirements of the social world – become charged with distress of 'unpleasure' and have to be barred from consciousness in the process of repression.

The psychoanalytic process relies on attaining an understanding of the operation of repression. It does not give access to the unconscious as such; it merely recognises symptoms of it when they surface, in the form of dreams, puns, parapraxes (examples of which include deliberate mistakes, forgetting specific things or names, misspellings and slips of the tongue) and hysterical or neurotic disorders, and offers a narrative about what may have been repressed to cause a specific set of symptoms. The unconscious does not operate according to the same set of paradigmatic and syntagmatic rules that govern conscious thought and language. Its associations and substitutions are quite different, and are specific to individuals rather than shared by a linguistic community. For example, narratives are traditionally ordered syntagmatically, according to a temporal of linear model of cause and effect: 'I went shopping and bought some cat food; then I went home and called Felix in from the garden'. In a dream, this structure might be disorderly, with the cat being fed *before* the tin of kitty nibbles has been purchased or the cat food might be used to feed a tortoise instead of Felix. The structure of the dream is formulated according to the associative patterns of the drea-mer's experience, rather than according to any normative assump-tions of what is appropriate. It is during analysis that such individual patterns of associations (such as inappropriate food being served, or the recurrence of voracious reptiles) become clear, and can then be made sense of in terms of the dreamer's experience. This analytic practice has been transcribed directly into the study of literature, with critics looking for recurring imagery, scenes or character types in a writer's work, and drawing conclusions about what these patterns say about the author.

The forms in which the unconscious makes itself known are radically modified, and deliberately 'in disguise'. The traumas that have been repressed are extremely painful and damaging: the unconscious acts as a protective mechanism to prevent the sub-ject's realisation of these agonies. In dreams, the process that the repressed undergoes, before it surfaces in the remembered dream, is called 'dream work', and it is considered to operate in a fashion analogous to the creation of art or literature. The 'dream work' is the transformation of the repressed, forbidden or taboo thoughts or desires, into the manifest. The manifest elements are what a dreamer remembers, but they are equivalent to what slips off the tongue by mistake, or an hysterical crying fit, or a panic attack. The latter symptoms are less approachable for literary analysts, who are used to narrative, poetic and other linguistic forms, so it is the process of dream interpretation that we will consider in more detail here.

Some of the basic processes of the dream work, the trans-formation of the latent content into the manifest dream, are as follows:

condensation: This is the compression of two or more elements into a single form. It is a process of over-determination: Freud's analogy is with a double or multiple exposure in photography. Freud argues that condensation has the function of representing a large amount of latent material in a small, manifest space: 'the manifest dream has a smaller content than the latent one, and is thus an abbreviated translation of it' (1973a: 205). The familiar dream image Freud uses as an example is a person who: 'may look like A perhaps, but be dressed like B, may do something that we remember C doing, and at the same time we may know that he is D' (206).

There must always be some connection between the figures that become collapsed into one another and Freud stresses that no matter how unfamiliar the resulting condensed image or narrative might be, it has been made out of something that the dreamer knows. He insists, importantly for the literary critic, that 'the "creative" imagination, indeed, is quite incapable of *inventing* anything; it can only combine components that are strange to one another' (206). Condensation is essentially a production of private signifying chains, the whole of which can be invoked by one image. This image may appear original, but its constitutive components are familiar ones to the creator. In terms of literary analysis, the process of condensation is often linked with the operation of metonyms, where there are connections between the image and the thing for which it stands.

displacement: This is a process of transferral or substitution, whereby elements in the manifest dream come to replace elements in the latent dream as a method of disguise. Its function is that of censoring sensitive latent material so that 'the allusions employed for displacement in dreams . . . are connected with elements they replace by the most external and remote relations and are therefore unintelligible' (1973a: 208–9). Freud explains that the process of displacement has two main aspects: firstly, 'a latent element is replaced not by a component part of itself but by something more remote – that is, by an allusion' (208); secondly, 'the psychical accent is shifted from an important element on to another which is unimportant, so that the dream appears differently centred and strange' (208). An important object can be replaced by something neutral, and an unimportant object becomes charged with the energy or trauma that really belongs to something which is taboo or repressed. The process of displacement is often linked with the operation of metaphor in literature.

considerations of representability: Dream thoughts achieve representation in the dream through images. For example, abstract thoughts can be represented by sounds or scenes. Similarly, spatial relationships (such as an arrangement of cakes on a dish) can come to stand for chronological ones (such as a series of meals over several years), or vice versa.

secondary revision: This is most easily explained by reference to the retelling of a dream verbally. The dream is reordered and certain parts of it are selected and given emphasis as we turn it into a story that can be recounted when we are awake. The blur that is the dream has to undergo a form of translation, and we know from experience that, as we become conscious, the dream begins to slip away from our memory, at least in its original form.

The following quotation comes from a science fiction novel, *The Wanderground*, by Sally Gearhart. Science fiction can often be decoded as though it were a dream, since the texts are constructed out of a present reality but are altered in such a way as to make the constructed world unrecognisable. In this novel, the characters have an advanced intellectual state which enables a meeting of minds with those of other people and of animals. The action quoted here takes place in a 'remember room', which offers a guided trip into the memory (very much like the process of psychoanalysis):

> At first there was only the tumult of sounds, voices, colours, scraps of a thousand memories in swift succession. '. . . the mask immediately to your face. Cover your mouth and nose with the mask and dream normally. Again, we welcome you aboard Flight . . .' Sandalwood and wine, with the purple candle spilling its yellow insides all over the phone bill and the dresser cloth. The wires outside the window intersect at

small and large angles all over the sky. A man calls my name and I answer. He is at the door smiling. A tall bearded smile. He lies down beside me here on the low bed . . . 'At a speed of ten point six times the square root of the air pressure in the tyres a car will hydroplane on wet or frosty pavement . . .' Inch high steaks. Fat and dripping grease. High flames and waves of heat. 'I'll quit if he doesn't get the fan going by tomorrow . . .' 'Liz, Rosie's won! The Amazons are city champions! I was out stealing third by we recuped [*sic*]. The party's tonight . . .' There he comes again stumping through the hall with that walker. I can't stand it another minute. I'll tell Jim we'll have to call the nursing home tomorrow . . . Heavy rhythms, roaring ears, flashing coloured lights, a hundred sweating undulating bodies, bending, turning, stomping, clapping, rushing, shouting. Next time I can't wear this damned brassiere . . . [ellipses in original text]

(Gearhart 1985: 152)

i) How does the narrative style suggest a dream or memory sequence? (Refer to the explanation of 'secondary revision' and 'considerations of representability' above.)

ii) This is a science fiction text. What are the implications of looking at the unconscious of the narrative (rather than of the character or author) in such an instance?

(iii) Do any of the images have particular resonance for you as a reader? Does this self-analysis add to your ability to understand the text?

iv) Look again at the explanations of condensation and displacement. How might some of the images in this text be working to disguise or connect with something significant? (It is not possible to get the exact connections without reading the novel, but the object here is to understand the operation of the dream work.)

The next question that needs to be addressed is the following: how useful is the understanding of the dream work to an analysis of literature? In terms of the relationship between psychoanalysis and literature, there are a number of conflicting issues. Literature and other forms of art can be seen as incidences of the return of the repressed, just as dreams are. They are the result of neurotic infantile wishes or traumas which resurface without the control of the writer or artist. In fact, the author's work becomes precisely something which has evaded his or her control. This tends to produce the kinds of readings whereby the task of the critic is to attain the 'true' and 'latent' meaning of a text, which consists of the private fantasy of the author.

Alternatively, fantasy and fiction can be seen as controlled and manipulated eruptions of the repressed. The ego of the writer is seen as coherent, able to control the unconscious impulses, and supported in this control by social and cultural standards of decency and sanity. The text becomes something which has been created out of the *manipulated* fantasies of the writer to produce particular effects. The kind of psychoanalytic reading here would tend to focus on the text or on echoes that a text produces in the reader, the extent to which the reader recognises his or her own fantasies and repressed desires in the work being read as constitutive of culture generally.

4 Sexual identity and psychoanalysis

Probably Freud's most well-known theory is that of the development of sexual identity. The Oedipus complex, a concept that is widely known and which is often used to explain family conflicts, arrives out of analogy with classical myth. It is used to explain how a sexualised and gendered subject comes to take his or her place in the world. This theory has been redefined and criticised more than any other Freudian concept, and more details of this criticism will be given in the section on Lacan later in this chapter.

In the Theban tragedy of Oedipus, King Laius banishes his infant son Oedipus because of a prophecy that the son will kill the father. During a chance encounter, Oedipus kills his father without knowing Laius' identity, then marries his victim's wife Jocasta, without knowing that she is his mother. Oedipus' discovery of his guilt of parricide and incest causes him to blind himself and flee.

This seems an unlikely and unpromising way to begin discussion of how all children become socially adjusted. However, it is Freud's assertion that sexual identity is constructed on a basis of guilt and repressed incestuous desires. According to Freud, the gender of a child is not solely dependent on her or his genitalia, but on the development of her or his psyche.

> What constitutes masculinity or femininity is an unknown characteristic which anatomy cannot lay hold of.
>
> (Freud [1933] 1973b: 147)

According to the explanation offered by the theory of the Oedipus complex, the sexual development of boys and girls differs, although both begin by desiring the mother, their first love-object, who is seen as all-powerful and capable of fulfilling the desires of the child. Eventually, the boy child begins to see the father as a sexual rival for the mother, but, being small and relatively helpless, he fears castration by the father as punishment for his unacceptable desires and represses them, later to transfer them on to other women when he reaches puberty.

The sexual development of the little girl is different. This is how Freud describes it:

> The little girl's clitoris behaves at first just like a penis, but by comparing herself with a boy playfellow the child perceives that she has 'come off short', and takes this fact as ill-treatment and as a reason for feeling inferior. For a time she still consoles herself with the expectation that later, when she grows up, she will acquire just as big an appendage as a boy. . . . The female child does not understand her

actual loss as a sex characteristic, but explains it by assuming that at some earlier date she had possessed a member which was just as big and which had later been lost by castration.

(Freud 1969: 274)

The girl discovers that she has suffered castration already; she lacks the penis, and the masculine power that this represents. The solution to this lack, says Freud:

> is far simpler, far less equivocal, than that of the little possessor of the penis . . . it seldom goes beyond the wish to take the mother's place, the feminine attitude towards the father. Acceptance of the loss of a penis is not endured without some attempt at compensation . . . [the girl's] Oedipus-complex culminates in the desire which is long cherished, to be given a child by her father as a present, to bear him a child. One has the impression that the Oedipus-complex is later gradually abandoned because this wish is never fulfilled.
>
> (Freud [1924] 1969: 275)

The Freudian psychoanalytic model relies heavily on the conflicts of the family situation, and on the differentiation between the sexes. In considering literature, therefore, it is not surprising that the most interesting texts for analysis are those which use a transgressive family as a focus for attention. The classic examples of texts which have been subjected to Freudian psychoanalysis include D.H. Lawrence's *Sons and Lovers*, the Oedipal conflict here indicated in the title; and Shakespeare's *Hamlet*, which both Freud and Lacan use as a clear example of a son with unresolved desires toward his mother and in sexual rivalry with his stepfather. Here is an extract from one of these standard literary examples for psychoanalysis, *Sons and Lovers* (1913). Paul and Miriam are involved in a sexually charged relationship, but both are denying their attraction at this stage. They are in the garden at Paul's family's house, and he is making her a posy of sweet peas:

Miriam laughed. She thought flowers ought to be pinned in

one's dress without any care. That Paul should take pains to fix her flowers for her was his whim.

He was rather offended at her laughter.

'Some women do – those who look decent,' he said.

Miriam laughed again, but mirthlessly, to hear him thus mix her up with women in a general way. From most men she would have ignored it. But from him it hurt her.

He had nearly finished arranging the flowers when he heard his mother's footsteps on the stairs. Hurriedly he pushed in the last pin and turned away.

'Don't let mater know,' he said.

Miriam picked up her books and stood in the doorway looking with chagrin at the beautiful sunset. She would call for Paul no more, she said.

'Good evening, Mrs Morel,' she said, in a deferential way. She sounded as if she had no right to be there.

'Oh, is it you, Miriam?' replied Mrs Morel coolly.

But Paul insisted on everybody's accepting his friendship with the girl, and Mrs Morel was too wise to have any open rupture.

(Lawrence [1913] 1980: 215)

i) What does the difference in beliefs about how the flowers should be arranged suggest about Miriam's and Paul's view of women?

ii) What is suggested by Mrs Morel's attitude to Miriam (and Paul's secrecy about the nature of their relationship)?

iii) What might be the problems with choosing an *obvious text* for a psychoanalytic approach?

This is how D. H. Lawrence explains his novel *Sons and Lovers* in a letter to Edward Garnett:

A woman of character and refinement goes into the lower class, and has no satisfaction in her own life . . . as her sons grow up she selects them as lovers – first the eldest, then the

second [Paul]. These sons are *urged* into life by their reci-
procal love for their mother – urged on and on. But when
they come to manhood, they can't love, because their mother
is the strongest power in their lives . . . As soon as the young
men come into contact with women, there's a split . . . [Paul]
gets a woman who fights for his soul – fights his mother. The
son loves the mother – all the sons hate and are jealous of the
father. The battle goes on between the mother and the girl,
with the son as object. The mother gradually proves the
stronger, because of the tie of blood.

(Lawrence [1922] 1967: 13)

iv) Does awareness of the Oedipus complex give us insight
into the unconscious world of the writer here, or into an
unconscious level of the narrative?
v) Or, on the contrary, is the Oedipal plot so obvious that we
should be looking for something else?

As well as Lawrence, Shakespeare and other family sagas,
fairy-tales and dramas for children have also been the focus of
much interest to psychoanalysis. Children's literature has been
understood by analysts either as a means of socialising children
or as a means of illustrating their fears and fantasies in a safe way,
to help resolve them.

Peter Pan has been produced in several versions as a play, film
and novel. Peter is the protector of the Lost Boys in Never Land,
and it becomes his (paternal) duty to find a mother for them, but
also for himself. He loves stories and listens at the nursery window
of the Darling children, and at one stage his shadow is severed as
he leaves the windowsill. The shadow is rescued, rolled up and
stored in a drawer. Peter goes in search of his shadow and asks
Wendy, only girl in a family of three, to sew it back on for him. He
then asks her to come to tell stories and perform other 'feminine'
duties for the Lost Boys. Peter teaches Wendy, and her brothers
John and Michael, to fly, and they go to Never Land, where they

get involved in traditional boys' adventures with pirates and 'Redskins', with Wendy presiding over them all, telling them stories and doing the sewing and cleaning. The children, and particularly Peter, are pursued by the threatening Captain Hook, and many of their adventures involve them eluding his grasp. The Darling children return to the nursery after becoming afraid that their mother will forget them and bar the window against them. There is a joyful family reunion, with a mournful Peter shut out at the window. Peter eventually returns, a long time later, to find Wendy a grown woman with a baby of her own, and it is Jane, Wendy's daughter, that Peter claims as his new 'mother' to fly to Never Land, to tell stories to the Lost Boys.

Before we offer a few brief suggestions about how *Peter Pan* might be approached in the light of Freudian psychoanalysis, you might want to consider the following issues (we assume here some prior knowledge of the story and the traditions that surround its performance):

vi) What is the relationship between Peter and Wendy?

vii) What does the story suggest about childhood (relationships between children, between children and adults)?

viii) What is the role of Captain Hook?

ix) Is there anything that can be suggested about the writer from *Peter Pan*?

x) What is expected *by* the audience when seeing the pantomime? What is expected *of* the audience? What do we have to believe about the performance?

xi) How might we explain Peter's detachable shadow through psychoanalysis?

Peter's invitation to Wendy to come with him takes the form of a seduction which can not be fulfilled, for Peter is ever a boy. He tempts her with promises of mermaids and flight, but his biggest lure is the promise that Wendy can tuck the boys in at night. Peter recognises sexual attraction only in the form of mothering. He wants only mother-love: all women are, for him, substitute mothers. The extract below, cut from later versions of the play script, demonstrates this quite clearly:

PETER: Now then, what is it you *want*?
TIGER-LILY: Want to be your squaw.
PETER: Is that what you want, Wendy?
WENDY: I suppose it is, Peter.
PETER: Is that what you want, Tink?

Bells answer.

PETER: You all three want that. Very well – that's really wishing to be my mother.

(J.M. Barrie, *Peter Pan*, Act 2 Sc. 3 quoted in Rose 1984: 37)

The complex substitutes that operate in the play, with the Darling children being 'mothered' by Nana the dog, and Peter playing first mother then father to the Lost Boys, then Wendy 'mothering' Peter, open the play out to a reading through the Freudian Oedipal model. There is an effacement of any father-figures in the text: although Peter plays at being father of the Lost Boys, with Wendy as the mother, he does not really want it to be so:

'I was just thinking,' he said, a little scared. 'It is only make-believe, isn't it, that I am their father?'
'Oh, yes,' said Wendy primly.
'You see,' he continued apologetically, 'it would make me seem so old to be their real father.'

(Barrie [1906] 1987: 113)

Mr Darling is portrayed as feeble and powerless in the domestic sphere, failing to prove himself a man because he will not take his medicine, and eventually ending up in Nana's kennel when the children have flown. Captain Hook is the most prominent adult male in the text, and he desires and pursues Peter in a relentless and quite disturbing manner, with his protruding and threatening false hand.

Jacqueline Rose's analysis of *Peter Pan* (1984) is an outstanding example of psychoanalytic criticism, which takes on the writer, the text, the readers/audience and the characters in its discussion of the sexualisation of the child. Rose discusses the changing views towards child sexuality in the late nineteenth century, which corresponded with the development of Freud's theories, and the conflicting ways in which this is represented in literature of the time, notably *Peter Pan*. Rose suggests that the most acutely distressing point of the play, which therefore becomes the symptom to which psychoanalytic critics must pay most attention, is the final scene where:

> Peter Pan returns to the nursery after many years and finds Wendy a grown woman with a child. Faced with the 'living proof' of the irreducible difference between them (the fact of growing up and of passing time), Peter goes to Wendy's daughter, Jane, with a dagger . . . This version copes with the crisis by having the child wake up and address Peter Pan with exactly the same words that Wendy had used in the opening scene of the play which then sets off the whole cycle again. This in itself shows how repetition . . . serves above all to ward off something with which it is impossible to deal.
> (Rose 1984: 38)

Rose here suggests that this whole scene is like a psychic 'crisis' or hysterical symptom which is 'coped with' or repressed, and therefore subject to repetition. The 'irreducible difference' between Peter and Wendy is not only, as Rose comments, that she ages and he does not, of course. The issue of sexual difference is crucial here, for when Peter's desires for Wendy (the mother) are thwarted, he transfers the attention of his phallic knife to the more appropriate 'love-object', Jane. In some ways then, this scene shows that Peter *has* grown up: his transferral of desire from mother to daughter seems to show his resolution of the Oedipal stage. Yet Peter is doomed to repeat this stage, as long as he continues to periodically leave the homosocial environment of the Lost Boys and peer in at the window of the female-dominated sphere of the nursery.

The above reading of *Peter Pan* argues that the relationships between the characters both exemplify *and* problematise the structural relations between members of the family, or those who play certain familial roles. It also throws certainty about sexual difference and sexual development into question. The applications of such methodologies do not 'explain away' the drama: rather, they help us account for the enduring popularity of the Peter Pan story, and its potential to move and disturb us, even into adulthood.

5 Lacanian psychoanalysis

Jacques Lacan was a practising psychoanalyst whose writing was first published in the 1930s, but whose impact has grown since the publication of *Écrits* in 1966 (of which only selections are available in English). He founded several schools for training analysts and caused immense controversy with both his style of teaching and of practising psychoanalysis. Lacan provides a radical rereading and rewriting of the texts of Freud, particularly those relating to the coming-into-being of the 'self'. He was a pioneer of the current tradition of reading Freud as a creative writer, rather than as a constructor of a rigid science. In terms of cultural studies, the most important, interesting and vital debates over the work of Lacan have been produced by feminist engagements with his theory. This is an enormous and still-growing field of criticism, and it is inevitable that our discussion of Lacan is filtered through these feminist discourses.

The main reason that Lacan's writing is so important to feminist criticism is due to his controversial discussion of the (metaphorical and physical) figure of 'woman', and his location of this figure as somehow outside or 'other' to cultural structures such as language. Lacan's recognition which is so important to a discussion of subjectivity is his understanding that identity is constructed badly; that is, it falls apart *not* just in the psychotic

161

or disturbed patient, but as a condition of normal social development. Crucially however, Lacanian theory suggests that identity is
constructed (badly) in *gendered terms*.

Within literary studies, Lacan is discussed in relation to his
theories of language. He reconsiders Saussure's model of the
relationship between the signifier and the signified, and what
impact this has on meaning. However, it is important to stress
that the Lacanian critique and construction of linguistic theories is
not the only part of his work that has significance for literary
critics. Juliet Flower MacCannell argues forcefully that Lacan's
theory has a much wider impact:

> It is literature and not language or linguistics that is the
> proper model for figuring Lacan. Although it has been the
> usual practice to apply structuralist versions of language to
> Lacan and to reduce his method to the metaphor/metonymy
> opposition, it is not enough to do so without paying strict
> attention to the form of the *social ties* these figures make.
> (MacCannell 1986: 14)

We will be considering what MacCannell calls the 'metaphor/
metonymy opposition', but we do not want to stress the linguistic
aspects of Lacan at the expense of his contributions to the understanding of the status of the subject or 'the form of social ties'.

It is Lacan's account of the attaining of a gendered subjecthood that needs elaboration first of all. We should state that
Lacan's writing is notoriously 'difficult': it is wayward, impenetrable, elliptical, highly suggestive, and never open to a single
interpretation. We have used Lacan's own writings and a variety
of secondary sources to produce this account, but it is by no
means an authoritative version. Lacan deliberately refused such
certainties, and produced lectures and essays that mimicked the
operation of the unconscious, so that the student of psychoanalysis, at whom much of Lacan's writing is aimed, is obliged to
undertake the role of analyst rather sooner than she or he might
wish. Here, for example, is his self-conscious commentary on his
own style, in his essay 'The Agency of the Letter in the
Unconscious or Reason Since Freud':

Writing is distinguished by a prevalence of the *text* in the sense that this factor of discourse will assume in this essay a factor that makes possible the kind of tightening up that I like in order to leave the reader no other way out than the way in, which I prefer to be difficult. In that sense, then, this will not be writing.

(Lacan 1977: 146)

This extract is from something which was originally given as a lecture, published in a collection titled *Écrits* ('Writings'). Lacan argues that he likes his writing to be inaccessible: the reader has no option (no other way out) than to get into the text, but this entrance is difficult. The fact that these comments are made by Lacan about his writing, but he is making them at the beginning of a lecture, complicates matters further. The fact that we are unsure as to how we are to gain access to any certain meaning seems to put us precisely where Lacan wants us to be.

For Freud, as we have seen, all infants are supposedly bisexual and their sexuality is only determined after they have experienced and resolved their Oedipal conflicts. This has proved problematic, in ways we have already discussed. During the period of sexual definition, according to Freud, the girl sees the penis and desires it, feeling her own inadequacy; the little boy sees the female lack of penis and becomes afraid for the safety of his own. The most forceful objection to this account of sexual development is that it reduces sexual determination to a matter of which genitals can be seen and which are 'invisible' or perceived as absent. Despite Freud's attempts to give an account of the *psyche*, his explanation of the Oedipus complex comes down to fairly basic biological essentialism, and it privileges the penis, against which women are judged as inadequate or lacking.

Lacan offers an account of the development of the subject, reading Freud's account at the level of the figural rather than the literal, on the level of the linguistic rather than the anatomical. For Lacan, it is not only the female subject who is defined against what she lacks: he suggests that all subjectivity is based on loss, absence and failure. Like Freud, he uses terms developed in quite specific ways to illustrate his explanation of the socialisation of the subject, a process that he calls the transition from the Imaginary to the Symbolic through the process of the Mirror Stage.

According to Lacan, all infants are born into the realm of the Imaginary, the main feature of which is the symbiotic relationship of the infant with the world. The baby's early experience is as a mass of drives, as a mass of psychic pulsions (to be distinguished from physiological instincts such as suckling, crying and so on). The infant has no awareness of the physical boundaries of its body. The Imaginary used within Lacanian discourse, then, is not simply that which is imagined or fictitious. It relates to the operation of the psyche.

The first difference that the infant learns is of the absence or presence of satisfaction (of the breast, and then later, of the mother). This difference, between absence and presence, then comes to be recreated in language. The symbiosis of the infant with the world, its non-differentiation, is disrupted by the intervention of a third term, that of the patriarchal law, or the Name of the Father, the *nom du père*. This authoritative intervention is about locating the infant within an already existing societal frame. It can be represented in a variety of ways, but its operations are those which assert identity, stable meaning and normalisation. There is a pun in French on the sound of the word *nom* which is indistinguishable from the word *non* when spoken. The *name* of the father is also the *no* of the father. This figure is a repressive one, then, but it is also what guarantees sanity. It is in the Name of the Father that meaning is, however provisionally, fixed. Just as the familial metaphor suggests, the paternal figure who orders and controls wayward children is necessary if that child is going to grow up properly adjusted. The fact that it is the *father* that is invoked, rather than the mother, is to do with the patriarchal nature of Western culture, with men as legislators.

What is instituted at the moment of disruption of the Imaginary by the *nom du père* is Desire, a drive or urge to return to the utopian state of the Imaginary, of coherence, of oneness, from which the subject has been banned. Unfortunately, one can never fulfil one's Desire. The loss of the Imaginary is a permanent one. Once the division is made, there is no concealing the cracks. But this Desire is repressed, and this act of repression brings the unconscious into being. Lacan's own synopsis of this process is concise, if rather coded:

> The development is experienced as a temporal dialectic that decisively projects the formation of the individual into history. The *mirror stage* is a drama whose internal thrust is precipitated from insufficiency to anticipation – and which manufactures for the subject, caught up in the lure of spatial identification, the succession of phantasies that extends from a fragmented body-image to a form of its totality . . . and, lastly, to the assumption of the armour of an alienating identity, which will mark with its rigid structure the subject's entire mental development.
>
> (Lacan 1977: 4)

From the point of the Mirror Stage, the subject becomes established in the realm of the Symbolic, the realm of language and representation, and this relies on the recognition of the figurative construction of the world: the crucial recognition of the Other in the mirror, that is both oneself and not-oneself, is a representative figure for the entry of the subject into the Symbolic. The concept of self-recognition in the mirror is an analogy for the process of gaining subjectivity: the infant does not literally have to see its reflection in order for it to pass through the Mirror Stage. The reflection of the infant in language is an example of the same operation. Entry into the Symbolic is the recognition that the 'I' that is spoken is not the same as the subject that actually speaks that 'I'. The nominal identity, the 'I', is always a misrecognition of the subject as unified and coherent. Contained within the misrecognition is always the reminder of the original loss that caused entry into the signifying chain of language in the first place. The image of the infant in the mirror and the child which actually sees that image become severed. The 'individual' can no longer be spoken, since we know precisely that the subject *is* divided. This play on the subject suggests that the 'I', as well as being the subject of her own perceptions, 'is subject in another sense, "subject" to the authority and prescriptions of someone or something. That something . . . is precisely the Symbolic order, or language.' (Cameron 1985: 119).

The image of the mirror – both the reflection in the mirror, and the representation of the mirror itself – is a frequent one in literature, and a character's examination of herself or himself in the glass often marks a textual turning point, but the reflection of the self mirrored by the Other that is, precisely, *not* the self (because it is a reflection) does not have to occur in a mirror, or even a photograph or portrait. Frequently, the not-self is given back to the self by another person: that is, subjecthood is dependent on the definition provided by an Other.

In Charlotte Brontë's *Jane Eyre* (1847), the construction of the subjectivity of Jane, under a Lacanian analysis, turns out to be at least partly constructed by 'the madwoman in the attic'. The raging and howling Bertha Mason, the first wife of Mr Rochester, appears as the savage counterpart to the domesticated Jane, Mr Rochester's wife-to-be. Bertha can be read as representing the psychotic side of womanhood, a lesson in what happens to those who evade the patriarchal law of the father, what Jane might potentially turn into if she were to become 'intemperate and unchaste' like Bertha. Jane's first encounter with Bertha in the flesh (although she has heard her inarticulate, pre-Symbolic utterances before) occurs in a dream-like sequence, which Jane retells to Mr Rochester:

> 'It seemed, sir, a woman, tall and large, with thick and dark hair hanging long down her back. I know not what dress she had on: it was white and straight; but whether gown, sheet or shroud, I cannot tell.'
>
> 'Did you see her face?'
>
> 'Not at first. But presently she took my veil from its place: she held it up, gazed at it long, and then, she threw it over her own head, and turned to the mirror. At that moment I saw the reflection of the visage and features quite distinctly in the long glass.'
>
> 'And how were they?'

'Fearful and ghastly to me – oh, sir, I never saw a face like it! It was a discoloured face – it was a savage face. I wish I could forget the roll of the red eyes and the fearful blackened inflation of the lineaments! . . . the lips were swelled and dark; the brow furrowed; the black eyebrows widely raised over the bloodshot eyes.'

(Brontë [1847] 1966: 311)

In this excerpt, Mr Rochester takes on almost the analyst's role, questioning Jane about her terrifying vision of a monster she claims is like 'the foul German spectre – the vampire'. But this disturbing image provides Jane with a picture of her other self, a repressed and monstrous Other that appears during the liminal sexual state of a woman immediately prior to her marriage. The monstrous Bertha throws Jane's veil over her own head, demonstrating not only her memories of her own wedding, but also indicating to Jane what she might possibly become. It is thus a reflection of both herself and not-herself that Jane sees in the long mirror: it is Bertha and herself defined by Bertha that Jane recognises.

In quite a literal way, Jane's identity is dependent on this Other: because Bertha is still married to Mr Rochester, Jane cannot become Mrs Rochester; she must remain Jane Eyre. However, her identity as a sane, white woman also depends on her distinction from this mad animal from the tropics. Jean Rhys's *Wide Sargasso Sea* (1966) emphasises and develops aspects of the cultural as well as gendered Other that operate within *Jane Eyre*. Bertha Mason represents not only the eruption of the Imaginary into the Symbolic, the Otherness of femininity, but she also functions as a metonym for cultural Otherness, too.

Bertha Mason comes from a Creole background of some uncertainty, originating in the West Indies; her mother has a history of mental illness and promiscuity and this is cited as explanation for her disturbed behaviour in *Jane Eyre*. The history of 'Bertha' is (re)created in Rhys's novel as the story of Antoinette Cosway, a young woman caught in a complex familial and cultural exchange process. Mr Rochester's power to define is emphasised by his renaming of Antoinette, making her into the monstrous Bertha. Rochester demonstrated the Symbolic in operation in his patriarchal naming power, his ability to transform identities through his words.

Both these novels are now taught regularly, and in conjunction, in schools and at degree level. It has become almost impossible to consider one without taking into account the other. The relationship between the two novels illustrates the relationship between self and Other, and between the Imaginary and the Symbolic, in a Lacanian analytical system. *Wide Sargasso Sea* has become the Other of *Jane Eyre*, each text redefining the meanings of the other, each text dependent upon the other for its identity.

The following is an extract from *Wide Sargasso Sea*. It is followed by some questions that might help you consider some of the issues raised so far in this section. The narrator of the passage is the young white Creole, Antoinette Cosway. Tia is the daughter of Christophine, the domestic worker at Antoinette's parents' house, and up until this point has been the playmate of the young Antoinette. The scene occurs just after the family house has been burned to the ground.

> Then, not so far off, I saw Tia and her mother and I ran to her, for she was all that was left of my life as it had been. We had eaten the same food, slept side by side, bathed in the same river. As I ran, I thought, I will live with Tia and I will be like her. Not to leave Coulibri. Not to go. Not. When I was close I saw the jagged stone in her hand but I did not see her throw it. I did not feel it either, only something wet, running down my face. I looked at her and I saw her face crumple up as she began to cry. We stared at each other, blood on my face, tears on hers. It was as if I saw myself. Like in a looking glass.
>
> (Rhys [1966] 1988: 38)

i) What is the significance of the narrator wanting to return to Tia and her mother?

ii) What can we say about the 'mirroring'? (Think about differences of class and race here, as well as the implications for the coherence of the subjectivity of the narrator.)

iii) What does this quotation indicate about power relations between the characters?

iv) How does this scene, the childhood story of the woman who is to become the mad Bertha Rochester, affect our reading of *Jane Eyre*?

v) How might a Freudian reading differ from a Lacanian reading of the text?

6 Lacan and language

Probably Lacan's most famous comment, for literary theorists at least, is that 'the unconscious is structured like a language'. The significant property of language to psychoanalysis is as that which established order through systems of syntax, and polarities through systems of semantics. Through language, the subject learns and internalises the structures of society, and, more specifically, the differences of gender. The position and identity of the subject is constituted by language. So, if a subject is put within a given gender, she or he identifies with that position in one-to-one correspondence. But this is to miss a crucial point concerning the instability of the subject. If we use the Saussurean model of the signifier attached closely to its signified, there is an immediate and limited identification of the subject with one position (see Chapter 2), whereas within post-structuralist analyses of language, of which Lacanian psychoanalysis is one example, one signifier relates to another along a constantly shifting, open-ended chain (see Chapter 5, Deconstructing the Text, pp. 215–221).

For example, in the structuralist model, the one-to-one correspondence model, the 'individual' misses the fact that she or he is part of a signifying chain. For example, the signifier 'woman' is seen to 'mean', reductively and intransigently, a biological female. What becomes buried, repressed if you like, are all the other cultural and ideological associations and differences that go to make up the term, such as femininity, fertility, heterosexuality, XY chromosomes and so on. Although it is not usually acknowledged that all the latter associations (and more) are part of our understanding of the signifier 'woman', how else would it be possible to say, for instance, of lesbians, as it is possible to say in this culture, that they are not real women? How else would it be possible for women to experience themselves as desexed or neutered after a hysterectomy? What Lacan is at pains to emphasise is that this chain effect of signifiers is linguistic, but that language profoundly affects our experience of our bodies and minds. Even our experience of our own sexuality is bound by the function of language.

The slippery operation of the signifier within the cultural context within which it is learned and used is illustrated by Margaret Atwood's novel *Cat's Eye* (1989). In this extract, the protagonist, Elaine Risley, is walking on a Toronto street, and ahead of her she sees a body lying on the pavement:

> When I get up even, I see that this person is a woman. She's lying on her back, staring straight at me. 'Lady,' she says. 'Lady. Lady.'
>
> That word has been through a lot. Noble lady, Dark Lady, she's a real lady, old-lady lace, Listen lady, Hey lady watch where you're going, Ladies' Room, run through with lipstick and replaced with Women. But still the final word of appeal. If you want something very badly you do not say *Woman, Woman*, you say *Lady, Lady*. As she is saying now. . .
>
> 'Here,' I say. I fumble in my purse, find a ten, crumple it into her hand, paying her off. I'm a sucker, I'm a bleeding heart. There's a cut in my heart, it bleeds money.
>
> 'Bless you,' she says. Her head rolls from side to side, back against the wall. 'God bless you lady, Our Lady bless you.'
>
> (Atwood 1989: 152–3)

Atwood's list of variations on the term 'lady' places it within its learned context, and gives it meaning by differentiation (for instance, by contrasting it with the signifier 'woman'). 'Lady' does not simply correspond to a biological female: it has other political and linguistic 'baggage'. Whilst one signifier always has dominance, in this case the polite, begging appellation 'Lady', the alternatives potentially disrupt it. The chain of differently inflected invocations of the signifier 'Lady' are made explicit by Atwood, and even if they aren't reiterated, they cannot be completely obliterated, just as the unconscious can always be suggested or invoked in the conscious mind, as a disruptive, but ever-present force.

i) Try to make a similarly explicit chain with the word 'man'. (You could also try it with the term 'gentleman' – it's an instructive, if short, exercise!)

Lacan shows that the same signifier can be attributed to different signifieds, and that the only way of understanding which signified is being invoked is to look at the relation between the two *signifiers*. The classic example is that of two public toilet doors, otherwise entirely identical, but one marked 'Ladies' and the other marked 'Gentlemen'. The signifier is the only means of telling them apart, and in this context the terms 'Ladies' and 'Gentlemen' only make sense in relation to one another. Why, otherwise, would two identical things be labelled differently, except when they operate as part of a cultural system in which difference is meaningful? The cultural system in this example is that of gender, and the edict that in Western societies women and men must use segregated lavatories in public. Through this example, Lacan insists that language operates with the signifier in a position of authority over the signified, and he associates this operation with the condition of the Symbolic. This is how he actually describes the relationship between signifier, signified and speaking subject:

the signifier has an active function in determining certain effects in which the signifiable appears as submitting to its mark, by becoming through that passion the signified.

This passion of the signifier now becomes a new dimension of the human condition in that it is not only man who speaks, but in man and through man *it* speaks (*ça parle*), that his nature is woven by effects in which is to be found the structure of language, of which he becomes material, and that therefore there resounds in him, beyond what could be conceived of by a psychology of ideas, the relation of speech.

(Lacan 1977: 284)

What is evident here is the *passive* construction of the subject: 'it speaks' *through* the subject, rather than the subject speaking though it. The Symbolic system predates the subject and speaks it, not the other way around.

The law of the signifier over the signified cannot be forgotten by the subject. It is a constant reminder of the loss of the Imaginary and its accompanying state of blissful coherence. The substitution of the Symbolic, the metaphoric level where language stands in for what has been lost, is hardly an adequate replacement. The knowledge of difference, of the self and the Other, cannot be eradicated once the subject has entered the Symbolic realm. In the Symbolic, language is always representative, a re-presentation, a figuration. Language never quite speaks the subject: it can only operate in metaphoric or metonymic terms. It can only remind the subject that there is an Other out there that it must depend on for its self-definition since it has lost its coherence after passing out of the Imaginary state.

Lacan represents the distinction between genders through metaphor and metonymy of an imbalanced kind. He takes the phallus (*not* the penis, the flesh and blood thing itself, but its symbolic representative) as the 'privileged signifier' to show the *division* between gendered subjects – as opposed to showing their *relationships*. Lacan substitutes one sexual part, the phallus, and he makes it stand for the whole of sexuality. A metonymic signifier, claims Jane Gallop, should have a varied definition with many sorts of relations between signifier and signified, whereas Lacan shows metonymy as merely one part standing for the whole. The word 'whole' can be used to demonstrate the operation of a complex chain of signifiers: the whole – fullness, completeness – is what the phallus stands for, as well as coming to stand for gender in its entirety. But the word is also a homonym for (that is, it sounds the same as) 'hole'. This 'hole' then comes to stand for the feminine side of the equation, indicating both female genitals – the vagina, since Freud, is perceived as a lack, a hole – and the absence of the phallus, which is the affliction of all subjects, male and female, within the Symbolic realm.

Why should the phallus be chosen as the privileged signifier? Lacan writes that he chooses this particular signifier as 'what stands out as most easily seized upon' (1977: 82). Although the phallus is not the same as the penis, and although neither men nor women 'have' the phallus (they both lack it and desire it, for it offers stability and authenticity of meaning, as well as authority and power), Lacan's comment on its visibility links the phallus more closely with the male subject: men can identity with the phallus in a way that women cannot.

The phallus marks a *point de capiton*: in translation, these are the buttons on a mattress that stop the stuffing sliding around too much. For Lacan, the term means a 'moment in language', a temporary fixing of meaning. It is the phallus that fixes meaning (temporarily) when the infant enters the Symbolic and the world of language. But at this point, the woman's relation to that signifier also becomes fixed. She becomes 'Other', not to be understood because she is not linked to the phallus, and therefore only understood because she is not linked to the phallus. The woman is only understood negatively. Lacan puts 'woman' in the position of the excluded term. He explains that the position is not inherent, that it is linguistically, rather than biologically, determined.

The feminine terrain of lack, of marginality, in relation to the phallus is supposedly open to men and women alike. This mobility of the subject position in relation to the phallus allows access to *'jouissance'*. *Jouissance* (conventionally translated as a kind of orgasmic pleasure) is beyond the phallus, beyond man, beyond

representation and therefore can disrupt and undermine all representation. It is the qualities of excessiveness and defiance that give
it value within the Symbolic system: it is lawlessness under an
otherwise repressive legalistic regime. *Jouissance* is where the
phallus is revealed as completely arbitrary rather than being a
transcendental signifier of difference. In the Lacanian system, the
unconscious, from which *jouissance* emerges, is a feminine space;
it is the space of the Other, the women's room. It is from this
starting point that much feminist commentary upon, and development of, Lacanian precepts takes off (see Chapter 6).

7 A Lacanian reading

Although it must be stressed that *Peter Pan* is not *the* privileged
text in relation to psychoanalytic discourse, the reading of it here
is offered as a helpful contrast to the Freudian reading of the play
which was given in the earlier part of this chapter. This might help
to identify the differences between the two kinds of analytic
procedure.

Marjorie Garber, in her *Vested Interests*, provides a critique
of representations of transvestism in culture. She argues that the
issue of the woman cross-dressed to play Peter on the stage
becomes a central, not a marginal, issue. For Garber, the way to
fix the meaning of *Peter Pan* is less through the presence of the
phallus than through the absence of the penis. Peter is granted
power by virtue of his masculinity:

> That Peter is a kind of Wendy Unbound, a re-gendered,
> not-quite-degendered alternative persona who can have
> adventures, fight pirates, smoke pipes, and cavort with red-
> skins is certainly one feasible way of understanding him –
> and her. Peter can do all kinds of things that Wendy, Victor-
> ian girl-child that she is, is forbidden.
>
> (Garber 1993: 168)

In Garber's interpretation, Peter becomes the Other of Wendy,
called up in her dreams as her alter-ego. He is a phallic Wendy,

both Wendy's imagined version of herself, and, in ?
tion, a woman accorded masculine power by virtue
ance. The woman who plays Peter, nevertheless, can
lacking the penis, when she comes off stage and
clearly demonstrates the Lacanian insistence that the penis anu ...
phallus must be distinguished, and however it might appear, no
one ever possesses the phallus (it is only Wendy's dream version of
herself as Peter). This also demonstrates the power accorded to
those *supposed* to have possession of the *penis* – they can fly, fight
with pirates and so on.

In the words of Soloman Caw, a resident rook in Kensington
Gardens, Peter is a 'Betwixt-and-Between', not quite human, not
quite bird, not quite fairy, and Garber asserts that Peter's sexual
and gendered identity is likewise neither one thing or the other. It
is appropriate to introduce here a metaphor that Lacan uses to
discuss certain recurring images in the discourses of his patients,
which he labels *le corps morcelé*, the fragmented body. He claims
that this image 'usually manifests itself in dreams when the movement of analysis encounters a certain level of aggressive disintegration' (Lacan 1977: 4). This symptom can appear in the form of the
internal body organs imagined on the outside, or other kinds of
evisceration, the loss of limbs and the growing of wings. In the Peter
Pan story, we witness both the growing of wings on the 'Betwixt-
and-Between', and also the severing of Peter from his shadow early
in the narrative; we also see the reintegration of that dark part of
Peter Pan through the efforts of Wendy. Peter could, then, be
interpreted as the symptom of an imagination at a point of crisis,
the product of a mind in a state of 'aggressive disintegration'.

i) Think of some other examples of le *corps morcelé* the
fragmented body (either in this text – what about Hook? – or
in others with which you are familiar). Are they helpful in
offering interpretations of the text?

Below is an extract from Kate Chopin's novel, *The Awakening* (1899), on which you can practise your skills at psychoanalysis.

The novel was controversial when it was first published in 1899 because it depicts a married woman, a mother, who is estranged from her husband and who becomes involved in a romantic infatuation with one man and a purely sexual liaison with another. This extract is from the end of the novel, when the protagonist Edna Pontellier has recognised that her desires for a perfect union with a man are hopeless. Although there are various interpretations of this ambiguous final scene, it is generally agreed that Edna drowns herself.

> The water of the Gulf stretched out before her, gleaming with the million lights of the sun. The voice of the sea is seductive, never ceasing, whispering, clamouring, murmuring, inviting the soul to wander in abysses of solitude. All along the white beach, up and down, there was no living thing in sight. A bird with a broken wing was beating the air above, reeling, fluttering, circling disabled down, down to the water.
>
> Edna had found her old bathing suit still hanging, faded, upon its accustomed peg.
>
> She put it on, leaving her clothing in the bath-house. But when she was there beside the sea, absolutely alone, she cast the unpleasant, pricking garments from her, and for the first time in her life she stood naked in the open air, at the mercy of the sun, the breeze that beat upon her, and the waves that invited her.
>
> How strange and how awful it seemed to stand naked under the sky! How delicious! She felt like some new-born creature, opening its eyes in a familiar world that it had never known.
>
> The foamy wavelets curled up to her white feet, and coiled like serpents about her ankles. She walked out. The water was chill, but she walked on. The water was deep, but she lifted her white body and reached out with a long, sweeping stroke. The touch of the sea is sensuous, enfolding the body in its soft, close embrace.
>
> She went on and on. She remembered the night she

swam far out, and recalled the terror that seized her at the fear of being unable to regain the shore. She did not look back now, but went on and on, thinking of the bluegrass meadow that she had traversed when a little child, believing that it had no beginning and no end.

(Chopin [1899] 1979: 189–90)

ii) Attempt a psychoanalytic reading of this passage. It could incorporate both Freudian and Lacanian features. Some aspects to consider include:

The significance of Edna's solitude

The importance of recalling a childhood fear (and overcoming it)

The sensual descriptions of the sea

The importance of Edna shedding her clothing

What problems might the mention of the 'soul' cause psychoanalysis?

You might also like to refer back to the broader questions asked in Literature and Psychoanalysis earlier in this chapter.

Glossary

condensation: (Freud) In dreams, a multiple or compound image.

le corps morcelé: (Lacan) Translates as 'the fragmented body', and refers to a common obsessional fear of losing coherence and self-identity, which is represented in the imagination as a disintegration or chopping-up of the body.

Desire: (Lacan) Produced by the gap between a fundamental need and the inability of language to articulate a demand to see the need is met. Desire is effected by the transition from the Imaginary into the Symbolic: it is the mark of the failure of language and of the loss of the undifferentiated pre-Symbolic state of the infant.

displacement: (Freud) In dreams, it is a method of disguise, analogous to the operation of metaphor, where something comes to stand for another, entirely unrelated object, person or emotion.

dream work: (Freud) The transformation of repressed or taboo thoughts into the manifest elements that the dreamer remembers.

ego: (Freud) A controlling or pacifying function of the id, a mediator between what is acceptable and unacceptable.

id: (Freud) The instinctual drives of the body.

Imaginary: (Lacan) The pre-Symbolic state, dominated by a non-differentiation of the subject from the world. It is a dimension of unconscious and conscious images, experienced or fantasised, which cannot be told apart.

jouissance: (Lacan) Orgasmic or supreme joy. It has a transgressive aspect: it defies representation in the Symbolic and is, for that reason, associated with the feminine.

latent: (Freud) The repressed material to which there is no access, except in the modified form of the manifest; the latent material is the stimulus of the dream.

manifest: (Freud) The translated form of the latent traumas, a selective and coded appearance of repressed material that can be accessed by the subject.

Mirror Stage: (Lacan) The transition from the Imaginary to the Symbolic, the acquisition of subjectivity, language and awareness of differentiation.

Name of the Father (*nom du père*):   (Lacan) The third term or figure of law that is a feature of the Symbolic. It is a repressive figure, but also a guarantor of meaning, and therefore of normality or sanity.

Oedipus complex: (Freud) The normalising description of process of a subject taking up a sexualised identity, by transferring affections from the mother on to non-family members of the opposite sex.

Other: (Lacan) The realm of femininity, the realm outside the Symbolic, the unrepresentable and therefore associated with the unconscious.

other (*objet petit a*):   (Lacan) The object, the version of itself that is received back by the subject from others, the marker in the Symbolic realm of the relationship between subject and object. (The *petit a*, or 'little a' refers to the French word for other, *autre* – the English equivalent would be 'little o', but Lacan insists that the term should not be translated.)

parapraxes: (Freud) Evidence or symptoms of the unconscious – slips of the tongue, nervous tics, patterns of forgetting or repeating, obsessions, etc.

point de capiton: (Lacan) A point of temporary fixity of meaning.

phallus: The transcendental signifier, the marker of gendered difference, a symbol of power and authenticity.

repression: The disappearence of a memory into the unconscious.

secondary revision: (Freud) The re-translation of a dream by the dreamer once she or he is awake.

super-ego: (Freud) The representative of external forces, of paternalistic controls and norms, which imprints itself on the ego.

Symbolic: (Lacan) The realm of language and representation.

transference: This characterises the relationship between the analyst and analysand.

unconscious: Probably Freud's single most important discovery, it is the result of the negative constitution of the conscious mind (through repression and denial). All that is negated takes up a parallel existence in the unconscious, which operates according to an entirely different logic and mode of representation to the conscious mind.

Select bibliography

1 Defining subjectivity

Kaja Silverman's *The Subject of Semiotics* (1983) is a clear introduction to psychoanalysis, structuralism and deconstruction. Most of the analyses are of film rather than literature, but it is a clearly organised book, and although quite sophisticated, it is not unmanageable for a newcomer. Paul Smith's *Discerning the Subject* (1988) is one of few books solely on the issue of the subject. It assumes a reader who is already well-acquainted with post-structuralist theory and so is not a text for beginners. The text contains a bitter rather than enlightening critique of Jacques Derrida which undermines some of the more helpful aspects of the argument. Mühlhäusler and Harre's essay on 'I: The Indexicalities of Responsibility and Place' in their *Pronouns and People* (1990) is probably not ideal for the general reader because of its base in advanced linguistics, but it does have an unusual emphasis on issues of morality and responsibility which are useful in discussing the role of the author.

2 Literature and psychoanalysis

Elizabeth Wright's introduction, *Psychoanalytic Criticism: Theory in Practice* (1984) covers not only Freud and Lacan, but others such as Jung, Laing and Reich. Her book is aimed towards students of Cultural Studies and is an excellent starting point. Wright has also edited *Feminism and Psychoanalysis: A Critical Dictionary* (1992) is probably the most useful single text that can be recommended; it is indispensable for anyone working with psychoanalytic theory, not just feminists. It contains entries from many of the best writers on the area, and it is comprehensively cross-referenced and clearly written, without losing any complexity. Shoshana Felman's (ed.) collection of essays, *Literature and Psychoanalysis* (1982), includes her crucial introduction to the relationship between analyst, client, reader and text, as well as her definitive paper on Henry James's *The Turn of the Screw*. It also includes Lacan's essay on *Hamlet*, and although it is a predominantly Lacan-oriented study, there are also essays on Freud.

3 Freudian psychoanalysis

Freud himself is the best starting place. His writing is elegant and entertaining, despite its contradictions. Begin with the *Introductory Lectures on Psychoanalysis* for an understanding of the basic principles. *Freud For Beginners* (1992) by Richard Appignanesi and Oscar Zarate is a cartoon introduction to Freud; its strength is that it gives a Freud chronology, making it easier to follow the transitions in his ideas. Jeffrey Masson's *The Assault on Truth* (1992) sets out, unashamedly, to destroy Freud's reputation. It is avowedly anti-Freud, but it does help to put him into an historical perspective, and severely questions some of the foundations on which the Freudian clinical tradition has been built. Whatever you are inclined to believe, Masson's work is a lucid piece of social history and a remarkable document of archival research. *In Dora's Case* (1985), eds Charles Bernheimer and Claire Kahane, contains a variety of essays on one of Freud's most well-known case-studies, that of 'Dora'. It not only sheds light on the issue of transference, but also records the historical reception of Freud's work within cultural studies.

4 Sexual identity and psychoanalysis

Jane Gallop's introduction, *Feminism and Psychoanalysis: The Daughter's Seduction* (1992), has become a classic work in its consideration of feminist criticism and Lacanian psychoanalysis. Gallop adopts a symptomatic approach to Lacan's writings, and to the writings of Irigaray, Cixous and Kristeva, analysing the theoretical work of these critics as though their texts were transcripts of sessions from the couch.

5 Lacanian psychoanalysis

Malcolm Bowie's introduction, *Lacan* (1991), is thorough and erudite, and it situates Lacan's work within analyses of literature and art. It is one of the few that is not primarily feminist in approach (although it is by no means anti-feminist). Bowie does a splendid job of introducing Lacan without bamboozling the reader, and without doing Lacan an injustice. Juliet Mitchell and Jacqueline Rose's (eds) *Feminine Sexuality: Jacques Lacan and the école Freudienne*' (1985) contains two essays on Lacan, one by each of the editors, and contains translations of some of Lacan's controversial seminars on female sexuality. This is an important resource for anyone interested in Lacan's contribution to the construction of subjectivity, and to his importance for feminism.

6 Lacan and language

Deborah Cameron's *Feminism and Linguistic Theory* (1985) has a brief (and fairly damning) analysis of Lacan, but Cameron does make things extremely clear where others are foggy. For a more sophisticated reading, see Gallop (1992).

7 A Lacanian reading

Juliet Flower MacCannell, in *Figuring Lacan: Criticism and the Cultural Unconscious* (1986), produces Lacanian readings of Lacan himself, and identifies where his theories are useful for cultural analysis. *Lacan and Narration: The Psychoanalytic Difference in Narrative Theory*, ed. Robert Con Davis (1983), contains Lacanian readings of a variety of texts, from Sophocles through Shakespeare to Stendhal. It is certainly not a volume for beginners, but is useful in the respect that it shows Lacanian psychoanalysis in action on literary texts.

Chapter 5

Reading, writing and reception

1 The role of the reader

W HAT PART DOES the reader play in the creation and realisation of the meaning of a text? What is the role of the reader's own personality in the interpretation of a text? If the meaning of a text is 'personal', is there an unlimited number of possible readings? How accurate is it to speak of *interaction* between text and reader, or between author and reader? Is there a range of possible meanings which are prescribed in a culture?

This chapter is primarily concerned with the reading and interpretative processes. Here, we look at the personal, social and cultural aspects of constructed readings of texts and at the role of the author in the situation of meaning. We look at those theories, notably deconstruction, which seek to read the text not as a unified whole, but as fractured, self-referential and contradictory.

The following quotations are concerned with the way readers make sense of texts:

> This 'I' which approaches the text is already itself a plurality of other texts, of codes which are infinite or more precisely, lost (whose origin is lost). *Objectivity* and *subjectivity* are of course forces which can take over the text, but they are forces which have no affinity with it. Subjectivity is a plenary image, with which I may be thought to encumber the text, but whose deceptive plenitude is merely the wake of all the codes that constitute me, so that ultimately my subjectivity has the generality of stereotypes.
>
> (Barthes 1974: 10)

Barthes here considers the reader, or the '"I" which approaches the text', to a be a compound of other texts, not a uniquely experiencing individual 'I'. The origins of these texts that consti- tute the 'I' are not simply or immediately discernible. The sub- jectivity with which one might normally consider functioning in relation to a text is merely an image; its plenary quality, that is, its completeness, its lack of limitation, is a function of these lost origins. The subject that encounters the text is not the stable, unique 'I', but a stereotype constituted from various other textual codes.

> one text is potentially capable of several different realisa-
> tions, and no reading can ever exhaust the full potential for
> each individual reader will fill in the gaps in his own way,
> thereby excluding the various other possibilities.
>
> (Iser 1974: 271)

The question exists, of course, as to how many 'realisations' are possible. Iser suggests 'several', but this is vague and unsubstantiated. What form might these realisations take? Iser seems also to suggest that far from being reducible to just 'several' readings, or realisations, the text's 'full potential' is made possible by an infinite number of readers. What exactly are the 'gaps' of which Iser speaks?

> The text provokes certain expectations which in turn we
> project onto the text in such a way as to reduce the
> polysemantic interpretation in keeping with the expecta-
> tions aroused, thus extracting an individual, configurative
> meaning.
>
> (Iser 1974: 279)

Here, Iser talks about the text 'provoking' responses. But how can we separate that which the text 'provokes' from that which readers map on to the text?

> The reader, of whose responses I speak, then, is this
> informed reader, rather an abstraction, not an actual living
> reader, but a hybrid, a real reader (me) who does everything
> in his power to keep himself informed.
>
> (Fish 1980: 49)

If an abstracted, informed reader becomes the basis for reader-response criticism, are the responses ever likely to be empirically valid? One problem with positing an abstracted reader is that

185

individual readings are given the authority of generalities, and conventional criticism is merely given a gloss as 'reader-based'.

> The Affective Fallacy is a confusion between the poem and its results (what it is and what it does) . . . It begins by trying to derive the standards of criticism from the psychological effects of the poem and ends in impressionism and relativism. The outcome is that the poem itself, as an object of specifically critical judgement, tends to disappear.
>
> (Wimsatt and Beardsley 1954: 21)

This statement represents the theory of the so-called 'New Criticism', which dominated in the middle part of the century. New Criticism rejected the claims of the author and focused on 'the words on the page'. The 'meaning' of a text was to be found in the arrangement of the words of the text and not in other factors such as the reader's psychology, the author's intention or the historical context. The objectivity of the text is sanctioned by Wimsatt and Beardsley: if the effect of the text on the reader is taken into account, 'impressionism and relativism' ensue.

> We do not judge students simply on what they know about a given work; we presume to evaluate their skills and progress as readers, and that presumption ought to indicate our confidence in the existence of public and generalisable operations of reading . . . it is clear that any literary criticism must assume general operations of reading: all critics must make decisions about what can be taken for granted, what must be explicitly argued for, what will count as evidence for a particular interpretation and what would count as evidence against it. Indeed, the whole notion of bringing someone to see that a particular interpretation is a good one assumes shared points of departure and common notions of how to read. In short, far from appealing to 'the text itself' as a source of objectivity, one must assert that the notion of 'what the text says' itself depends upon common procedures of reading.
>
> (Culler 1981: 125)

Culler in this extract focuses not on the individual reader as a source of meaning, but on the reading community. Reading is a learned and interpersonal activity, and because it is so rooted in societal education there are bound to be 'common procedures' in the reading process. Why is it, then, that no reading ever 'exhausts' a text – that there never seems to be a 'final' reading? Although there may be common ground among readers, the range of reading groups and personalities seems too large to accommodate clear and definite agreement on the interpretation of a text. It is more likely that groups of readers would perform similar interpretative moves, but even then those moves would be offset not only by the personalities of the individual readers, but also by the context in which they are performed. Similarly, readings of texts by cultures change over time, and an interpretation that may seem definitive for one generation can be discarded in the next.

A writer has a number of forces and constraints acting upon him or her. It is useful to consider whether these same elements act upon the reader. The elements would include the following, as noted in Chapter 2, Structures and Intention:

Language itself (it imposes its own rules: we have to conform grammatically, to be understood)
Tradition and genre
Unspoken assumptions of society in which the author is a part
Unconscious desires
Class
Race
Gender
The process of publication and editing

You might consider these in relation to the reading process:

Language: Any articulation of response is subject to the same forces and constraints as any texts.
Tradition and genre: We read within traditions of reading, and our assumptions are based on those traditions. Genre expectations create meaning.

Unspoken assumptions: These are part of the ideology we bring
   to a text.
Unconscious desires: We read what we want to read but we think
   we don't.
Class, Race and Gender: All beyond the individual's control.
The process of editing and publication. Analogously, something
   must take place in the mind between responding, articulating
   and formally criticising.

One important basis for many theories of reading is the
philosophy of *phenomenology*. Phenomenology refers to those
things in the world which are perceived by human consciousness,
and is particularly associated with the philosopher Husserl. For
Husserl, objects in an external world do not have independent
existence, but are always processed and mediated through the
conscious mind. The kind of literary criticism influenced by
phenomenology is one which sees literature as a relation between
the textual object and a generalised 'consciousness'. In terms of a
theory of reading, it is most productively expressed in the work of
Roman Ingarden. His two massive volumes *The Literary Work of
Art* and *The Cognition of the Literary Work of Art* have been very
influential upon later theorists such as Wolfgang Iser. Ingarden's
most fundamental notion is the distinction between the text as
object and its 'concretisation'. The act of reading is a concretisation of the consciouness of the author: like a musical score, it has
intention and form, but is only realised in the act of performance.
However, it is not, for Ingarden, merely the performance (or
reading) that exists. The score, or text, has form, patterning
and structure, and these are aids to the concretisation of the
consciousness of the text. Ingarden states:

> During our reading we . . . try to push away, as possible
> distractions, events and concerns that in themselves are quite
> negligible (hence we look for a comfortable position, a quiet
> setting, etc.). This aloofness from our real surroundings
> leads, on the one hand, to the situation that the represented
> objectivities that are depicted constitute a separate world for

us, one that is distant from actual reality; on the other hand, it enables us to assume an attitude of pure beholding with respect to the represented objectivities and to enjoy fully the aesthetic values that appear in the work. It is because of this, among other things, that we achieve the specifically 'aesthetic' ('beholding') attitude that is absolutely necessary for the apprehension of, and vital communion with, works of art.

(Ingarden 1973: 355)

For Ingarden, the literary reading experience is materially different from other kinds of reading experience: the reader must achieve a certain attitude that will enable the consciousness of the text to be realised.

Let us now look at a literary text and try to assess the reading process in the light of a general theory of reading. Consider the following passage from John Fowles's *The Magus*:

Alison was always female; she never, like so many English girls, betrayed her gender. She wasn't beautiful, she very often wasn't even pretty. But she had a fashionably thin boyish figure, she had a contemporary dress sense, she had a conscious way of walking, and her sum was extraordinarily more than her parts. I would sit in the car and watch her walking down the street towards me, pause, cross the road and she looked wonderful. But then when she was close, beside me, there often seemed to be something rather shallow, something spoilt-child, in her prettiness. Even close to her, I was always being wrong-footed. She would be ugly one moment, and then some movement, look, angle of her face, made ugliness impossible.

When she went out she used to wear a lot of eyeshadow, which married with the sulky way she sometimes held her mouth gave her a characteristic bruised look; a look that subtly made one want to bruise her more. Men were always aware of her, in the street, in restaurants, in pubs; and she knew it. I always used to watch them sliding their eyes at her as she passed. She was one of those rare, even among already pretty, women that are born with a natural aura of sexuality: always in their lives it will be the relationships with men, it will be how men react, that matters. And even the tamest sense it.

(Fowles 1977: 31–2)

i) Consider the possible meanings and resonances of the following words and phrases: always female, betrayed her gender, like so many English girls, beautiful, pretty, fashionably thin, contemporary dress sense, wonderful, shallow, spoilt-child, ugly, eye-shadow, sulky, bruised look, natural aura of sexuality.

The above expressions have been selected because we consider them to be crucial to our understanding of the text. Is there any sense in which a group of readers would agree with our choices? Do you disagree with some of them?

ii) How different do you feel that men's and women's responses to the text would be? What exactly are you responding to if you are responding 'according to gender'?

iii) Is the wearing of 'a lot of eye-shadow' a significant metonym (a telling detail) for you? If so, what is it supposed to suggest about Alison?

iv) How would you characterise the narrator? What phrases, words or other linguistic elements of the text can you explicitly cite as evidence for your characterisation?

v) Iser speaks of 'gaps' in the text that must be filled in by the reader. Consider what these gaps might be in the light of a sample sentence from the text: 'She would be ugly one moment, and then some movement, look, angle of her face, made ugliness impossible.'

Any response to this sentence is already 'primed' by the existence of prior co-text. In response to this co-text we will have built up an idea not only of the character of Alison, but also of the narrator, for it is his monologic view of Alison that we receive. The reception of *how* the narrator describes Alison (rather than *what* he says) will affect our understanding of that narrator's motives, which will in turn have bearings on our idea of the relevance and 'truth' of the portrayal. If we trust the narrator, we trust and believe the descriptions presented. In first person narratives, however, the narrator becomes a character in a more obvious sense than is the case with third person fiction, for the narrator is both teller and participant. In the above sentence we have speculations on a possible 'event', and a judgement upon it; but we have no real means of checking the veracity of the narrator's pronouncements. If a narrator says something is 'ugly' (or not) we only have further descriptions (possibly) to help us decide whether we agree or not. But in this case we are not being *shown* that Alison is either ugly or not ugly: we are being *told* about a possibility relating to her physical appearance. The co-text *may* assist us here, but if we look back we find that we have to focus on the role of metonyms such as 'a lot of eye-shadow'. Even then, this may not help us a great deal in processing Alison's potential 'ugliness'.

Of course, this is to assume already that Alison's physical appearance is important to our undestanding of the text; it may be that such a statement is primarily emitting a lateral message about the narrator. What our brief reading has shown is that it is a basic interpretative move to look for thematic coherence in a text. In picking out the salient words and expressions, as we have done, we have already presupposed a particular reading of the text. Thus the reading, or interpretative, process is circular and paradoxical. Our interpretation is based on salient aspects of the text, but they are only salient because they form the basis of our interpretation. In this manner the psychology of the interpretation can be glossed over because the interpretative moves are backed up by 'objective' features of the text. But these features are only the result of an initial interpretation.

2 Reading and identity

In the above exercise we suggested that reading and interpretation were cyclical processes. But how can we describe the processes involved in the activity of reading if this is the case? Critics and theorists such as Stanley Fish and Wolfgang Iser posit the notion of a generalised reader in order to make statements about the reading process. Michael Riffatere, in *The Semiotics of Poetry* (1978) talks about the reader who is is propelled along textual and intertextual networks and who constantly encounters and overcomes hurdles of interpretation. Iser makes a distinction between the 'implied reader', which is essentially a function of the text, and the 'real' reader. But the issue remains as to what such generalised and idealised readers have in common with 'real' readers. What are the benefits for criticism in describing and analysing the activities of readers? Would not an emphasis on the psychology of the individual lead to 'impressionism and relativism' as Wimsatt and Beardsley (1954: 21) suggest? One critic who attempted to give psychological reasons for the responses of readers is Norman Holland. Working from the assumptions of American ego-psychology, Holland sees texts as setting into motion in the reader an interplay of fantasies and defences against those fantasies. Transmuting Freudian theories into critical practice, Holland seeks out the unconscious world of the text, the language of which is subjected to the same scrutiny as the Freudian patient. The analyst/critic looks for dichotomies, ambiguities, absences and repetitions. Although this may sound like pure textual criticism (that is, with no account taken of the reader), Holland takes this further to say that the unconscious sub-text interacts with the sub-text (unconscious) of the reader. The reader who encounters this sub-text is one possessed of a unique 'identity theme', an element which organises the interpretation of a text according to that theme . The text is read in order to 'replicate' the mind of the reader. In an influential and highly idiosyncratic essay 'Unity Identity Text Self', Holland considers responses to the following clause from a short story by William Faulkner, 'A Rose for Emily':

> he who fathered the edict that no Negro woman should
> appear on the streets without an apron

Varying responses to the word 'fathered' were taped by Holland,
and he comments:

> Obviously, since the text presents just the one word 'fath-
> ered', one cannot explain by means of the text alone why one
> reader would find that word heroic, another neutral and
> abstract, and a third sexual. To be sure, differences in age,
> sex, nationality, class or reading experience will contribute to
> differences in interpretation. Yet it is a familiar experience in
> the world of literary or clinical interpretation to find people
> similar in age, sex, nationality, class and interpretive skill
> nevertheless differing radically over particular interpreta-
> tions. And one finds the opposite situation: people super-
> ficially diffferent agreeing on interpretations. Certainly, the
> hundreds of psychological experiments inconclusively corre-
> lating such variables with interpretation give little hope that
> they will provide an answer. At the Center for the Psycho-
> logical Study of the Arts, we have found that we can explain
> such differences in interpretation by examining differences in
> the personalities of the interpreters. More precisely, *inter-
> pretation is a function of identity*, specifically, identity con-
> ceived as variations upon an identity theme.
>
> (Holland 1980: 123)

One of the problems with the kind of conclusion that Holland
reaches is that literary study is carried on in institutions and has
public, political and socio-cultural functions. If interpretation is
always a function of personality, then to study literature is only to
replicate one's personality (Holland himself uses the term 'replicate'). If literary studies is to be seen as an 'academic' subject, in
that it takes place within the academy, then surely it must have
standards of criticism which are in some way objective or public,
and not merely the realisations of the idiosyncratic personalities
of individual readers? How can we reconcile 'personal' interpretation with public standards?

It is fair to say that many theorists have shied away from the tricky problem of identity and instead focused on the relationship between formal features of a text and the reader's construction of meaning. Stanley Fish is one such critic. Fish's early criticism was based on a simply stated theory: the text is not an objective entity, nor is it the critic's task to describe this entity. Rather, criticism must be:

An analysis of the developing responses of the reader in relation to the words as they succeed one another in time.

(Fish 1980: 387–8)

Here is a quotation from his essay 'Interpreting the Variorum'. He is discussing lines from Milton's 'Lycidas':

The first passage (actually the second in the poem's sequence) begins at line 42:

The willows and the hazel copses green
Shall no more be seen,
Fanning their joyous leaves to thy soft lays.

(l. 42–44)

It is my thesis that the reader is always making sense (I intend 'making' to have its literal force), and in the case of these lines the sense he makes will involve the assumption (and therefore the creation) of a completed assertion after the word 'seen', to wit, the death of Lycidas has so affected the willows and the hazel copses green that, in sympathy, they will wither and die (will no more be seen by anyone). In other words at the end of line 43 the reader will have hazarded an interpretation, or performed an act of perceptual closure, or made a decision as to what is being asserted. I do not mean that he has done four things, but that he has done one thing the description of which might take any one of four forms – making sense, interpreting, performing perceptual closure, deciding about what is intended. (The importance of this point will become clear later.) Whatever he has done (that is, however we characterise it) he will undo it in the act of reading the next line; for here he discovers that his closure, or making of sense, was premature and that he must make a new one in which the relationship between man and nature is exactly the reverse of what was first assumed . . . Rather than intention and its formal realisation producing interpretation (the 'normal' picture), interpretation creates intention and its formal realisation by creating the conditions in which it becomes possible to pick them out. In other words, in the analysis of these lines from *Lycidas* I did what critics always do; I 'saw' what my interpretive principles permitted or directed me to see, and then I turned around and attributed what I had 'seen' to a text and an intention . . .

This, then is my thesis; that the form of the reader's experience, formal units, and the structure of intention are one, that they come into view simultaneously, and that therefore the questions of priority and independence do not arise.

(Fish 1980: 162–5)

i) Compare Fish's documented reading experience of the lines to your own.

ii) What do you understand by the term 'interpretive principles'? Does this in any way encapsulate any point in the reading process?

iii) How can Fish know that such structures of the reading process come into view simultaneously?

iv) Considering the possibility that Fish's model may be 'what happens' when we read and try to make sense of texts, what are the likely consequences for criticism?

v) Is the model Fish proposes restricted to one genre? Are features that are created likely to be different in a novel, drama or even a different kind of poetry?

The notion of 'interpretive principles' is problematic. It is not clear from Fish's argument whether they are broad psychological impulses, or responses engendered by the genre of the text being read. His 'principles' direct him to see certain things, but then Fish must posit another set of principles which have to do with the defeating of those principles of expectation. Although Fish suggests that structures and the reading of those structures come into play at the same moment, his interpretation seems to suggest that formal features do account in some way for his 'interpretive principles'. Fish always, ironically, expects the same things to happen, and he never learns from the experience of reading. His imagined reader replicates the same reading pattern time and time again. The problem with trying to account for what happens when we read is that the reader ends up accounting for what happens when we try to account for the reading experience. The reading experience may be one thing, but the documentation of that experience produces another text – and, crucially, another reader. As Jonathan Culler states in *On Deconstruction*:

> Each time it is possible to interpret the end of a line of verse as completing a thought, he [Fish] does so only to find, in numerous cases, that the beginning of the next line brings a change of sense. One would expect any real reader, especially one striving to be informed, to notice that premature guesses often prove wrong and to anticipate this possibility as he reads. Stanley E. Fish, after all, not only notices this possibility but writes books about it. We can confidently suppose that as Fish reads he is on the lookout for such cases and is pleased rather than dismayed when they occur. The conclusion seems inescapable: what Fish reports is not Stanley Fish reading but Stanley Fish imagining reading as a Fishian reader.
>
> (Culler 1983: 66)

Culler highlights a significant problem for any kind of criticism based on the reader's response. To talk about response is always to do so retroactively. An initial response to a text may be one thing, but the documentation of that response is far from simple. We can never see raw 'response': and its documentation and transcription give us not only another text, but also another reader, for the articulated response is materially different from the response itself. Further, we can only talk about response once we have interpreted the text. What arises here is what is known as the 'hermeneutic circle': we cannot speak of 'gaps' in the text, for instance, unless we have an idea of the textual whole; but the whole cannot be understood without an understanding of its parts, and therefore of its gaps. This was suggested earlier in our reading of the extract from Fowles's *The Magus*.

3 From micro- to macro-reading

In this part we will look at the process of reading in more detail, beginning with the analysis of a very short text and concluding with a case-study of readings of William Blake's 'London'. First, however, here is Noam Chomsky on how we understand sentences:

> in order to understand a sentence it is necessary to know the kernel sentences from which it originates . . . and the phrase structures of each of these elementary components, as well as the transformational history of development of the given sentence from these kernel sentences . . . The general problem of analyzing the process of 'understanding' is thus reduced, in a sense, to the problem of explaining how kernel sentences are understood, these being considered the basic 'content elements' from which the usual, more complex sentences of real life are formed by transformational development.
>
> (Chomsky 1957: 92)

Chomsky's comments on the understanding of individual sentences seem rather abstract, but his essential thesis is that each sentence is derived from a core or 'kernel' sentence. If we wish to understand how we understand, then we have to look at these more basic, if idealised, sentences. One problem with such an approach is that we rarely respond, either in reading or listening, to single sentences, and it is not clear that larger discourses are merely 'long sentences' (see Chapters 1 and 2). The 'more complex sentences of real life' presumably refers to those uttered in spoken discourse, and the recognition of their complexity is based on their relation to original kernel sentences. But this presupposes that the language of spoken discourse is homogeneous, and that it has a special authority and credibility. However, it is only the existence of fuller, idealised and abstracted forms that gives credence to the 'complex' forms that are spoken. Are written texts subject to different processing procedures, and if so, is there an implication that written language itself is 'different' from spoken? Is 'literary language' different still? Consider the sentence:

See you down the pub later?

This piece of language is recognisable and familiar, even if we do not know who is speaking, who is being addressed, where 'the pub' is or how long 'later' is. The ellipted declarative form of the sentence is offset by the question mark, and we would suggest that we have little difficulty in reconciling the form (declarative) with a range of functions (interrogative, enquiry). What this means is that, given such a sentence, we have little difficulty in creating an interpretative context whereby it not only makes sense semantically (that is, we 'understand' the sentence) but also pragmatically – we create a suitable *use* for it. Now, the sentence could be uttered in a threatening manner; it could be ironic, or sarcastic; it could be a hidden command; it could be uttered by someone unlikely ever to visit a pub. All these are possibilities, but we suggest that we 'round off' the pragmatic possibilities to an appropriate, likely context – that is, two young adults in polite discourse. There is no necessary reason for this, and we are not suggesting that we all create the same context, only that we create an accessible, plausible one given our own identities and knowledge. We would all, no doubt, have different mental representations of speaker and hearer. It is suggested that there are certain textual clues which assist in the construction of possible contexts, but this is not very complex given the short, abstracted example. Given that the sentence is also more likely to feature in spoken discourse we would have access to extra-linguistic elements to assist us in our context-creation and interpretation. These elements will not simply explain away the meaning of a sentence – a relevant context still has to be constructed – but we are likely to draw on the signal given in the immediate discourse environment for help. In any written text there is rarely an immediate discourse environment. Written discourse is less context-bound. In a semi-public domain such as that which pervades Jane Austen's novels, however, the written is context-bound.

Consider the following poem, William Blake's 'London' (1793). You should read the poem one line at a time and cover the rest. Although this is of course an artificial reading process, it will be useful for the analysis of response.

> I wander thro' each charter'd street
> Near where the charter'd Thames does flow,
> And mark in every face I meet
> Marks of weakness, marks of woe.
>
> In every cry of every Man,
> In every Infant's cry of fear,
> In every voice, in every ban,
> The mind-forg'd manacles I hear.
>
> How the Chimney-sweeper's cry
> Every black'ning Church appalls;
> And the hapless Soldier's sigh
> Runs in blood down Palace walls.
>
> But most thro' midnight streets I hear
> How the youthful Harlot's curse
> Blasts the new-born Infant's tear
> And blights with plagues the Marriage-hearse
>
> (Blake 1986)

i) What kinds of expectations are set up by the opening line? Are these expectations sentence-based, expression-based, or based on any other elements, such as individual words?

ii) Is there a word or phrase which seems crucial to the understanding of a line?

iii) What kinds of extra-textual knowledge do you think are needed in order to make sense of the text?

iv) Can you locate elements of your response which might be said to be more 'personal' than others? Is this to do with your evaluation of the text?

v) Is it possible to distinguish between those aspects of the text's meaning that seem to you personal, and those which are part of the text's 'immanent' meaning – that is, parts which would mean the same to everyone?

vi) How close is the one-line-at-a-time approach to reading to your own reading?

Jonathan Culler in *The Pursuit of Signs* (1981) discusses the various readings of the poem, and in particular the interpretative move of seeking *unity*. He states:

> In general the interpretations of the poem show, as one would expect, that the reading process involves the attempt to bring together the various sights and sounds according to one of our models of unity. The model most frequently used here is that of the synecdochic series, where a list of particulars are interpreted as instances of a general class to which they all belong. Critics name this class in different ways – social problems of eighteenth-century urban life, evils produced by the artificial impositions of Reason, generalized human suffering – and their interpretations explain, where it is not obvious, how each of the sights and sounds fits into the class so named.
>
> The other model of unity that appears in interpretations of the poem is what one might call the *pattern of alethic reversal* [alethic = relating to truth]: first a false or inadequate vision, then its true or adequate counterpart. By

this model, more common in interpretations of other works, one unifies the poem by identifying a shift.

(Culler 1981: 69)

The kind of shift Culler refers to at the close of the quotation might be something stylistic. For example, the repetition of prepositional phrases such as 'In every' ceases in the final stanza, and the conjunction 'But' introduces the final movement of the poem. Of course the conjunction need not signify a reversal of any sort. Although this might represent a shift of some kind, it is also a *development* of the argument. A central difficulty, noted by many of the critics that Culler cites, lies in the lines:

How the Chimney-sweeper's cry
Every black'ning Church appalls

The chimney sweeper is presumably the innocent victim here, yet his cry 'appalls' the church. Culler suggests that 'no critic accepts this statement at face value . . . each finds a way round it' (70). If the church 'appalls' the cry of the sweeper, there are three obvious interpretative choices to be made, once we have agreed on the grammar of the proposition. First, the Church itself is guilty – organised religion is guilty of hypocrisy, ostensibly caring, but effectively 'appalled' at the sweeper. Second, the church is shocked that something like the sweeper's condition could exist. Finally, we could read 'the church' as the building itself, where the clergymen are *not* guilty. This sets up an opposition between the institution as represented by the physical existence of the building, and the clergymen who represent and inhabit the building.

vii) Given the obvious prescriptions noted above, can you decide on a particular interpretation?

viii) State as explicitly as possible the criteria by which you made the interpretative decision.

4 Open and closed texts

The way a text is read within a culture has political significance. The history of literature is littered with cases of attacks on, and defences of, particular works which seem to threaten the dominant politics of a given time. The critic's task in these cases is seen as one of correction – making the text in question acceptable or unacceptable to its assumed naive readers. But this is not a question of exposing absolute truths that a culture has misread, for instance. Meaning is a political variant, and is so precisely because the literary work can never (or rarely) be corrected, but only interpreted. The text itself cannot be corrected, but readings of it can.

Reception theorists such as Karlheinz Stierle (1980) suggest that popular literature serves to perpetuate and produce naive readings: the reader collaborates with the text and the text collaborates with the reader in the production of a self-fulfilling illusion. This is attained without complex aesthetic procedures. The semiotician Umberto Eco makes a distinction between *open* and *closed* texts in his work *The Role of the Reader: Explorations in the Semiotics of Texts* (1979). Eco stresses that 'the reader as an active principal of interpretation is part of the picture of the generative process of the text' (5). His theory of open and closed texts rests on the assumption of what he calls the 'Model Reader'. He states:

> To organize a text, its author has to rely upon a series of codes that assign given contents to the expressions he uses. To make his text communicative, the author has to assume that the ensemble of codes he relies upon is the same as that shared by the possible reader. The author has thus to foresee a model of the possible reader (hereafter Model Reader) supposedly able to deal interpretatively with the expressions in the same way as the author generatively deals with them.
>
> (Eco 1979: 7)

A Model Reader for closed text is described as follows:

In the process of communication, a text is frequently interpreted against the background of codes different from those
intended by the author. Some authors do not take into
account such a possibility. They have in mind an average
addressee referred to a given social context. Nobody can
say what happens when the actual reader is different from
the 'average' one. Those texts that obsessively aim at arous-
ing a precise response on the part of more or less precise
empirical readers . . . are in fact open to any possible
'aberrant decoding'. A text so immoderately 'open' to every
possible interpretation will be called a *closed* one.

(Eco 1979: 8)

Eco suggests that Superman comics and the novels of Ian
Fleming are closed texts, ironically open to aberrant interpretations. These texts seem to propel the reader along a predetermined
path, but can be read for different ideological purposes.

The Model Reader for closed texts is described in the
following manner:

When reading a Fleming novel or a Superman comic strip,
one can at most guess what kind of reader their authors had
in mind, not which requirements a 'good' reader should
meet. I was not the kind of reader foreseen by the authors
of Superman, but I presume to have been a 'good' one . . .
On the contrary, when reading *Ulysses* one can extrapolate
the profile of a 'good *Ulysses* reader' from the text itself,
because the pragmatic process of interpretation is not an
empirical accident independent of the text *qua* text, but is
a structural element of its generative process.
      . . . The 'ideal' reader of *Finnegans Wake* cannot be a
Greek reader of the second century BC or an illiterate man of
Aran. The reader is strictly defined by the texical and the
syntactical organisation of the text: the text is nothing else
but the semantic-pragmatic production of its own Model
Reader.

(Eco 1979: 9–10)

Here are extracts from the kinds of texts Eco discusses. 'Bomb Then, Bomb Now' by Bruce Andrews:

> what is it? The influence of envy in secretarial work, nutrition's affection for the body swallows these expectations, my name is on high. Monster goo urbanism that spurts a valet; my epoch's not up yet – some deft tuck no longer setting out for the hacienda, then the single women got tied up to watch the divorcees. There is no such thing as an emergency in the world, resuscitation won't work – & yet bodies keep swarm, that's gangland slang, hypnosis surveillance kill a crustacean for Christ's criminology a nobody treachery hope. We must reject into account; true, not truth – resumes for Reagan. Castigate masters – can't a man flout a goat? At last, a chewing gum for the bellybuttons of the rich; couple talk is coop talk
> mirandized him – pump iron to be bright
> her usual spinster tourist spitfire *fantasy causes stress* . . .
> (Andrews 1994: 535)

Now, Fleming. The following is from *Thunderball* (1961):

> It was one of those days when it seemed to James Bond that all life, as someone put it, was nothing but a heap of six to four against.
> To begin with he was ashamed of himself – a rare state of mind. He had a hangover, a bad one, with an aching head and stiff joints. When he coughed – smoking too much goes with drinking too much and doubles the hangover – a cloud of small luminous black spots swarm across his vision like amoebae in pond water. The one drink too many signals itself unmistakably. His final whisky and soda in the luxurious flat in Park Lane had been no different from the ten preceding ones, but it had gone down reluctantly and had left a bitter taste and an ugly sensation of surfeit. And, although he had taken in the message, he had agreed to play just one more rubber. Five pounds a hundred as it's the last one? He

had agreed. And he had played the rubber like a fool. Even now he could see the queen of spades, with that stupid Mona Lisa smile on her fat face, . . .

(Fleming 1978: 9)

i) What kinds of stylistic differences between the two texts can you detail?

ii) To what extent is style (complexity or simplicity) dictating model readerships.

iii) Given that Fleming text is 'easier' to read than Andrews's, and more clearly follows certain generic conventions, can you account for the fact the latter's reader is 'strictly defined'?

Like Eco, Roland Barthes also makes a distinction between two kinds of text; but for Barthes it is not a distinction between the 'open' and 'closed' but between the readable and unreadable. In *S/Z* (1974) Barthes discusses those texts which are traditionally intelligible (*lisible*) and those which, though written, cannot be properly read (*scriptable*). For Barthes, a Fleming novel would be an example of the *lisible* text (texte de plaisir) and *Finnegans Wake* (Or 'Bomb Then, Bomb Now') a *scriptible* (texte de jouissance) one. However, this is not a straightforward binarism, and it is better to think of the difference operating in degrees rather than being one of kind. The distinction between a James Bond novel and *Finnegans Wake* is an extreme version of the binarism. Of the 'pleasure of the text', Barthes states:

> . . . what I enjoy in a narrative is not directly its content or even its structure, but rather the abrasions I impose upon the fine surface: I read on, I skip, I look up, I dip in again. Which has nothing to do with the deep laceration the text of bliss inflicts upon language itself, and not upon the simple temporality of its reading.
>
> Whence two systems of reading: one goes straight to the articulations of the anecdote, it considers the extent of the text, ignores the play of language (If I read Jules Verne, I

go fast: I lose discourse, and yet my reading is not hampered by any verbal *loss* in the speleological sense of that word); the other reading skips nothing; it weighs, it sticks to the text, it reads, so to speak, with application and transport, grasps at every point in the text the asyndeton [a rhetorical figure] which cuts the various languages – and not the anecdote: it is not (logical) extension that captivates it, the winnowing out of truths, but the layering of significance; as in the children's game of topping hands, the excitement comes not from a processive haste but from a kind of vertical din (the verticality of language and of its destruction); it is at the moment when each (different) hand skips over the next (and not one *after* the other) that the hole, the gap, is created and carries off the subject of the game – the subject of the text.

(Barthes 1975: 11–12)

Ever mindful of the readers of his own text, Barthes speaks of reading not as if it were some complete, objective process with each element given equal weight and consideration, but as a subjective, transient and pleasurable activity. We do not read each part of the text with equal interest or involvement, but rather miss out bits and gloss over others. In criticism generally, the pleasure of the text is very rarely noted; it is not seen as a fit topic of critical discussion. But if we are to suggest that readers actively make meaning, and make that activity the focus of criticism, then we must take into account the fact that reading is a much looser and more haphazard activity than at first it would seem.

5 Deaths of authors, births of readers

At the close of his infamous essay 'The Death of the Author' (1968, in Barthes 1977) Roland Barthes states that 'the birth of the reader must be at the cost of the death of the author'. Structuralism, though heavily text-centred, paved the way for the reintroduction of the reader as a site of critical interest because it focused on the systems which made meanings possible. If the text is a 'tissue of quotations', it is the reader who must process and ultimately realise its culture. But that reader, as we have seen, is difficult to define or to locate. For the structuralists, however, the reader was less a real entity than a *function* – a semiotic, idealised site where meaning ultimately resides. Barthes states:

> We know now that a text is not a line of words releasing a single 'theological' meaning (the 'message' of the Author-God) but a multi-dimensional space in which a variety of writings, none of them original, blend and clash. The text is a tissue of quotations drawn from innumerable centres of culture.
>
> Once the author is removed, the claim to decipher a text becomes quite futile. To give a text an Author is to impose a limit on that text, to furnish it with a final signified, to close the writing . . . In the multiplicity of writing, everything is to be *disentangled*, nothing *deciphered*; the structure can be followed, 'run' (like the thread of a stocking) at every point and at every level, but there is nothing beneath: the space of writing is to be ranged over, not pierced; writing ceaselessly posits meaning ceaselessly to evaporate it, carrying out a systematic exemption of meaning. In precisely this way literature (it would be better now to say *writing*), by refusing to assign a 'secret', an ultimate meaning, to the text (and to the world as text), liberates what might be called an anti-theological activity, an activity that is truly revolutionary since to refuse to fix meaning is, in the end, to refuse God and his hypostases – reason, science, law.
>
> (Barthes 1977: 147)

The 'Author-God' here is replaced by an intertextual reader. There is no 'secret' meaning in a text which can be extrapolated Barthes' pronouncements have a political edge, for he sees the refusal to see meaning as both 'ultimate' and author-centred as a refusal to accept traditional Western power structures. His essay is the *locus classicus* of anti-authorial statements, but Northrop Frye had also come to be suspicious of the 'authority' of the author. Something of a hybrid critic, Frye is sometimes reviled as a New Critic, along with Cleanth Brooks, Allen Tate and W.K. Wimsatt, and sometimes lauded as a proto-structuralist for his theories of modes and genres in *Anatomy of Criticism* (1957). Here is an extract from the 'Polemical Introduction' to the book:

> The axiom of criticism must be, not that the poet does not know what he is talking about, but that he cannot talk about what he knows. To defend the right of criticism to exist at all, therefore, is to assume that criticism is a structure of thought and knowledge existing in its own right, with some measure of independence from the art it deals with.
>
> The poet may of course have some critical ability of his own, and so be able to talk about his own work. But the Dante who writes a commentary on the first canto of the *Paradiso* is merely one more of Dante's critics. What he says has a peculiar interest, but not a peculiar authority. It is generally accepted that a critic is a better judge of the *value* of a poem than its creator, but there is still a lingering notion that it is somehow ridiculous to regard the critic as the final judge of its meaning, even though in practice it is clear that he must be. The reason for this is an inability to distinguish literature from the descriptive or assertive writing which derives from the active will and the conscious mind, and which is primarily concerned to 'say' something.
>
> (Frye 1957: 5)

i) What do you understand by the statement 'the axiom of criticism must be, not that the poet does not know what he is talking about, but that he cannot talk about what he knows'?

ii) Do you consider the author to the most valuable insight into his or her own work?

iii) What is Frye saying about the differences between literary writing and other kinds of writing?

The following statements are concerned with the power and authority of the author. With which of the following do you agree?

The author is the sole source and arbiter of meaning.
The author is source of meaning only in the sense that he or she is in a privileged position of knowledge about the text.
The author is the source of meaning but cannot always know that meaning.
The author is the initial source of meaning, but meaning becomes public at the point of publication.
The author is a cultural construction.

There are various positions that the critic can take regarding the problem of where meaning resides. They can be stated very simply:

The author
The text (as in New Critical Practice)
The reader

However, there is another approach, adopted by some reader-response theorists, in which meaning is seen as a product of the interrelationship between textual features and reader knowledge. The following is an extract from Wolfgang Iser's essay 'Interaction Between Text and Reader':

> Communication in literature . . . is a process set in motion and regulated, not by a given code, but by a mutually restrictive and magnifying interaction between the explicit and the implicit, between revelation and concealment. What is concealed spurs the reader into action, but this action is also controlled by what is revealed; the explicit in its turn is transformed when the implicit has been brought to light. Whenever the reader bridges the gaps, communication begins. The gaps function as a kind of pivot on which the whole text–reader relationship revolves. Hence, the structured blanks of the text stimulate the process of ideation to be performed by the reader on terms set by the text. There

is, however, another place in the textual system where text and reader converge, and that is marked by the various types of negation which arise in the course of the reading. Blanks and negations both control the process of communication in their own different ways: the blanks leave open the connection between textual perspectives, and so spur the reader into coordinating these perspectives and patterns – in other words, they induce the reader to perform basic operations *within* the text. The various types of negation invoke familiar and determinate elements or knowledge only to cancel them out. What is cancelled, however, remains in view, and thus brings about modifications in the reader's attitude toward what is familiar or determinate – in other words, he is guided to adopt a position *in relation* to the text.

(Iser 1980: 111–12)

The reading process for Iser is characterised by the *response* to the structures of the text and a realisation or actualisation of its gaps. Reading is therefore a dynamic process. It is neither predetermined by generic conventions nor open to infinite interpretation. The advantage of Iser's theory is that the text is seen not as fixed and absolute, but as a fluid entity, although he does not go as far as Barthes in his assessment of the reader's 'struggle' with the text. One possible problem, however, lies in the assessment of what the text provokes and what the reader concludes: traditional text-focused criticism may survive but accompanied by a new terminology.

In *Aesthetic Experience and Literary Hermeneutics* (1982a) Hans Robert Jauss suggests that differences in readings of texts, not only between individuals but also across time, cannot be accounted for by differences in personality alone. Similarly, generic conventions cannot be said to fully determine the reading process if readings of texts change to a significant extent. The genre may help to *contain* those responses, but it will not prescribe them. Thus Jauss speaks of 'paradigms' and the 'horizon of expectations'. A paradigm is similar to a theory, but it contains both implicit and explicit cultural assumptions. In the same way that a theory will only accommodate a world view and therefore seem 'truthful' until a new theory arrives to displace it, the cultural assumptions of an historical paradigm are only relevant until such changes cause it to shift. The contemporary readers of Elizabethan sonnets, for instance, were subject to a different paradigm to that which modern readers are subjected, and that accounts, in part, for the production of different readings. Each culture in each paradigm has a 'horizon of expectations' – a set of assumptions which will contribute to the production of certain kinds of readings. This may well account for the fact that some writers seem to be 'out of time' – either reviled by their contemporaries and lauded by a later culture or praised by contemporary readers and neglected later. Paradigm shifts have brought about shifts in the readings of the texts: different 'horizons of expectations' prevail. Ironically, however, Jauss's theory turns out to be ahistorical. The 'horizon' is constructed in three ways:

> First, through familiar norms or the immanent poetics of the genre; second, through the implicit relationships to familiar works of the literary-historical surroundings; and third, through the opposition between fiction and reality, between the poetic and practical functions of language, which is always available to the reflective reader during the reading as a possibility of comparison.
>
> (Jauss 1982a: 24)

Jauss cites generic, literary-historical and linguistic aspects of the 'horizon', but purely historical aspects are absent. The text is still primarily a 'literary' phenomenon, and the horizon of expectations, though determined by cultural assumptions, is filtered through a text which maintains its aesthetic autonomy

iv) Is it possible to add to Jauss's points? What other elements might usefully be cited as relevant to the 'horizons of expectations'?

6 Anti-formalisms, structures and Gestalt

Both linguistic and literary formalisms betray a belief in the dominance of form and the primacy of structure over any individual realisation of that structure. Thus Chomsky's theories are based on the concept of an underlying grammatical structure the reconstruction of which is seen to be the task of the analyst (see Chapter 1). In literary theory, formalist analyses concentrate on the notions of cohesion and unity, and in some cases attempt to reconstruct abstract grammars of cultural artefacts (see Chapter 2). Much modern theory, both linguistic and literary, has turned away from the pervasive formalisms of the middle part of the century. The so-called 'Geneva School' of theorists in the 1940s and 1950s, which drew on the work of the phenomenologist Husserl, shifted the focus on to the relationship between consciousness and text, rather than focusing on immanent objective structures, and this is the basis of much modern reader-response theory. The object, or text, is contingent on the subject, or conscious mind, for its realisation. Geneva theorists such as George Poulet and Maurice Blanchot talk about the relation between object and subject, and how the subject, the reader, takes on the thoughts of another, the world of the text. Poulet states:

> because of the strange invasion of my person by the thoughts of another, I am a self who is granted the experience of thinking thoughts foreign to him. I am the subject of thoughts other than my own.
>
> (Poulet 1969: 56)

Reader-response theorists do not necessarily reject the idea of formal patterning inherent in texts. Fish's model in 'Interpreting the Variorum' is an extreme case of reader-focused criticism; in his later work, Fish focused on the meaning texts have for particular 'interpretive communities', and abandoned the idea of the reader being solely responsible for meaning. As we have seen, Ingarden and Poulet also focus on the interaction between textual form and readerly consciousness. These perspectives highlight the difficulties involved in separating formal features from interpretative procedures, and separating generalised readers – or readers within a given community or culture – from 'actual' readers.

In the discussion of Norman Holland's theories of interpretation and identity (see Reading and Identity, p. 192), it was suggested that there exists a tension between the socio-cultural and public demands of interpretative procedures within the academy and the personal readings of texts based on subjective identity. Writing is a more public activity than reading, and the transcription of interpretation brings with it a different set of norms, expectations and constraints. To take a simple example based on Holland's work: even if an individual reader considers the word 'father' in the Faulkner novel to be 'sexual' or 'neutral' she or he may not reveal this in any formal, written discussion of the work, because that writing is public (at least, it is not private, as a private thought might be). The interpretation may be tempered to conform to accepted criteria, whether implicit or explicit. A focus on the formal features of a text, couched in objective or quasi-objective terms, is thus the least overtly political kind of criticism, although of course it hides a dominant ideology by maintaining the status quo. If formal features can be recognised and described, they must be 'in' the text; and if they are in the text, then some kind of textual meaning must be stable; if textual meaning is relatively stable, we can set criteria for the description and evaluation of that meaning. Formalist criticism is, then, the critical practice most readily institutionalised, for if meaning is unstable and constructed in the minds of readers, what aspects of that text can be 'taught'?

We have talked about the reader's search for 'unity' in a text, with reference to Blake's 'London' (see from Micro- to Macro-Reading, p. 199–201), and the ways in which the parts of a text are conceived and integrated into an idea about the text as a whole. We shall discuss a more specific theory related to this idea, Gestalt, before looking at the theory that seeks to display meaning as unstable, shifting and displaced: deconstruction.

In Gestalt psychology, originating in the work of Fritz Perls in the early twentieth century, the human mind is seen as having a tendency to construct coherent wholes out of parts, these wholes not merely being the sum of those parts. *Gestalt* means 'form', and reflects the mind's predisposition to construct formal coherence, and to seek 'closure' – the sense of completion or the 'rounding off' of phenomena such as interpretations of texts. One part of a text, for instance, may lead to the construction of a particular gestalt, a grasping of wholeness. But further reading and information will lead to the construction of further gestalten and the earlier one will be built upon, or modified. Interpretation is therefore made up of layers of gestalten, each rehearsing some form of closure. Essentially, this means that new information is processed in the light of old, and new 'wholes' are constructed as the reader proceeds through the text. For theorists such as Iser, multiple gestalten are facilitated by 'textual strategies' – the roles of the narrator, the characters, the plot and the reader. These help control the possibilities for interpretation. However, a 'final' gestalt is never formed. As William Ray explains:

> The reader must make constant decisions in order to affect any closure: 'a gestalt can only be closed if one possibility is selected and the rest excluded' . . . This choice represents a kind of commitment and involvement. But the reader's 'entanglement' can never be complete, because it is open to revision when excluded possibilities re-emerge as viable choices.
>
> (Ray 1984: 35–6)

In the theory of Gestalt represented by Ray here, there are contradictory impulses: the reader is searching for closure in the construction of gestalten; but the gestalten, represented by the corollary of the reader's involvement, can never be fixed. Interpretation can be characterised, in this model, as a search for an ever-elusive final meaning, and it is this relation between closure and elusive meaning that, in part, characterizes the theory and practice of deconstruction, though it has no direct relation to Gestalt theory.

7 Deconstructing the text

There are many commentaries on, and explanations of, deconstruction available. Indeed, for both the professional critic and the
student, deconstructive practice has proved curiously accessible,
despite the fear shown in some quarters of its principal theorist,
Jacques Derrida. Deconstruction has a positive face for many
students because it is, in one form, fairly 'easy' to apply and
therefore to see working in texts (theoretically any text). This,
however, is also its main drawback (it deconstructs itself pedago-
gically) because its very applicability belies the strength and
complexity of its philosophical base. Put simply, the practice of
deconstruction, particularly in its 'Yale' form (deconstruction
practised by imitators of Geoffrey Hartman and J. Hillis
Miller), can lead to naive readings of texts and the automatic
application of a seductive methodology.

Deconstruction attacks Western metaphysical thought by
showing how it privileges certain ideas and concepts. The kinds
of metaphysical concepts analysed by deconstruction are characterised by the assumption of ultimate sources of meaning which
are encoded linguistically (God, Reason, Law, etc.). These concepts are anchors which, if you buy into their belief systems,
cannot be dislodged. Reworking Saussure's theory of binary
oppositions, Derrida shows that in each pair one element is
suppressed and one privileged. Derrida tried to show how the
privileged term depended for its meaning upon the suppressed
one. Language is ultimately arbitrary, being a purely unstable
differential system. Meaning is further suspended in the process
of reading; and because language is subject to temporal processes
something is always deferred – meaning is always 'in process' and
not fixed. Every text is subject to a kind of generalised absence.

Structuralism, at its most conservative, is an interpretative
practice that seeks order and intelligibility amongst the many
possible patterns a text holds. A structuralist critic is supposed
to be able to pick out significant patterns of signs, and draw
conclusions from such patterns about the culture that is being
investigated. Saussure advanced the proposition that language is

215

made up of a differential network, at both the level of the signifier and the signified. We can show a straightforward linguistic analogy here, developing the example used in Chapter 2. The phonemes /p/ and /b/ are closely related: they share the same place and manner of articulation. They are both bilabial (sound made with both lips) and plosive (produced with a sudden expulsion of air). They are in binary relation, differentiated by virtue of the voiced/voiceless binarism. /b/ is voiced, /p/ is voiceless. Yet /b/ would not be called 'voiced' if there were not a phoneme with a lack of voice to oppose it. The voiced phoneme might be called 'privileged' because it is the one which is defined by a characteristic possession: it 'has' voice, or 'is' voiced. The /p/ phoneme, however, is differentiated by virtue of what it lacks: the voice. The voiced phoneme claims its centrality by being defined in terms of what the suppressed term is not. Part of its 'meaning', or function, is embedded in its voiceless counterpart.

It is to these proliferating differences that Jacques Derrida gives the term *différance*. This term connects both with the process of differing, as /p/ differs from /b/, and to the process of deferring, as the definition of one signified necessarily and endlessly refers to other signifieds, and to the whole system of signifieds that constitutes language. The term *différance* in its composite structure not only points out these processes of difference and deferral, but also offers its own unstable meaning. The word *différance* itself is a graphic example of the process at work: a deconstructionist can never settle on either one meaning or the other for the invented term – she or he shifts between difference and deferral endlessly. Derrida's own exploration of *différance* is at its most concise in his essay of the same title, which appears in *Margins of Philosophy*. He explains:

> There is no essence of *différance*; it (is) that which only could never be appropriated in the *as such* of its name or its appearing, but also that which threatens the authority of the *as such* in general, of the presence of the thing itself in its essence. That there is not a proper essence of *différance* at this point, implies that there is neither a Being nor truth of

the play of writing such as it engages *différance* . . . 'There is no name for it' – a proposition to be read in this *platitude*. This unnameable is not an ineffable Being which no name could approach: God, for example. This unnameable is the play which makes possible nominal effects, the relatively unitary and atomic structures that are called names, the chains of substitutions of names in which, for example, the nominal effect *différance* is itself *enmeshed*, carried off, reinscribed, just as false entry or a false exit is still part of the game, a function of the system.

(Derrida 1982: 27)

We have argued that the process of deconstruction is illustrated in the word *différance*. How does the quotation above support this argument? Derrida's definition of the term is a non-definition; he says that 'there is not a proper essence of *différance*'. He argues that its function in language is that which makes possible 'nominal effects', nominal effects being what we conventionally understand as linguistic meaning. Crucially though, he argues that the term *différance* is not privileged above other linguistic signs or nominal effects. *Différance* itself is subject to the same effect that the term delineates; the term is 'enmeshed', differing and deferring along a signifying chain. Although it is a term that we have singled out for attention, Derrida is at pains to point out that this should not be the case. It is one more 'false entry' into the game, or into deconstruction.

It is possible that at this point you are beginning to be frustrated by this activity which defies your quest for understanding. But Derrida explains that this is the nature of the procedure. In the following quotation he articulates the difficulty of the undertaking of deconstruction:

We have no language – no syntax and no lexicon which is foreign to [this] history; we can pronounce not a single destructive proposition which has not already had to slip into the from, the logic, and the implicit postulations of precisely what it seeks to contest. To take one example from many: the metaphysics of presence is shaken with the help of the concept of the sign. But . . . as soon as one seeks to demonstrate in this way that there is no transcendental or privileged signified and that the domain or play of signification henceforth has no limit, one must reject even the concept and word 'sign' itself – which is precisely what cannot be done. For the signification 'sign' has always been understood and determined in its meaning, as a sign of, a signifier referring to a signified, a signifier different from its signified. If one erases the radical difference between signifier and signified, it is the word 'signifier' itself which must be abandoned as a metaphysical concept . . . The concept of the sign, in each of its aspects, has been determined by this opposition throughout the totality of history. It has lived only on this opposition and its system. But we cannot do without the concept of the sign, for we cannot give up this metaphysical complicity without also giving up the critique we are directing against this complicity, or without the risk of erasing difference in the self-identity of a signified reducing its signifier into itself, or, amounting to the same thing, simply expelling its signifier outside itself.

(Derrida 1978: 280–1)

What Derrida is reiterating here is the complicity of the critic in the process of deconstruction, the way in which any writer is bound up in the forms that she or he seeks to challenge. If we wish to give up this complicity, we must also give up the challenge, and the result of this is the expulsion of the 'signifier outside itself'. Although Derrida's argument is very abstract, his suggestion that we are always colluders in the construction of meaning, no matter how we want to unpick the process, is an important one for literary critics to remember. Every time they approach a poem to root out its hidden meaning they are are putting that meaning together as much as pulling it apart.

Consider the following poem by Philip Larkin:

The Winter Palace
Most people know more as they get older:
I give all that the cold shoulder.

I spent my second quarter-century
Losing what I had learnt at university

And refusing to take in what had happened since.
Now I know none of the names in the public prints,

And am starting to give offence by forgetting faces
And swearing I've never been in certain places.

It will be worth it, if in the end I manage
To blank out whatever it is that is doing the damage.

Then there will be nothing I know.
My mind will fold in on itself, like fields, like snow.

(Larkin 1988: 211)

One way of deconstructing the poem is to fix on binary oppositions and allow the suppressed or marginalised term to subvert the
dominant. Larkin's poem dramatises memory and knowledge. In
terms of the signification of the poem itself, memory loss and
unknowing are privileged ideas, even if in society as a whole this is
not so. The concepts of loss and lack of knowledge being foregrounded and privileged is apparent in the noun groups that
Larkin uses. These tend to be verbose and vague. For example:
'my second quarter-century' 'what I had learnt at university', 'the
public prints' 'certain places', 'what had happened since', 'whatever it is that is doing the damage'. The poem seems to be a
wholesale rejection of knowledge and of memory, written in, at
times, colloquial style. The penultimate line produces a startling
realisation of the rejection of knowledge and memory:

Then there will be nothing I know

Here an initial affirmation, 'there will be . . .' is subverted by the
appearance of the word 'nothing' (as extensive complement, see
Chapter 1). The affirmation/denial binarism is realised syntactically and formally, as the sentence would be quite different if it
were to read 'Then I will not know anything'. The persona at this
stage seems to be able to enact linguistically the very negation he
craves.

The final line contains the *aporia*, or moment of crisis. As the voice asserts that his mind will 'fold in on itself', we might expect that same syntactic realisation. But at that moment of folding, of the mind at last not knowing, not remembering, not being, that very act is, for the first time in the poem, couched in overt metaphor. At the very moment of the persona's psychic collapse it uses the metaphors of fields and snow. At the moment of psychic despair, the deconstructive *aporia* folds not into negation but poetic affirmation.

But it is impossible for the deconstructive critic to stop at this point of poetic affirmation. Looking again at that simile in the final line, we can see that the trope fails. The folding inward is figured in the poem by external images. At the height of introversion the reader is offered the stimulus of the outside world. In a poem of vagueness the reader is offered the most vivid vision when there is supposed to be only blankness. Does the poem, then, enact the failure of which the persona speaks? Is it the case that all that has been learned has deserted the writer. Or, on the contrary, are we being shown a formal *pièce de résistance*, where the structure of the poem reinforces the content? As critics, too, we are being asked to question ourselves what there is to know of a poem that is so resolutely oblique. By finalising our commentary upon it, we are at risk of undermining the effects of disorder and collapse that we ourselves have read into the poem. So we reach a critical impasse, which is the celebrated effect of deconstruction.

A different kind of deconstructive reading can be shown in an analysis of the following lines from Yeats's 'Among School Children':

> O chestnut tree, great-rooted blossomer,
> Are you the leaf, the blossom or the bole?
> O body swayed to music, O brightening glance,
> How can we know the dancer from the dance?

(Yeats 1987: 217)

A conventional reading would assume that the final line is a rhetorical question; it is a recognisable lyric trope. Such questions are not really questions at all, but betray some other kind of pragmatic activity. We might assume that the line says that we *cannot* know the dancer from the dance. But we can read the line literally, and take it as an actual question. In other words we can focus on the *locution* of the utterance rather than the *illocution*. Paul de Man in *Allegories of Reading* (1979) takes the dancer and the dance to stand for grammatical structure and rhetorical performance (roughly *locution* and *illocution*). The question for de Man is then 'how can we tell grammatical form from rhetorical performance?' But to treat the line as a rhetorical question is to assume that we *can* tell the difference. Indeed the reading of the rhetorical trope is proof of this. The convention of rhetorical questioning itself leads us to the opposite view. Read rhetorically the question is a statement to the effect that we cannot tell form from function; but if we read it rhetorically we have already been able to make that distinction. As de Man states:

> . . . the authority of the meaning engendered by the gram-matical structure is fully obscured by the duplicity of a figure that cries out for the differentiation it conceals.
>
> (de Man 1979: 12)

What is shown in de Man's analysis and our discussion of the lines from 'Among School Children' is that the reader is caught between the literal and figurative meanings, not only in the poem but in language as a whole.

Glossary

affective fallacy: Wimsatt and Beardsley's statement in *The Verbal Icon* (1954) that elements relating to emotional effects should not and cannot be part of criticism. The focus on the reader's response would lead to 'impressionism and relativism'.

alethic: Relating to truth. Fiction and other kinds of literary discourse are said to operate in a non-alethic system.

aporia: In rhetoric, a moment of deliberation or hesitation on the part of the speaker. In deconstructive terms, the moment when the text's logic undoes itself.

closed text: For Eco (1979) a text is paradoxically open to aberrant readings.

closure: Resolution or completion at the end of a work.

différance: Derrida's term combining two senses of the verb *différer*; to differ and to defer. The new word points out how language never contains full meaning: it is always deferred and *different*.

formal feature: Any feature of a text which can be noted as immanent. This includes arrangement on the page, structure and formal semantic relations.

gaps: For Iser, the gaps in a text are those elements which are indeterminate and which the reader has to fill. These might include macro-gaps, such as plot enigmas, and micro-gaps, such as the relation between the proposition contained in one clause and that contained in another.

hermeneutic: Concerning interpretation.

horizon of expectations: Jauss (1982a) claimed that every text was read against a set of cultural expectations which change through time. The 'horizon of expectations' is a pragmatico-cultural frame through which meaning is generated.

identity theme: Norman Holland suggested that every reader comes to a text possessed of his or her unique identity theme – a psychological condition which dictates the interpretation of texts.

interpretative strategy: Implicit and largely unconscious strategies the reader constructs to make sense of texts.

interpretive community: An homogeneous community or group of readers where particular interpretations are sanctioned. See in particular Culler (1981) and Fish (1975).

kernel sentence: (Chomsky) 'Core' sentence upon which the complex sentence of ordinary discourse is founded.

lisible: 'Readable', for Barthes. This is like Eco's closed text.

locution and illocution: See Chapter 1, Speech Acts.

metonym: A 'telling detail', normally a nominal, of a text. Elements such as descriptions of clothes, furniture and others relating to appearance are invariably metonymic. See in particular David Lodge's *The Modes of Modern Writing* (1977).

New Criticism: A critical practice that dominated the middle part of the twentieth century. Central figures include Wimsatt and Beardsley, Cleanth Brooks and Allen Tate, all conservatives from America's Southern States. Their central tenet was that the meaning of a text lies in the arrangement of the 'words on the page' and they rejected the notion that the author was the sole source and arbiter of meaning.

open text: Eco's well-defined text, such as Joyce's *Finnegans Wake*.

phenomenology: Philosophy associated with Husserl, who said that objects do not have independent existence, but are filtered through human consciousness.

polysemantic: Having many possible meanings.

reception-aesthetic: Theory of the reception and interpretation of texts based on the work of Jauss and Gadamer in particular.

scriptible: 'Writable'. The modernist and postmodernist text, which awaits a competent readership.

synecdoche: A part-to-whole relationship in language. An element is referred to through reference to a part of it ('all *hands* on deck'). Synecdoche is very closely related to metonymy.

transformation: (Chomsky) All derived sentences are transformations of kernel sentences.

Select bibliography

1 The role of the reader

Roland Barthes' highly idiosyncratic *S/Z* (1974) has much to say about how readings are constructed, and looks forward to deconstruction. Wolfgang Iser's *The Act of Reading: A Theory of Aesthetic Response* (1978) and *The Implied Reader: Patterns of Communication in Prose Fiction* (1974) contain discussions of all the relevant issues. Jane Tomkins' (ed.) collection of essays *Reader Response Criticism* (1980) contains Fish's 'Affective Stylistics'. Wimsatt and Beardsley's *The Verbal Icon* (1954) is *the* New Critical statement, and contains 'The Affective Fallacy' and 'The Intentional Fallacy'. Jonathan Culler's *The Pursuit of Signs: Semiotics, Literature, Deconstruction* (1981) is not as compelling as his earlier *Structuralist Poetics* (1975) but has good discussions of the major response theorists. William Ray's *Literary Meaning* (1984) also contains clear summaries of important theories, and suggests ways in which such theories can be rendered more 'useful'.

2 Reading and identity

Norman Holland's essays are contained in the Tomkins (1980) volume cited above. The discussion of identity is taken up by Culler in *On*

Deconstruction (1983). Karlheinz Stierle's essay, 'The Reading of Fictional Texts' (1980) contains a discussion on readers' identification with texts and is featured in Suleiman and Crosman's collection *The Reader in the Text: Essays on Audience and Interpretation* (1980). The volume also has essays by Todorov, Culler, Iser, Holland and Brooke-Rose. Fish's discussion of 'Lycidas' is in an essay entitled 'Interpreting the Variorum' and is to be found in his volume *Is There a Text in this Class?* (1975).

3 From micro- to macro-reading

Chomsky's famous *Syntactic Structures* (1957) set the programme for linguistics for the following decades, with its focus on 'competence' rather than 'performance'. An excellent, linguistics-based analysis of a particular phenomenon of reading is Catherine Emmott's 'Frames of Reference: Contextual Monitoring and the Interpretation of Narrative Discourse' in Malcolm Coulthard's (ed.) *Advances in Written Text Analysis* (1994).

4 Open and closed texts

Umberto Eco's *The Role of the Reader: Explorations in the Semiotics of Texts* (1979) is very dense in places, but is thought-provoking, showing how semiotics and reader-response criticism are related. Roland Barthes' *The Pleasure of the Text* (1975) is a typical Barthesian hybrid, but still one of the few texts to take reading pleasure, paradoxically, 'seriously'. Analysis of the roles of popular narratives in culture (and attendant 'pleasure') is presented in Derek Longhurst's (ed.) (1989) *Gender, Genre and Narrative Pleasure* .

5 Deaths of authors, births of readers

Barthes' 'The Death of the Author' is taken from *Image/Music/Text* (1977) containing essays selected and translated by Stephen Heath. Frye's *Anatomy of Criticism* (1957) is erudite, but very readable. His theory of modes is inverted to a readers' perspective by Jauss in *Toward an Aesthetic of Reception* (1982). Iser's 'Interaction Between Text and Reader' is from Suleiman and Crosman's volume (1980), cited above. A clear discussion of reception theories and reader-response criticism is to be found in Robert Holub's *Reception Theory* (1984). Response is dealt with in more detail in Elizabeth Freund's *The Return of the Reader* (1986).

6 Anti-formalisms, structures and gestalt

Russian formalism is defined and expressed in Victor Erlich's *Russian Formalism: History-Doctrine* (1955). A conservative intentionalism is to be found in E.D. Hirsch Jr's *The Aims of Interpretation* (1976) and *Validity in Interpretation* (1967). The Poulet (1969) quotation comes from the inaugural issue of *New Literary History*, October 1969. A clear, though not sympathetic, discussion of phenomenology and related issues appears in Terry Eagleton's *Literary Theory: An Introduction* (1983).

7 Deconstructing the text

Culler's *On Deconstruction* (1983) and Christopher Norris's *Deconstruction: Theory and Practice* (1982) are good introductions, with Culler's being the more demanding text. Paul de Man's *Allegories of Reading* (1979) is usefully read alongside his *Blindness and Insight* (1983). Derrida's 'Structure Sign and Play in the Discourse of Human Sciences' is ubiquitously anthologised, and appears in his *Writing and Difference* (1978). His *Margins of Philosophy* (1982) contains a collection of essays which address some of the key concepts of his work, and is an easier place to start than most. David Lehman's *Signs of the Times* (1991) attacks deconstruction generally and Paul de Man in particular, but he nevertheless spells out some of the aims and pitfalls of deconstruction in a helpful fashion.

Chapter 6

Feminism, literature and criticism

1 Defining feminism

T O NAME ONESELF a feminist in the current social climate is likely to provoke a query about what one means by the term 'feminist'. It is certainly no longer possible to call oneself an 'unqualified' feminist critic: one has to be a deconstructionist feminist, a Marxian feminist, a lesbian feminist, a materialist feminist or a combination of these labels. It might even be possible to be a male feminist, although that is a debate that is still raging (and will be explored in the last section of this chapter). Whilst many literary critics, students and academics may not have an opinion on certain theoretical discourses – for example, deconstruction or psychoanalysis – so great is the contemporary significance of feminist debates in literature and criticism that few people would admit to not having the first idea of what feminist criticism is about. Whether or not this is an *accurate* idea of what some feminist critics think they're about is another matter entirely.

i) Read the following definitions of feminist criticism and list any major issues that they have in common.

The feminist reader is enlisted in the process of changing the gender relations which prevail in our society, and she regards the practice of reading as one of the sites in the struggle for change.

(Belsey and Moore 1989: 1)

Most feminist critics speak . . . like people who must bear witness, people who must enact and express in their own lives and words the revisionary discovery that the experiences of women in and with literature are different from those of men.

(Sandra Gilbert, quoted in Showalter 1986: 5)

Feminist critics generally agree that the oppression of women is a fact of life, that gender leaves its traces in literary texts and on literary history, and that feminist criticism plays a worthwhile part in the struggle to end oppression in the world outside of texts . . . feminists are always engaged in an explicitly political enterprise, always working to change existing power structures both inside and outside academia. Its overtly political nature is perhaps the single most distinguishing feature of feminist scholarly work.

(Warhol and Price Herndl 1991: x)

Feminism is a politics. It is a politics directed at changing existing power relations between women and men in society. These power relations structure all areas of life, the family, education and welfare, the worlds of work and politics, culture and leisure. They determine who does what and for whom, what we are and what we might become.

(Weedon 1987: 1)

Feminism has developed . . . a political language about gender that refuses the fixed and transhistorical definitions of masculinity and femininity in the dominant culture.

(Kaplan 1986: 6)

[Feminist critics insist on] the need for all readers, male and female alike, to learn to penetrate the otherwise unfamiliar universes of symbolic action that comprise women's writings, past and present.

(Kolodny 1986: 149)

From the above quotations then, it is possible to identify some issues that are of central concern, and constant debate, to a variety of feminist literary criticisms. Some of the issues are as follows (you may have noted others):

The definition and stability of a gendered identity
The distinctive character (or lack of it) of women's writing
The gender-based struggle for power over definition and meanings
   and recognition for these definitions and meanings

229

Beyond these few points it becomes more difficult to generalise. Each of the following sub-sections gives a discussion of a distinctive version of a feminist critical approach. Different historical periods, different sexual orientations, different cultural identities, different social classes, all suggest a particular focus for the work of feminist critiques. This diversity of viewpoints is commonly seen as infighting and as a lack of cohesion that has a consequent lack of power. However, many feminist critics see this diversity as one of the major *strengths* of feminist approaches and the reason for its continued success, although not without struggle, within literary studies.

2 The second wave

The 'First Wave' of feminism, although it is not always referred to as such, was the activism in the early part of the century that led to the enfranchisement of women. The period of dramatic change in the influence of feminism that took place in the late 1960s and after has therefore become known as the 'Second Wave', but even the historical era to which it refers is open to debate. There is even less agreement on any key critical texts that were associated with the Women's Liberation movement which gathered strength in this period, but the usually cited writers include Simone de Beauvoir, Ann Oakley, Kate Millett, Juliet Mitchell and Germaine Greer. The concerns of these writers were not solely, or even primarily, focused on literature or cultural activities: as the introductory section has already suggested, political motives are the life and soul of any feminist critical activity. Nevertheless, their writing *did* inform the theoretical positions of those working in the literary field and became the basis of the current framework that supports feminist criticism.

The focus of literary critics had several main concerns:

The continued exclusion of writing by women from publication and mainstream academic study

Representations of women in (usually canonical) texts by writers
of either gender
The representation of women's unique experience in their own
writing
The development of appropriate modes of language and form to
represent these unique experiences

The issue of exclusion of texts by women from mainstream
English Studies survey courses is an obvious starting point for
feminist criticism. In the 1970s and early 1980s, the burning
question centred around why it was that only the famous few
women got taught as part of compulsory options for literature
students, these few being: for prose, George Eliot, either Charlotte
or Emily Brontë (not usually both), Jane Austen and sometimes
Virginia Woolf; and for poetry, Emily Dickinson, Christina Ros-
setti or Elizabeth Barrett Browning (not usually both) and Sylvia
Plath (if lucky). Joanna Russ, in her book *How to Suppress
Women's Writing* (1984) gives a list of reasons frequently given for
the exclusion of women's writing from mainstream consideration:

> She didn't write it.
> She wrote it, but she shouldn't have.
> She wrote it, but look what she wrote about.
> She wrote it, but 'she' isn't really an artist and 'it' isn't really
> serious, of the right genre, i.e. really art.
> She wrote it, but she wrote only one of it.
> She wrote it, but it's only interesting/included in the canon
> for one, limited reason.
> She wrote it, but there are very few of her.
>
> (Russ 1984: 76)

The main implications of these comments are, firstly, that there
are fewer women writers than men, and secondly, that the quality
of their work is somehow inferior. The first of these accusations
has been answered by innumerable feminist scholars rediscovering
'lost' (suppressed) texts by women. Texts that have been out of print
for many years, or works that have not received due recognition
have been given a new lease of life through the attentions of

feminist scholars: anthologies of works by women, edited by women, and the rise of women-only presses have promoted texts which would otherwise have been neglected. The Virago 'Modern Classics' series is one of the most well-known sources of 'undiscovered' writing by women.

The accusation that women's texts are 'worse' than those by men has been challenged by the re-examination of the kind of critical judgement being passed. Feminists have argued that women's writing is not inferior men's writing, merely that it does not correspond to the same evaluative criteria. Feminist critics have therefore constructed new sets of criteria that *are* appropriate. The defence mounted against the 'suppression' of women's texts on the grounds of inferiority or scarcity has resulted in a real increase in the range of texts available, and often in forms which do not usually come under the scrutiny of the critic, such as diaries and journals, letters, travelogues, autobiographies and oral histories.

The need to include texts by women about women into mainstream survey courses on literature may seem obvious, but the reasons had to be articulated clearly by those struggling for the recognition of women's writing in the academic arena in the 1960s and 1970s. Lillian S. Robinson states:

> For more than a decade now, feminist scholars have been protesting the apparently systematic neglect of women's experience in the literary canon, neglect that takes the form of distorting and misreading the few recognised female writers and excluding the others. Moreover, the argument runs, the predominantly male authors in the canon show us the female character and relations between the sexes in a way that both reflects and contributes to sexist ideology – an aspect of these classic works about which the critical tradition remained silent for generations.
>
> (Robinson 1986: 106)

Robinson argues for what can be referred to as the 'images of women' version of feminist criticism, which looks at the representation of women, usually in canonical texts written by both men and women, and suggests how repetition of particular roles and character types for women can contribute to our construction of what women should be like and how they should behave in the world outside the text. Much of 'images of women' criticism focuses on stereotypes that constrain women. Thus, a common argument rehearsed by this kind of criticism is that women's sexuality defines them: they are either virgins or whores. Either women characters are seductresses who lead to the downfall of the male protagonist or they are innocent of all matters sexual and material and they have to be protected from the wickedness of the world by men. In the following extract from Mickey Spillane's *I, the Jury* (1947), we have an example of a woman serial killer. The detective and narrator, Mike Hammer, has worked out that the woman, Charlotte, is the killer he has been seeking, but as he makes his accusations to her, she takes off her clothes:

> (Her thumbs hooked in the fragile silk of the panties and pulled them down. She stepped out of them as delicately as one coming from a bathtub. She was completely naked now. A sun-tanned goddess giving herself to her lover. With arms outstretched she walked over toward me. Lightly, her tongue ran over her lips, making them glisten with passion. The smell of her was like an exhilarating perfume. Slowly, a sigh escaped her, making the hemispheres of her breasts quiver. She leaned forward to kiss me, her arms going out to encircle my neck.)
>
> The roar of the .45 shook the room. Charlotte staggered back a step. Her eyes were a symphony of incredulity, and unbelieving witness to truth. Slowly she looked down at the ugly swelling on her naked belly where the bullet went in. A thin trickle of blood welled out.
>
> (Spillane [1947] 1973: 173)

i) How is Charlotte characterised?

ii) How does it compare with the way male serial killers are characterised?

iii) Is there anything significant about Charlotte's sexuality, her gender and the way in which she dies?

The stereotype is clear in this text: sexually assertive women are bad women, and they get their comeuppance, in this case by the penetration of a bullet. The more traditional feminine stereotype is of a passive creature who is vulnerable, dependent and not capable of violence or sexual desire. Germaine Greer argues that whatever the kind of feminine stereotype to which women are supposed to conform, it is necessarily a construction of patriarchal capitalism. Women are empty symbols, dolls, to be used to show off the wealth of their men:

> The stereotype is the Eternal Feminine. She is the Sexual Object sought by all men, and by all women. She is of neither sex, for she has herself no sex at all. Her value is solely attested by the demand she excites in others. All she must contribute is her existence. She need never give positive evidence of her moral character because virtue is assumed from her loveliness, and her passivity. . . There are stringent limits to the variations on the stereotype, for nothing must interfere with her function as sex object. She may wear leather, as long as she cannot actually handle a motorbike; she may wear rubber, but it ought not to indicate that she is an expert diver or water-skier. If she wears athletic clothes the purpose is to underline her unathleticism. She may sit astride a horse, looking soft and curvy, but she must not crouch over its neck with her rump in the air.
>
> (Greer [1971] 1993: 67–8)

There are limits to simply looking for stereotypes of women in fiction and the heyday of the 'images of women' kind of criticism is past; but despite criticisms about its reductive effects (the accusation that it merely exposes sexism in one work of literature after another), it remains an important practice. An awareness of how women are forced into fixed roles as characters in literary works allows readers to consider how similar stereo-typical roles constrain women within their real lives.

An alternative practice to criticising images of women retro-actively, and a way of challenging the representation of women by the traditional white heterosexual male writer, is for women to represent themselves positively. This may be done in terms of the forms women writers use for expression of their distinctive experi-ence (see below), or it may be in terms of content. To alter the stereotyped visions of women, female characters are depicted as strong, active heroes rather than passive sidekicks to the great male protagonist. Genres that are conventionally male-dominated, such as Chandleresque detective fiction, may be subverted by having a tough female private eye, for example. In the case of novelist Aritha Van Herk, she subverts the male-centred work of the beats (such as Jack Kerouac) in her road novel *No Fixed Address* (1989). In this work, it is an independent woman who fetishises a motor vehicle and picks up men on a regular basis. In the following scene, the protagonist, Arachne, shows her skill at attracting men in the unlikely setting of a provincial museum:

> Arachne sniffs the air, the neat recycled air, and falls behind a tall German tourist. She does not know he is a German tourist, but he has a very large camera. He wants to take pictures of the pictures on display here, but the light is wrong, fuzzy and gray. Arachne brushes his thigh. He moves away. She follows, close behind. He can feel her breath on the back of his neck.
>
> (Van Herk 1989: 51)

iv) Do you find this scene comic or threatening?

v) Would you respond differently if Arachne wore a man and the tourist in this scene were a woman?

An alternative way of transforming literary works, rather than switching the gender of the protagonist from male to female, is to create literature which focuses on a distinctive area of importance for women. Many writers have begun to represent certain experiences of what it means to be a woman which may be ignored in writing by men. Many feminists argue that the representation by women writers of experiences such as childbirth or rape gives a uniquely female view of the world.

vi) Can only women write convincingly about women's lives and experiences?

vii) What might be the wider implications of your answer to this question? (That is, if you answer yes, does that mean that male writers of texts about women are always failures, or are there exceptions? If you answer no, does that mean there is no difference between women's construction of female characters and men's construction of them?)

Women's writing about women for women is not necessarily always a politically radical or confrontational act aimed at achieving gender equality. Popular romances of the Mills and Boon or Silhouette range, for instance, are almost exclusively written by women and are largely focused on the consciousness of a female protagonist, but they do not always promote role-models for assertive women. For instance, in a romance novel called *The Love of Dugan Magee*, the heroine Sarah Haywood is a modern, independent woman with her own flat and a job working for a 'Crimestoppers' organisation. She is a rape victim, but has struggled hard to overcome her fears and make a new life. Despite these promising signs of liberated womanhood though, the reader knows that Sarah is healed only at the end when her lover is able to 'take' her forcefully without her flinching, only when he is able to, as she puts it, 'love me the way we both want you to'. This is the final scene in the novel. Dugan and Sarah are in bed where he is 'pressing against her, crushing her into the mattress':

'Now that I've got you right where I want you, are you going to marry me? You'd better say yes, woman, because I warn you right now, nothing else is acceptable.'

Her eyes dancing, she reached up to tangle her fingers in his hair. 'Oh, it's not, is it? Then I guess I'd better say yes'
. . .

She was still whispering yeses when his mouth covered hers and he slowly entered her, still whispering yeses when he tumbled with her over the edge into ecstasy moments later. A soft, dreamy smile playing about her kiss-bruised mouth, she hugged him close and floated back to earth.

(Turner 1994: 250–1)

The rhetoric of Sarah's 'seduction' is revealing: she is 'pressed' and 'crushed', she is bullied into consenting to marriage (albeit playfully), her mouth is 'kiss-bruised'. For a character who has survived rape, it is important for her consent to be established in any sexual encounter, hence the emphasis on her many 'yeses'. However, all of the descriptions of passion are couched in metaphors of violence and this casts doubt on how freely her 'yeses' are given. This novel is part of the 'Silhouette Sensation' range of romances which are aimed at a younger, less-shockable audience, but it would seem that even in more forward-looking fiction, the narrative reverts to an aggressive man–submissive woman relationship at the conclusion.

In less conservative genres than romantic fiction, the contribution to raising feminist consciousness through the representation of women's experiences by women writers can still be questioned. In *Female Desire* (1984), cultural critic Ros Coward argues that 'woman-centred' novels may only be another version of conventional nineteenth-century realist fiction which replace the marriage at the centre of the narrative structure with a story about a woman's sexual development. Coward's essay refers to novels popular in the 1970s and early 1980s such as Lisa Alther's *Kinflicks*, Marilyn French's *The Women's Room*, Erica Jong's *Fear of Flying* and Marge Piercy's *Braided Lives*. She argues that these novels follow a very distinct formula:

In these novels where women's experience is highlighted, it has become a standing joke that we are to expect the first period, first kiss, first (fumbled) intercourse, first (disastrous) marriage, lesbian affair and usually lonely resolution. The end product is normally that the protagonist feels she has 'become her own person'. This disingenuous construction of an adolescent world derives precisely from the novel's attempt to create a higher realism. The complex family history and interrelations, the anecdotes presented as if passed from generation to generation, the eccentric view of the world, are all practices aimed at creating the sense of the autobiographical . . . Women-centred novels represent a fictionalised version of our culture's contemporary obsession with autobiography and with intimate revelations . . . The term 'women-centred' novels covers a multitude of sins. But at the heart of this multi-faceted phenomenon is one dominant convention, a type of narrative which corresponds to existing (and therefore problematic) ways of defining women through their sexual personhood. Because the whole issue of women's sexuality and changes in structures of living are crucial to our experiences now, these novels are sometimes able to explore the question of how female identity has been constructed and how this relates to society as a whole. Often though, the convention itself pulls the novels back into banal repetitions, asserting a world without fantasy where women struggle on, often grim, brutalised and victimised.

(Coward 1984: 181, 186)

Cowards central complaint is that 'woman-centred' novels are over-reliant on the construction of a narrative on the basis of a woman's sexual identity. If woman-centred fiction is about expressing uniquely female experiences, can it avoid the focus on sexuality? If not, then does this kind of fiction really transform the older stereotypes, such as those described by Germaine Greer earlier (see page 234).

In order for any women's writing about themselves to have an impact, it is necessary for their works to be read, and to be read in an appropriate way. The next step from the development of a literature about women is the establishment of a woman-centred critical practice, what Elaine Showalter has named 'gynocriticism' (1986). 'Gynocriticism' involves women reading about women's texts and constructing a largely sympathetic discourse about this body of work. Showalter explains:

> the program of gynocritics is to construct a female frame-work for the analysis of women's literature, to develop new models based on the study of female experience, rather than to adapt male models and theories. Gynocritics begins at the point when we free ourselves from the linear absolutes of male literary history, stop trying to fit women between the lines of the male tradition, and focus instead on the newly visible world of female culture.
>
> (Showalter 1986: 131)

The need for this kind of criticism is based on the idea that not only have women's works been systematically ignored by male critics and academics, but they have also been systematically misread, or read according to the expectations and values of the wrong gender. The argument of 'gynocriticism' is not only that women write about different subjects to men, but they also read and criticise them differently. Showalter argues in particular for a 'gynocritical' consideration of women's texts which subvert mis-ogynist myths: she rejects Sylvia Plath's *The Bell Jar*, which contains a mother-hating, suicidal protagonist, in favour of Margaret Atwood's *Surfacing*, which, she argues:

> goes beyond matrophobia [fear of the mother] to a coura-geously sustained quest for the mother . . . As the death of the father has always been an archetypal rite of passage for the Western hero, now the death of the mother as witnessed and transcended by the daughter has become one of the most profound occasions of female literature.
>
> (Showalter 1986: 135)

Here is a quotation from towards the end of Atwood's *Surfacing* (1972). The narrator is alone in a cabin in the Canadian wild-erness that was used by her family when she was a child. She has spent the summer there with her friends and vows not to return to the corruptive influences of the city:

> I try to think for the first time what it was like to be them: our father, islanding his life, protecting both us and himself, in the midst of war and in a poor country, the effort it must have taken to sustain his illusions of reason and benevolent order, and perhaps he didn't. Our mother, collecting the seasons and the weather and her children's faces, the meticulous records that allowed her to omit the other things, the pain and isolation and whatever it was she was fighting against, something in a vanished history, I can never know . . . I turn the mirror around: in it there's a creature neither animal nor human, furless, only a dirty blanket, shoulders huddled over into a crouch, eyes staring blue as ice from the deep sockets; the lips move by themselves . . . They would never believe it's only a natural woman, state of nature, they think of that as a tanned body on a beach with washed hair waving like scarves; not this, face dirt-caked and streaked, skin grimed and scabby, hair like a frayed bath-mat stuck with leaves and twigs. A new kind of centrefold.
>
> (Atwood [1972] 1979: 190)

viii) What does the narrator think about her mother?

ix) How does this compare with what she has discovered about her father?

x) Showalter wants to develop a framework for the analysis of women's literature based on female experience. How would this accommodate the fantasy elements of Atwood's novel (such as her 'natural woman')?

If the content of writing is subject to gender difference, certain feminist arguments insist that women also adopt, or are forced into, different literary forms. It has been claimed that women either choose, or are obliged to write in, genres other than the privileged modes of poetry and drama. Informal, 'private' and personal forms, such as diaries, journals, letters, travelogues and autobiography have traditionally been the refuges of women writers. Such genres are not designed for public performance or recital; they require no formal scholarship and training beyond literacy; they are much less ambitious, and are therefore seen as appropriate amusements for women, rather than ambitious career moves.

However, what is considered suitable for women writers is not immutable; rather, it is subject to historical flux. For instance, the eighteenth century witnessed a proliferation of 'lady-novelists' for whom novel-writing was seen as a wholly appropriate pastime, whilst in the nineteenth-century women were not encouraged to take up publication, leading novelists like George Eliot and Charlotte Brontë to disguise their gender through masculine pen-names. In the late twentieth century, literary fashions have made prose fiction by far the most popular literary medium for both men and women, although it is still a matter of debate as to whether women get equal recognition to men, even when using the same genre.

Despite the claims that women writers have been marginalised in the past, in the present they have revolutionised traditional forms. For instance, feminists have brought about a complete transformation of the academic essay, by the inclusion of autobiographical material as valid evidence, rather than excluding it as irrelevant and biased. A collection of essays, *Changing Subjects: The Making of Feminist Literary Criticism* (Greene and Kahn 1993), examines the progress of feminist criticism over twenty years or so, including essays which use autobiography to produce a critique of academic institutions and of feminism itself. Rachel Blau DuPlessis writes of her experience of finding her own place within feminist criticism:

> Suddenly, the feminist critical project extended to my creative work. Suddenly, on 2 January 1973, I awoke to my own poetry: 'Idea; to retell myths involving women as radical interpretations of them.' I began with Orpheus and Eurydice – he the figure of the poet, she a dead nothing. Where

241

had that come from? Where indeed. Experiences of anger.
The sense of being culturally marginal. Entombed. At a
career dead end. Couldn't write, no success with poetry,
none with critical book, none with jobs. A couple of mis-
carriages under my belt; there would be eight. The dream life
of the cave. My poem says it is not Orpheus who turns back
to Eurydice, but rather she who turns away from him, because
she wants to go deeper into the living cave . . . Working on
my own poem, I gained intellectual tread, formulated the
thesis of the revisionary relationship to hegemonic culture
that fuelled some of my critical work. Writing a (feminist)
poem allowed me to write (feminist) criticism . . .

(Blau DuPlessis 1993: 102–3)

xi) What are the 'personal' or autobiographical features of
this extract? (Think of style as well as content.)
xii) What is the critical argument in this extract?
xiii) How would the effect of the piece be changed if either the
autobiographical or critical arguments were removed?

Another less traditional, but still male-dominated, form,
that of science fiction, has also been transformed by the work of
women, who have moved the genre away from a focus on technol-
ogy, and have used the freedom of the form to create utopian
visions of a world not so dominated by patriarchy and gender
divisions. Joanna Russ characterises women's writing as 'vernacular', and suggests this is why their works are not often deemed
to be classic:

In the vernacular it's also hard to be 'classic', to be smooth,
to be perfect. The Sacred Canon of Literature quite often
pretends that some works can be not only atemporal and
universal (that is, outside history. . .) but without flaw and
without perceptible limitations. It's hard, in the vernacular,
to pretend this, to paper over the cracks.

(Russ 1984: 129)

Russ accepts here that such a position is an over-generalisation, but her argument is that whatever form it takes, women's writing cannot enter the realm of the classics unless it plays by the rules and pretends that it is a piece of timeless beauty.

3 Écriture féminine

In contrast to Russ's argument – that women need to conform, even in pretence, with masculine standards, if they want to achieve success – *écriture féminine* is a dramatic subversion of form and of traditional literary values. *Écriture féminine* has been (crassly) translated as 'women's writing'; it is more accurately rendered as 'feminine writing'; and glossed again, most helpfully, as 'writing-the-body'. The latter term is a useful one to remember because it is a reminder that this discourse is not only about femininity, and it is not necessarily about feminism either – or at least it has some arguments with the term. *Écriture féminine* is a discourse which is written out of a concern with subjectivity, sexuality and language. It maintains the belief that whatever symbolic systems currently exist – the most prominent of these systems being language – they are not adequate; they relentlessly place women within a restrictive system in which it is impossible for them to be active subjects. The force of patriarchy is always inscribed upon women, and upon men also, by the prevailing symbolic systems; it is a fundamental belief of *écriture féminine* that the only way to transform relations between the sexes is to transform the ways in which we *represent* these relations.

This discourse bases itself in the belief that women are different to men physically and that this has an influence on their relation to language. More significantly, femininity (as distinct from femaleness) is qualitatively different to masculinity and the proponents of *écriture féminine* suggest that there is a need for an alternative form of language in order to express this difference adequately, something which would benefit men and women: women are not the only sufferers from the marginalisation of the feminine. The change in language that is demanded by this discourse is not the same as the changes brought about by non-sexist language ('chair' instead of 'chairman', 'poet' instead of 'poetess', and so on). According to adherents of 'French feminism' as it has become known, it is the very *structures* of language which control the feminine unconsciously, positioning the feminine where it cannot be expressed.

Écriture féminine originates in the theories of Jacques Derrida and Jacques Lacan, and – paradoxically for a feminist theory – it cannot really be considered without reference to the works of these men, either implicitly or explicitly. But the criticism that has developed from psychoanalysis and deconstruction is not a passive acceptance of the theoretical premises of these discourses; rather, the feminism that has developed is, at its tamest, an animated dialogue with the 'founding fathers' of post-structuralism, and at its most extreme it is a bitter indictment of what these discourses say about women and femininity.

The most commonly cited names connected with *écriture féminine* are those of Hélène Cixous, Luce Irigaray and Julia Kristeva, but before we go on to give a short introduction to the theoretical stances of these writers, it is important to mention that there are many others who can be bracketed under the same heading: Nicole Brossard, Catherine Clément, Annie Leclerc, Michèle Montrelay, Lola Lemire Tostevin, and Monique Wittig, to name but a few. It is also important to stress that, although these theorists are all bundled together under the same heading, their particular discussions are quite distinct.

Hélène Cixous emphasises the hierarchical order of language, an order that privileges certain terms over others, and ultimately reduces these terms to a matter of the opposition between male and female. She argues that the feminine is absent from the patriarchal order of language; it is represented only in the negative. She poses the question 'Where is she?' (the pronoun referring to the Universal Woman) and offers the following hierarchical list, in which the feminine must be sought:

Activity/Passivity
Sun/Moon

Culture/Nature
Day/Night

Father/Mother
Head/Heart
Intelligible/Palpable
Logos/Pathos

(Cixous and Clément 1986: 115)

Cixous argues that such binary oppositions struggle with one another for supremacy, to create order through a fixed language, within which one side is always the winner (there is always a loser) and one is always the master (for which there must be a slave). This hierarchical, fixed structure of winner-takes-all is the characteristic of *logocentricism*. The fact that the winning half of the duo of terms is always the masculine is evidence of *phallocentrism* (and the combination of the two is referred to as *phallogocentrism*). These terms relate to Lacanian psychoanalysis (see Chapter 4), in which the stability of the signifier is guaranteed by the phallus. The operation of language is organised at a metaphorical level by the phallus, and Cixous argues that therefore Woman is always excluded from this operation, as her relation to the phallus is always one of lack.

Cixous insists that, in fact, either part of the binary of terms could be attributed either positive or negative status. Thus, passivity is linked with the feminine, but this could be seen as a positive term. Either men or women could identify with the feminine. Cixous maintains that the link between what we identify as feminine and biological females is an arbitrary one. This has the function, states Toril Moi, of displacing:

> the whole feminist debate around the problem of women and writing away from an empiricist emphasis on the sex of the author towards an analysis of the articulations of sexuality and desire within the literary text itself.

(Moi 1985: 114)

Although both men and women are capable of producing 'feminine' writing, Cixous allows that, under patriarchy, it is

245

mostly women that are the practitioners. She is, however, reluctant to state precisely what might be the features of what she labels 'feminine' writing. She states:

> It is impossible to define a feminine practice of writing, and this is an impossibility that will remain, for this practice can never be theorized, enclosed, coded – which doesn't mean that it doesn't exist. But it will always surpass the discourse that regulates the phallocentric system; it does and will take place in areas other than those subordinated to philoso-phico-theoretical domination. It will be conceived of only by subjects who are breakers of automatisms, by peripheral figures that no authority can ever subjugate.
>
> (Cixous 1981: 253)

i) What are the advantages and disadvantages to Cixous's strategy of refusing to define 'feminine writing'? Why might she not wish to define *écriture féminine*?

Whilst Cixous insists on the 'otherness' of feminine dis-course – on the way it is repressed by the fixed forms of phallo-gocentrism – philosopher, linguist and psychoanalyst Luce Irigaray insists on the subversive potential of women writers who must necessarily work *within* the symbolic system into which they are placed, but which they can effectively undermine by parody, dialogue or by filling in the spaces that male-dominated discourse has left blank.

Like Hélène Cixous, Irigaray believes that women are not adequately represented by existing symbolic systems. She argues that they are not given a proper place in a patriarchal world. Men inhabit, are able to live in, dwell in, 'grottoes, huts, women, towns, language, concepts, theories etc.' (Irigaray, quoted in Whitford 1989: 112), whereas the primary condition of women is one of 'déréliction'. However, Irigaray's method of dealing with this marginalisation of women is quite different to that of Cixous.

Irigaray uses mimicry and parody of masculine theorists and

their philosophical rhetoric as a way of expressing 'the feminine' in a position of resistance to the masculine symbolic. As we have seen, the phallus is chosen by Freudian and Lacanian psycho-analysis as the signifier of presence, the one, visible thing that must be there to allow positive definition of gendered identity and positive definition of meaning in language. In an act of subversion, which Irigaray believes is the only strategy for women within the masculine symbolic, she criticises the phallus as restrictive, mono-lithic, limitedly singular and fixed. She resists such a fixity of meaning that phallogocentrism implies. Instead of the singular phallus, Irigaray argues that women have the benefit of multiple sexual organs:

> As for a woman, she touches herself in and of herself without any need for mediation, and before there is any way to distinguish activity from passivity. Woman 'touches herself' all the time, and moreover no one can forbid her to do so, for her genitals are formed of two lips in continuous contact. Thus, within herself, she is already two – but not divisible to one(s) – that caress each other . . .
>
> Whence the mystery that woman represents in a culture claiming to count everything, to number everything by units, to inventory everything as individualities. *She is neither one nor two.* Rigorously speaking, she cannot be identified as either one person, or as two. She resists all adequate definition. Further, she has no 'proper' name. And her sexual organ, which is not *one* organ, is counted as *none.* The negative, the underside, the reverse of the only visible and morphologically designatable organ (even if the passage from erection to detumescence does pose some problems): the penis.
>
> (Irigaray 1985: 24–5)

Irigaray uses the female body as a counter-strategy to the ubiqui-tous use of the male body. Irigaray's assertion here is that male bodies and male sexual pleasure are distinct from female bodies and female sexual pleasure, but that doesn't mean they don't exist, and indeed, she suggests playfully, women have a lot to offer because they have more in the way of sexual pleasures – they don't just have the one thing! What Irigaray shows is that, just as it is the folly of patriarchy to define women according to their lack of the phallus, so it is equally mistaken to define their language, their existence under the symbolic system, according to the masculine model. Instead of the monologic, rational, fixed discourse of phallogocentrism, Irigaray suggests an alternative pattern for a feminine discourse:

> One would have to listen with another ear, as if hearing *an 'other meaning' always in the process of weaving itself, of embracing itself with words, but also of getting rid of words in order not to become fixed, congealed in them.* For if 'she' says something, it is not, it is already no longer, identical with what she means. What she says is never identical with anything, moreover; rather, it is contiguous. *It touches (upon).* And when it strays too far from that proximity, she breaks off and starts over at 'zero': her body-sex [emphasis in original].
>
> (Irigaray 1985: 29)

ii) Does Irigaray define écriture féminine?

iii) What is the relationship between what Irigaray says and the way that she says it?

Hélène Cixous argues that Woman must be represented outside the symbolic, in her own terms, in the terms of her body. Luce Irigaray argues that the masculine fails to adequately represent Woman, but, rather than accept this outside position, her strategy is to write the feminine into the masculine text by subverting traditional rhetorical strategies and putting a playful female body in the place of the serious male body. Julia Kristeva is perhaps more radical still, in her refusal to accept a definition of the term 'woman' at all; she rejects any essential identity between women, suggesting that the term can only be useful as an organisational category for political action, rather than as a meaningful term that should be accepted as self-definition by one half of the gendered divide:

> The belief that 'one is a woman' is almost as absurd and obscurantist as the belief that 'one is a man'. I say 'almost' because there are still many goals which women can achieve: freedom of abortion and contraception, day-care centres for children, equality on the job, etc. Therefore, we must use 'we are women' as an advertisement or slogan for our demands. On a deeper level, however, a woman cannot 'be'; it is something which does not even belong in the order of *being*. It follows that a feminist practice can only be negative, at odds with what already exists so that we may say 'that it's not' and 'that's still not it'. In 'woman' I see something that cannot be represented, something that is not said, something above and beyond nomenclatures and ideologies.
>
> (Kristeva 1981: 137)

Kristeva argues that language is crucial to the determination of subjectivity. She uses Lacan's term, the Symbolic, to designate phallocentric language, but she also introduces her own term, the 'semiotic', which represents the repressed, feminine aspect of language, which is always capable of disrupting or subverting the Symbolic. Evidence of the semiotic can be witnessed in pre-Oedipal infants, and in non-rational discourses that are marginalised by the Symbolic order, such as the ravings of the hysteric, the work of avant-garde artists, the discourse of a psychotic or schizophrenic patient, and so on. Although all subjects go through the semiotic stage, this aspect is always present (like the unconscious is always present) – it is simply more evident in some people, or at certain times, than others. Although the semiotic is representative of the repressed feminine side, it is present in both male and female subjects.

Kristeva insists on the instability of subjectivity, arguing that the co-existence of the Symbolic and the semiotic can only ever produce a subject that is *apparently* coherent. The semiotic can erupt at any time, and is capable of disrupting the stability and fixity represented by phallogocentrism. Kristeva is quite critical of of the women's movement, and of some feminist arguments for the need to establish relationships between women on the basis of their gender. Nevertheless, her arguments are still useful to feminism, as Chris Weedon points out:

> This radical alternative to the humanist view of subjectivity, in which it is self-present, unified and in control, offers the possibility of understanding the contradictory nature of individuals and of their dispersal across a range of subject positions of which they are not the authors.
>
> (Weedon 1987: 70)

iv) What problems are there in equating the semiotic and non-rational discourse with the feminine?

There is a risk that accompanies this kind of discourse. The danger is that these words will be taken as a reinforcement of old prejudices about women being worth no more than their reproductive organs, of them being either mother material or prostitute material, with all their value placed in their genitals. The emphasis on the woman's body, and the association that is given to the body with language, is a dangerous tactic, and it has been criticised as essentialist, relying on biology to define the position of women. The modes of argument incorporated into *écriture féminine* have also been criticised as impenetrable, élitist and impractical.

v) What does a feminist political activist or literary critic do with this kind of discourse?
vi) What kind of agenda does it set for feminism?

4 Writing lesbian

Just as the 'French Feminists' argue that there is not adequate representation of women's experience and of relationships between women, lesbian experience is also neglected. It is left out of legislative statutes, even in homophobic cultures that pass laws outlawing the sexual practices of gay men, and it is often ignored in cultural representations, or simply not recognised. Women being affectionate towards one another are more frequently deemed to be close friends than lovers, and literary representations of closeness between women are more often than not interpreted as platonic rather than sexual. Identifying the lesbian writer, and the lesbian in writing, becomes something of a problem and most critics agree that there is a need to define the term 'lesbian', and then examine its applicability to both writer and text. In her introduction to a collection of lesbian short stories, Margaret Reynolds offers her definition of lesbian writing:

> It is writing which exhibits, within the confines of the text itself, something which makes it distinctively about, or for, or out of lesbian experience. That element may lie in the plot, in the subject, in the theory, in the code or the genre, but it has to be there in the writing. The writer herself may never have kissed another woman. Even if she has, she may not call herself a lesbian . . .
>
> (Reynolds 1993: xxxii)

Reynolds here asserts that there must be something *distinctive* about writing to make it lesbian. Precisely what distinctive features might be lesbian are more difficult to define, especially given that many writers have had to be very subtle about mentioning sexual relationships between women for fear of publishing censorship or personal censure.

One crucial question that is repeatedly asked is whether, in order to make writing lesbian, there has to be representation of a sexual relationship between characters. Most critics now concur that in order to qualify as lesbian writing, relationships between women might be more part of what Adrienne Rich has called the 'lesbian continuum' which, at its broadest, can cover any woman-centred experience. However, instead of validating lesbian experience, this argument can have the effect of erasing it from recognition and representation yet again: if there is nothing to choose between the representation of the relationship between heterosexual women and between lesbians, any sense of lesbian identity might be lost. The definition of a lesbian identity is still being debated: is it a biological or genetic feature (as some scientists claim) or is it a result of psychosocial or historical features?

Another way in which critics have approached lesbian issues in literature is to look at the way they have been represented, as both positive and negative character types. Catharine Stimpson (1991) is able to identify several distinct styles of representation of lesbians in fiction. She points to the 'tortured lesbian', such as Stephen in Radclyffe Hall's *Well of Loneliness*, whose sexuality causes her to be at odds with herself and her society. There are also 'romantic lesbians', who are self-assured, beautiful, and so on, who triumph against all odds and find the perfect lover, evading stigma and self-contempt that characterises the 'tortured lesbian' narrative. Stimpson also identifies the lesbian as a figure from erotic or pornographic writing, who can be portrayed merely as a diversion, a 'sexual interlude' in an otherwise straight woman's life or whose sexual activities provide a spectacle for the voyeur.

The lesbian character type, whether it is a positive model or not, is only one feature of lesbian writing. It has also been argued that other, formal features have been seen to characterise lesbian writing, such as 'the use of the continuous present, unconventional grammar and neologism' (Zimmerman 1991: 128). Zimmerman also suggests that narrative themes, such as 'unrequited longing', flexible gender role-playing, gender ambiguity and 'a tension between romantic love and genital sexuality' are common in lesbian writing because they are also a feature in relationships between women. This does not mean that lesbian writing is always realist, and Zimmerman argues that lesbian writing is developing a unique symbolism, perhaps originating in the kind of codes used by lesbians to identify one another and talk about their experiences without facing homophobia.

For the critic of lesbian writing, there are a number of

questions that need to be asked. Many of them are put by Zimmerman, whose preliminary list includes:

> Does a woman's sexual and affectional preference influence the way she writes, reads, and thinks?
> Does lesbianism belong in the classroom and in scholarship?
> Is there a lesbian aesthetic distinct from a feminist aesthetic?
> What should be the role of the lesbian critic?
> Can we establish a lesbian 'canon' in the way in which feminist critics have established a female canon?
> Can lesbian feminists develop insights into female creativity that might enrich all literary criticism?
>
> (Zimmerman 1991: 117)

As well as establishing the function of criticism in relation to lesbian writing, questions must be asked about the political effects of lesbian texts. For example: How far is lesbian writing, because of its marginal status, always a form of resistance literature? Is lesbian writing necessarily transformational, radical or non-mainstream? What might be the advantages, and the difficulties, with a lesbian separatist politics in relation to literary criticism? (For instance, is writing by men completely banned from consideration by a lesbian poetics?)

5 'Post-feminism'

The success of feminism within the realms of literary theory has produced a change in the questions and difficulties faced by feminist critics in recent years. The issue of the 'Backlash', an aggressive response to women and feminism because of their achievements, is one such product. The argument that feminism is now unnecessary or passé, because equality has been achieved, is another. The changed position of feminist theories, and how these arguments must evolve accordingly, is the focus of this section.

There are at least two ways of interpreting the category of 'post-feminism', one meaning that we have somehow got beyond feminism to some other stage, and one suggesting the involvement

253

of feminism with other 'post' discourses. To deal with the latter form last, one of the most pressing current concerns for academic feminism is the question of what to do with 'post' discourses (post-structuralism, postmodernism, post-colonialism, post-Freudianism, etc.). All of these discourses challenge our understanding of knowledge of ourselves and of the world. They suggest that it is undesirable and impossible to fix definitions and explanations for things such as the subordination of women. 'What do we mean by the term "Woman"?' would be the 'post' response to an argument about women's oppression. 'You're talking about gendered power relations' would be the insistent 'post' response to an argument about men discriminating against women, keeping them out of high office and high-income brackets. In other words, the very ground that earlier feminisms have taken for granted – that is, that women are oppressed – has been challenged by new discourses and new ways of thinking. Judith Butler (1992) explains the problems of trying to define and represent feminism through the category of 'Woman':

> The minute that the category of women is invoked as *describing* the constituency for which feminism speaks, an internal debate invariably begins over what the descriptive content of that term will be. There are those who claim that there is an ontological specificity to women as childbearers that forms the basis of a specific legal and political interest in representation, and then there are others who understand maternity to be a social relation that is, under current social circumstances, the specific and cross-cultural situation of women. In the early 1980s, the feminist 'we' rightly came under attack by women of color who claimed that the 'we' was invariably white, and that that 'we' that was meant to solidify the movement was the very source of a painful factionalization. The effort to characterize a feminine specificity through recourse to maternity, whether biological or social, produced a similar factionalization and even a disavowal of feminism altogether. For surely all women are not mothers; some cannot be, some are too old or too young to

be, some choose not to be, and for some who are mothers, that is not necessarily the rallying point of their politicization in feminism.

(Butler 1992: 15)

The point here is that it is a mistake to try to find a single common point from which to start constructing a framework of feminist politics and criticism. Whichever point we choose, be it that of biology or social position, there will always be variations, and there will always be those who are not at that starting point with the others. Butler argues that different starting points, and disagreements about definitions of and within feminism, are not destructive, but that rather they prove that 'identity' – as stable, fixed and coherent – should not be claimed as the basis for feminism or any other politcal movement. She concludes:

Identity categories are never merely descriptive, but always normative, and as such, exclusionary . . . If there is a fear that, by no longer being able to take for granted the subject, its gender, its sex, or its materiality, feminism will founder, it might be wise to consider the political consequences of keeping in their place the very premises that have tried to secure [women's] subordination from the start.

(Butler 1992: 19)

One of the current debates in this area of unstable feminist identities, and which has significance for literary studies, emerges from earlier versions; it can perhaps be labelled as the 'reading as a woman' debate (named after an essay by Jonathan Culler [1983] which has become an important reference point). The debate in its earliest stages focused on whether it is possible to write as a woman. In other words, can a reader, ignorant of the gender of a writer, tell whether a piece of work was written by a man or a woman? Although both content and form of women's writing can be seen to be distinctive, 'post-feminists' see this as a matter of material circumstance rather than biological essence. In other words, women can write about the same things as men, and in the same styles if they choose. Their chosen form and subject-matter is to do with convention and personal interest rather than ability. The next obvious question, then – given the claim that women writers can produce the same kind of work as men – is whether women readers or critics are more sensitive or better equipped to deal with certain texts. Diana Fuss explains the debate in these terms:

> In the background of all of these investigations [into the 'reading as a woman' debate] lies the question of essentialism and the problem of the vexed relation between feminism and deconstruction. How and why have the current tensions between feminism and deconstruction mobilized around the issue of essentialism? Why indeed is essentialism such a powerful and seemingly intransigent category for both deconstructionists and feminists? Is it possible to be an essentialist deconstructionist when deconstruction is commonly understood as the very displacement of essence? By the same token, is it legitimate to call oneself an anti-essentialist feminist, when feminism seems to take for granted among its members a shared identity, some essential point of commonality?
>
> (Fuss 1990: 24)

i) Do women read differently from men? If so, what are the features that mark this difference?

ii) Can a man produce a feminist analysis of a text which is exactly the same as a woman's? What are the implications for feminist literary theory of your answer?

The difference in women's and men's language use, and the critical issues relating to readership are discussed in Chapter 1, Gender, pp. 32–6 and Chapter 5, The Role of the Reader pp. 184–92.

The work of Naomi Wolf, at least in her *Fire With Fire* (1993), could be seen as the other version of post-feminism. Some academic feminists are hostile towards Wolf's latest text, on the grounds that it is too moderate, liberal, middle class and pro-heterosexuality. What Wolf is attempting to do is to find a way of making feminism attractive in the face of the way the movement has been characterised by the popular media. Her thesis is a simple one: that women are colluding in their own oppression by failing to realise how much power they have won or by denying themselves and other women their successes. Wolf criticises what she calls 'victim feminism', a tendency to see women as victimised at all times, powerless and frail, unable to defend themselves appropriately without the intervention of a (patriarchal) state. There is a tendency in books like Wolf's to lament an incidence of the powerless plight of a woman/women and to call it 'victim feminism' (or 'rape crisis feminism' in Katie Roiphe's 1994 terms): they blame feminists for the position of women, when previously we may have blamed patriarchy. However, Wolf's book *does* allow for some of the complexities of the situation. In addition, she has something in common with the other kind of post-feminists when she offers the insight that often 'there is a search for a spurious authenticity – the most harmed woman is the *real* woman' (Wolf 1993: 217). Unless you're damaged, you can't be a real feminist, or even a real woman. She continues, 'Horrifying the world of sexism truly is, but this sometimes monolithic focus on the dire leads straight to burnout' (229). One strategy she recommends is to make use of popular women's magazine feminism as a way of mediating the depressing discourse of much academic feminism:

> The most effective option to offer women would bring the strengths of [women's magazine and academic feminist] cultures together: combining women's magazines' hopeful tone, and the self-help groups' faith in transformation with the clear political analysis and the organizing potential of the feminist movement. We should be able to look squarely at just how bad things can be for women without turning that ability into a kind of *machisma*, or ridiculing faith in potential change as being hopelessly naïve.
>
> (Wolf 1993: 229)

Tania Modleski opens her wittily titled collection of essays, *Feminism Without Women*, with a case-study of feminist critic

Elaine Showalter. Modleski explains that Showalter's career peculiarly mirrors the transition of academic feminism in the field of cultural studies. The movement is from gynocritics, which placed women's experience at its centre, to 'gender' studies, in which feminism becomes this thing which we can use to examine masculinity, instead of the (in her view, preferable) model which has 'men's studies' as a means of progressing feminism.

Questions have been raised about the usefulness of the term 'feminism' in critical studies now, on the grounds that it is too big and pervades everything, or, on the other hand, that 'gender studies' is more inclusive – feminism marginalises other issues around sexuality. Feminism has even been excluded on the grounds that it is passé – everybody knows about it, there's no need to teach it.

The problem with the term 'gender studies', as Modleski sees it being practised, is that:

It puts men centre stage (again).

It is very heterosexual – lesbians tend to get left out, although gay men usually have a place, alongside hard-done-by straight men.

Anthologies assume an equal weight is accorded to essays by men and women, straights and gays. Are they always read that way?

Modleski doesn't deny the need for a version of men's studies, but, she warns, we have to avoid the 'theories of male power [that] frequently work to efface female subjectivity by occupying the site of femininity' (Modleski 1991: 7). Instead, she wants to promote the kind of studies of masculinity that have a concern for the effects of masculine power on the *female* subject. What she wants to reject are what Nina Baym has called 'melodramas of beset manhood'. She wants to avoid, for instance, collections like Joseph Boone and Michael Cadden's (1990) which has an essay in which straight men complain how feminism has made them invisible.

6 'Men's studies'

The questioning of the term 'woman' by feminism, and the interest in 'gender relations' that is a result of challenging the category of woman, has produced a variety of responses to the challenges of feminism by men. There are a variety of these kinds of texts with quite distinct motives. There are texts which seek to redefine masculinity, those which seek to criticise feminism, and those which seek to understand the place of men within/alongside feminism.

Rowena Chapman calls the 'New Man' an invention of consumer capitalism. She identifies him as a figure from advertisements, popular cinema and women's magazines:

> He is everywhere. In the street, holding babies, pushing prams, collecting children, shopping with the progeny, panting in the ante-natal classes, shuffling sweaty-palmed in maternity rooms, grinning in the Mothercare catalogue . . . The new man is a rebel and an outlaw from hard-line masculinity, from the shirt-busting antics of the Incredible Hulk to the jaw-busting antics of John Wayne. He is an about-face from that whole fraternity of the Right Stuff from Eastwood to Stallone, with their staccato utterances and their castellated emotions.
>
> (Chapman 1988: 226)

Chapman argues that the New Man is a response to the pathologisation of masculinity by feminists, as well as a cynical effort to tap the lucrative, but previously difficult to target, market of upwardly mobile young men. Nevertheless, she agrees that he is a fictional character, 'an ideal that even the most liberated men would never lay claim to' (226). The New Man meets all the often-repeated demands of popular feminism, if it can be called that; *Cosmopolitan* feminism perhaps is a better term. He is involved with child-care, he is responsible for contraception, he cooks dinner and takes out the rubbish, he is a sensitive lover, he is supportive of his career-oriented partner. In other words, he is the choice romantic fantasy of the day.

259

The popular culture version of the New Man has a less idealised counterpart, the member of the men's group, whose views are represented in Victor Seidler's collection of essays entitled *Men, Sex and Relationships*. In his introduction to these essays written by members of the Achilles Heel men's collective, the book is described as containing writing which explores men's emotions and their (now stereotypical) inability to express them:

> *Achilles Heel*, the influential magazine of sexual politics first published in 1978, explored questions of masculinity from a standpoint which was sympathetic to the feminist critique of male power. This selection covers crucial issues in men's emotional and sexual lives and relationships, in particular the repressed aspects of their emotional involvement with others . . . [T]hese essays focus upon issues of childhood, sexualities and sexual identities, violence in its different dimensions, men's health, relationships and therapy. The writers are searching for an emotional language which could illuminate the contradictions of both love and power, fear and intimacy, autonomy and dependence, so that men can learn to communicate more openly and honestly within relationships.
>
> (Seidler 1992: frontispiece)

Seidler's volume of essays includes edited transcriptions of discussions on such things as politically incorrect sexual fantasies, personal responses to pornography, conversations about sex in long-term relationships, and autobiographical accounts of casual gay sex and getting tested for sexually transmitted diseases. Again, written in response to the common complaints about the insensitivity and inarticulacy of men, these writings assert that men feel emotion, too, and can sometimes manage to write about their pain.

Although it is entirely unacknowledged, the kind of 'explorations' that the essays in Seidler's volume perform mirror very closely the same kind of searches for self that were a feature of feminism in the 1970s. The 'men's group' is the masculine equivalent of the women's consciousness-raising groups that produced the slogan 'the personal is political' as a motivating force for feminists to include personal experience as appropriate data on which to form politicised attacks on patriarchy. The pioneering work of feminists to achieve some kind of acceptance for testimony within serious discussion goes overlooked by this volume, as indeed do recent problematisations by anti-essentialist feminists of calls to individual experience (see 'Post-Feminism' section).

Lynne Segal's full and clearly explained examination of many varieties of representations of masculinity, from tender father to sex beast, is introduced as follows:

> When men have written of themselves . . . they have done so as though presenting the universal truths of humanity, rather than the partial truths of half of it. And even now, when writing of men, women have done so more to expose the evils of their ways than to explore the riddles of 'masculinity' – its relation to, and dependence upon, 'femininity'.
>
> (Segal 1990: ix)

She identifies the new search for an understanding of masculinity within the context of the 'images of women' kind of feminist approach. Her suggestion, implied here, is that, instead of reading male characters in novels as human and gender-neutral, we see them as examples of a *constructed masculinity*, just as are the women characters who feature with them. Again, then, methodologies developed for feminist literary criticism are being applied in areas which had previously not been seen as being within feminists' remit. The question is, if the new object of this kind of Men's Studies (or Gender Studies as it is often called) is the old masculinity, how far have things changed? Is this any different when texts by men about men were the sole issue for discussion on English Literature degrees?

Susan Faludi's *Backlash* (1991) ensured a large amount of media attention for what she lists are the enormous number of unsympathetic responses to feminism that have become integrated into contemporary culture. 'Feminist bashing' (both literal and metaphorical) has become an established and popular sport (conducted by men and women alike). Consider, first of all, David Lodge's description, in *Nice Work* (1989), of his protagonist, Robyn Penrose, who is a lecturer in English Literature and a feminist:

> [Robyn] dresses herself in opaque green tights, a wide brown tweed skirt and a thick sweater loosely knitted in muted shades of orange, green and brown. Robyn generally favours loose clothes, made of natural fibres, that do not make her body into an object of sexual attention. The way they are cut also disguises her smallish breasts and widish hips while making the most of her height: thus are ideology and vanity equally satisfied. She contemplates her image in the long looking glass by the window, and decides that the effect is a little too sombre. She rummages in her jewellery box where brooches, necklaces and earrings are all jumbled together with enamel lapel badges expressing support for various radical causes – *Support the Miners*, *Crusade for Jobs*, *Legalize Pot*, *A Woman's Right to Choose* – and selects a silver brooch in which the CND symbol and the Yin sign are artfully intertwined. She pins it to her bosom.
>
> (Lodge 1989: 50)

Student and critic of feminism, Katie Roiphe, describes one of her feminist classmates as follows:

> As an undergraduate, Sarah wore baggy clothes in shades of brown and burnt orange. Looking at her, you couldn't see any curves or angles, just fabric. Her blond hair was short and she wore an earring in the shape of a woman symbol . . . When the papers brought news of a serial killer in Montreal shooting a group of women, Sarah wore black . . . She was somehow drawn to people who burst into tears all the time, or people who tried to kill themselves at parties. She was drawn to alcoholics and hypochondriacs . . . If you weren't on your guard and a word like 'freshman' or 'Indian-giver' slipped into your conversation, she would just walk away without a word.
>
> (Roiphe 1994: 115–17)

i) What kind of women are Robyn and Sarah supposed to be?
ii) How do they compare with other representations of women (for instance those discussed earlier in The Second Wave)?

The issue of men and feminism has become a pressing one for academics and others of late, mainly because of the increase of the institutionalisation of certain feminist ideas in the teaching of the humanities. Can men criticise texts using feminist methodologies as well as women, as *successfully* as women? What does this do to men, given that some feminisms ask them to take responsibility for the violence and oppressive behaviour meted out to women? What does it mean for women that men can teach and write about the way men have failed to represent women and have succeeded in excluding them from power and recognition?

The question of whether men are yet able to represent feminist ideas effectively is raised by Paul Smith's controversial remarks on the subject, some of which are quoted below, which have prompted an enormous amount of discussion. He is addressing a conference titled 'Men in Feminism', calling into question the position of men in relation to feminist discourses and he manages to choose precisely the wrong thing to say:

'Men in Feminism': the title for these two sessions and for which I have to take some large part of responsibility, has turned out to be at least provocative, perhaps offensive, at any rate troublesome for the participants. The provocation, the offence, the trouble that men now are for feminism is no longer – at least in the academy. . . simply a matter of men's being the object or *cause* of feminism (men's fault, feminism's cause; men as the agents of that which feminism seeks to change). Men, some men, now   and perhaps by way of repeating an age-old habit – are entering feminism, actively penetrating it (whatever 'it' might be, either before or after this intervention), for a variety of motives and in a variety of modes, fashions. That penetration is often looked upon with suspicion: it can be understood as yet another interruption, a

more or less illegal act of breaking and entering, entering
and breaking, for which these men must finally be held to
account. Perhaps the question that needs to be asked, then,
by these men, with them, for them, is to what extent their
irruption (penetration and interruption) is justified? Is it of
any use to feminism? To what extent is it wanted?

(Smith 1987: 33)

iii) What are the principal metaphors of this extract of Smith's
text?

iv) Why might they be considered problematic, even insensi-
tive, in the context of the work of feminists?

In addition to his role in the 'Men in Feminism' conference,
Smith has also written an essay called 'Vas' (1991) as a masculine
companion to the *écriture féminine*. His strategy in this essay is to
explore an alternative to the phallocentricism of masculine texts.
His term 'vas' invokes the *vas deferens* (the male vessel which,
during ejaculation, transports sperm from the testes to the ure-
thra), but also its Latin meaning of 'vessel' or 'baggage'. His essay
investigates the relationship between feminism and masculine
sexuality, but he tries to keep the term 'vas' operating as a
metaphor. He explains his choice of this term because it:

tries to avoid reducing male sexuality to the body itself: it
does not figure or suggest any specific organ in the way the
word 'phallus' ultimately does. It will be used instead to
describe a nexus of imaginary effects.

(Smith 1991: 1011–12)

Smith develops his essay into a critique of some feminist analyses
of pornography and cultural representations of male sexuality.
Whilst the objections to his work are clear – why should anyone
want or need another male-based metaphor for the cultural order
when the phallus is already so powerful? – Smith's work is
optimistic for feminism, too. He actively engages with feminist
analyses, for instance, and as well as criticising some feminist

work, he has also adopted feminist methodologies in an explicit way, rather than using feminist's work without giving credit. Work such as Smith's experimental essay is still in its early stages, but it is hopeful for the continuation of a feminism that is supported, rather than undermined, by men's studies.

Glossary

Desire: To be distinguished from straightforward sexual desire, Desire in the Lacanian scheme of things is a longing to return to a state of non-differentiation, of completeness. Once a subject has entered the Symbolic system, there is a schism between self and self-representation. This split is experienced as Desire for what is lacking (the phallus).

écriture féminine: A radical writing practice, the aim of which is to inscribe femininity. The feminine is excluded or repressed within the patriarchal, Symbolic order, and *écriture féminine* argues that existing linguistic structures are not sufficient for articulating the feminine: some new form of language has to be developed.

essentialism: Biological determinism; the denial of historical and cultural shifts in the human subject; the attribution of certain traits as unchangingly human, female, etc.

female: The biological basis of womanhood, argued as the grounds on which oppression of women, and the fight against this oppression, is based.

feminine: The cultural attributes of womanhood, as opposed to the biological, and which changes according to history and to cultural identity.

gynocriticism: A woman-centred critical practice which privileges women's criticisms of woman-authored texts, first promoted by Elaine Showalter.

logocentrism: This term is criticised by deconstruction as the philosophical understanding of words (*logos* means 'word') possessing metaphysical presence. Logocentricism is the belief that language can be authentic, fully representative and capable of producing fixed or certain meaning.

masculinity: The culturally acquired attributes of the male, assumed by

Freud as the norm against which feminine development has been judged wanting.

neologism: A new word.

patriarchy: Defined by materialist feminists as social and political domination by men, and by psychoanalytic feminists as the psychological, ideological primacy of the masculine over systems of representation.

phallocentrism: The ordering of Symbolic systems of difference around sexuality, where difference is determined according to possession or lack of the privileged signifier of the phallus. The term is mostly used in association with Lacanian discourse, and with the *écriture féminine*.

phallogocentrism: The connection of phallocentricism with logocentricism produces a system which privileges the phallus as both the main marker of sexual difference and as the guarantor of truth and meaning in language. (See Chapter 4 for further explanation).

semiotic: Not to be confused with semiotics (see Chapter 2), the semiotic is a term developed by Julia Kristeva, and indicates the pre-symbolic state of the infant, before its mind and body are regulated by language and the Symbolic order. The semiotic is the location of the feminine, after the subject has become integrated into the masculine order. The semiotic is not abolished with the entrance of the subject into the Symbolic; it remains in a repressed form, and is evident as a disruptive force, for instance, in moments of linguistic instability, in anti-social behaviour or transgressive and avant-garde art.

Symbolic: The order of language and representation. It is the order into which the subject must become integrated to gain recognition of its self, and to be recognised by others. It is also the order which depends on repression of disruptive forces. Feminists argue that the Symbolic order is a patriarchal one which needs to be transformed to accommodate feminine aspects.

Woman: A generalised woman, used by Jacques Lacan and the French Feminists to talk about the condition in which all women are placed and the way in which they are (inaccurately) represented by male-centred discourse. The term has been criticised as being essentialist, fixed and ahistorical.

Select bibliography

1 Defining feminism

The best anthology of American feminisms is called simply *Feminisms*, and is edited by Robyn R. Warhol and Diane Price Herndl (1991). As well as including some essays that have not been anthologised before, it contains helpful structures for organising ideas at the back, and is therefore very useful for teachers in course planning. Another anthology, confusingly also entitled *Feminisms* (1992), but edited by Maggie Humm, is oriented more towards a general Women's Studies market (rather than an English Studies audience). Its choice of texts is wide, and it contains very useful comments on the contributors. However, none of the inclusions are printed in full; it's not really a book that one can sit down and read from cover to cover, and it is rather frustrating as a reference text. Elaine Showalter's (ed.) *The New Feminist Criticism* (1986) was *the* course anthology in the mid-1980s. These days it is still useful, but more for helping students to catch up with older arguments, rather than offering the challenge of the new.

2 The second wave

Germaine Greer's notorious *The Female Eunuch* (1993) is forthright, brash, funny and still painfully relevant, although it was first published in 1971. Many others have tried to emulate Greer's account of how women and their bodies are manipulated by capitalist culture, but none have succeeded with such style. Sandra Gilbert and Susan Gubar's *The Madwoman in the Attic* (1979) contains radical readings of women's classics. It is much quoted and referred to, and is generally disliked by male tutors – if quoted by women students in their essays – who tend to think of it as extreme and slightly deranged. Ellen Moers's *Literary Women* (1976) and Elaine Showalter's *A Literature of Their Own* (1977) are more 'respectable' than Gilbert and Gubar, and also considerably less radical. *Feminist Readings, Feminists Reading*, by Sara Mills, Lynne Pearce, Sue Spaull and Elaine Millard (1989) contains readings of texts by women that are often taught on undergraduate degrees (such as *Jane Eyre*, *Wuthering Heights* and *The Color Purple*). It's a recent example of 'gynocriticism' and is a good text for beginners, who are looking for some idea of how to go about producing a feminist reading. Joanna Russ's witty *How to Suppress Women's Writing* (1984) argues polemically and convincingly about the continual neglect of women's writing.

3 Écriture féminine

The best starting point remains *New French Feminisms*, ed. Isabelle de Courtivron and Elaine Marks (1981). This is a 'beginners' anthology of very small extracts from a large number of the key writers, without much metacommentary. Ultimately, the brevity of the extracts is limiting, but it does give the reader an introduction to a range of writers in a manageable way. Toril Moi's *Sexual/Textual Politics* (1985) provides a thorough and informed introduction to the work of Irigaray, Cixous and Kristeva from a literary perspective. Susan Sellers' *Language and Sexual Difference: Feminist Writing in France* (1991) is more basic than Moi's, but also more readable, and she covers a much wider range of theorists. Chris Weedon's *Feminist Practice and Post-Structuralist Theory* (1987) is an extremely successful introduction to this area of feminism, as well as providing a helpful link between political commitment and otherwise male-dominated post-structuralist theories (such as psychoanalysis and deconstruction). Jane Gallop's *Feminism and Psychoanalysis: The Daughter's Seduction* (1992) provides a sophisticated introduction to Jacques Lacan, and also dedicates three full chapters to a critical discussion of the work of Luce Irigaray. Gallops text has become a classic of feminist psychoanlysis.

4 Writing lesbian

An excellent introduction to the range and history of lesbian writing can be found in *The Penguin Book of Lesbian Short Stories*, ed. Margaret Reynolds (1993). Reynolds introduces some of the main theoretical debates around lesbian writing in her foreword, which includes some valuable references to critical sources. Our chapter makes extensive use of two classic essays on lesbian writing: Bonnie Zimmerman's 'What Has Never Been: An Overview of Lesbian Feminist Literary Criticism' and Catharine Stimpson's 'Zero Degree Deviancy: The Lesbian Novel in English', both of which are anthologised in *Feminisms*, (eds Warhol and Price Herndl 1991, 117–37 and 301–15 respectively). Betsy Warland's *Inversions: Writings By Dykes, Queers and Lesbians* (1991) contains a wide range of essays by lesbians about their writing practice. Finally, reference should be made to Lillian Faderman's *Surpassing the Love of Men: Romantic Friendship and Love Between Women From the Renaissance to the Present*, (1981) and her more recent *Odd Girls and Twilight Lovers* (1992), both of which are impressive surveys of cultural representations of lesbians.

5 'Post-feminism'

Susan Faludi's, *Backlash* (1991) offers a large amount of evidence to support her argument that discrimination against women has taken on a disturbing new form as a response to the success of feminism. The enormous number of examples exposed by Faludi make the book an impressive journalistic feat and it is difficult not to be swayed in the face of so much documentation. Naomi Wolf's *Fire with Fire* (1993) has an entirely different agenda. Wolf argues that women have been alienated by 'victim' feminism, to the extent that they have failed to recognise the power that they already command. Like Faludi, she draws on a large range of contemporary examples to support her argument for a new kind of optimistic feminism for the future. Tania Modleski's *Feminism Without Women* (1991) is a collection of essays on cultural (mostly filmic) representations of gender relations. The collection is particularly valuable for the opening essay, which offers an extremely sharp analysis of current trends in feminist studies. Finally, *Feminists Theorize the Political*, eds. Judith Butler and Joan W. Scott (1992) is an excellent collection of varied essays, which shows how sophisticated, challenging and thought-provoking feminist criticism can be.

6 'Men's studies'

This is now a real growth area in publishing, and there are far more disappointing works than there are ground-breaking ones. The real forerunner of the marketing of men's studies was Robert Bly's *Iron John* (1991), which constructs a mythological, semi-psychoanalytical structure for understanding the condition of masculinity today. If you have embraced post-structuralist philosphies, Bly's use of archetypes and essences can be a bit wearing, but his work is a serious attempt to find a methodology to deal with the new conditions in which men find themselves. Unlike Bly, who has learned from feminism, Neil Lyndon's *No More Sex War: The Failures of Feminism* (1993) is unashamedly anti-feminist, aggressive in tone, containing much vitriolic diatribe and some very strained arguments and statistics. Lyndon's book was hugely hyped at the time of its publication, but is interesting mainly because it demonstrates the strength of anti-feminist feeling and the reality of the 'backlash'. Lynne Segal's *Slow Motion: Changing Masculinities, Changing Men* (1990) is a thorough, succinct and extremely clear-headed account of recent representations of masculinity and remains the best introduction to this area of gender studies. *Men In Feminism*, eds. A. Jardine and P. Smith (1987) remains a key text for theorising the position of men in relation to academic feminism. The essays assume a familiarity with deconstruction and psychoanalysis, and are not always the most approachable. However, the collection is useful in that it does explore the complexities of the relationship between men and the way feminism has been integrated into academic institutions, and offers hope for collaborative enterprises rather than competition and conflict.

Chapter 7

Cultural identity, literature, criticism

1 Challenging the canon

T HE TERM 'CANON' refers to a traditional core of literature, made up of works deemed 'great', 'valuable', 'universal' and 'timeless', and therefore worthy of continued academic study. The canon has never been completely formalised, with particular writers being *always* either in or out (probably Shakespeare would be the only writer who was always 'in' on English Literature courses). Fashions do change, but the range of what is counted as great remains restricted, and reliably reproduced, if only because teachers tend to teach what they are familiar with and publishers tend to publish what they know will sell. However, this simplistic answer skirts the issue of judgement, of how a text might qualify for greatness, universality and value. T.S. Eliot, in 'Tradition and the Individual Talent', posits his thesis for how traditions should be perpetuated by individual poets:

> The poet must be very conscious of the main current, which does not at all flow invariably through the most distinguished reputations. He must be quite aware of the obvious fact that art never improves, but that the material of art is never quite the same. He must be aware that the mind of Europe – the mind of his own country – a mind which he learns in time to be much more important than his own private mind – is a mind which changes.
>
> (Eliot 1975: 39)

Eliot makes both explicit and implicit points here. Explicitly, and perhaps these days uncontroversially, he suggests that the 'main current' of tradition is beyond the control of the individual, but it nevertheless influences what kind of art is produced. The less explicit points that can be gleaned from this small extract, though, are that poetry is what is important to artistic traditions, that poets are male, and most significant of all, poets are European. Such a position has not gone unchallenged, and some of this challenge has come from a liberalisation of the canon, an attempt to get a wider range of texts included on core literature courses, as well as the teaching of representative literatures, such as courses on women's writing, African-American writing and so on.

The inclusion of a wider range of texts to study is one response to the problem of an exclusive canon. But another question emerges from this debate: what is the effect of continuing to produce 'representative' canons that include the odd black writer or two, on the grounds that they are 'as good as' any of the white writers on the list? If one argues that one text is 'as good as' another, there must be a shared set of criteria on which that judgement is made. In other words, this makes alternative literatures conform to the same standards of a tradition that has excluded them.

Instead of simply saying that black writers should be included in the mainstream of literary study, it is perhaps more useful to consider what a literary canon which ratifies some works and not others does to our critical practice. What is the effect on critics' capacity to do their work, if they are used to reading only limited kinds of literature? Paul Lauter asks: 'How is *canon*, – that is, selection – related to, indeed a *function of* critical technique?' (1991: 228) He continues to question the ways in which the selective procedures govern the way in which we read and criticise. Try to answer Lauter's questions for yourself:

- can the canon significantly change if we retain essentially the same critical techniques and priorities?
- where do the techniques of criticism come from? Do they fall from the sky? Or do they arise out of social practice? And if the latter, from which social practice?
- out of what social practice, from what values, does the close analysis (disregarding other contextual factors) of complex texts (i.e. those deemed complex and valuable by the sustainers of the canon) arise?
- do we perpetuate those values in pursuing the critical practice derived from them?

- does such critical practice effectively screen from our appreciation, even our scrutiny, other worlds of creativity, of art?
- are there other worlds of art out there whose nature, dynamics, values we fail to appreciate because we ask the wrong questions, or don't know what questions to ask? Or maybe we shouldn't simply be asking questions.

[In other words] . . . the literary canon as we have known it is a product in significant measure of our training in male, white, bourgeois cultural tradition, including in particular the formal techniques of literary analysis. Other cultural traditions provide alternate views about the nature and function of art, and approaches to it.

(Lauter 1991: 228)

Lauter here is questioning the training and experience of literary critics and scholars, and suggests that the continual inscription of some texts as suitable for formal study and analysis, the continual delineation of others as unacceptable, is a self-perpetuating process. His questions ask critics to examine themselves and the answers suggest that who you are not only affects what you say, but it also affects who hears you and how they understand your work.

There is an undeniable Eurocentricism on English Literature core courses, certainly at degree level. It is not just that the 'essential' texts that students read year after year are predominantly by white writers, but also that the kind of issues that students are encouraged to examine do not engage with questions of cultural identity, racism, colonialism and marginalisation, of issues of home and abroad, and how the metropolitan 'home' is often constructed on the back of the colonised 'abroad'. To explain more fully what we mean, let us look at Jane Austen's *Mansfield Park* (1814) as it has been read by Edward Said. Said argues that the position of Sir Thomas Bertram at home cannot be understood without reference to his position as an absentee plantation owner on the Caribbean island of Antigua. Said quotes this scene from Jane Austen which establishes Sir Thomas's role as lord of Mansfield Park, and follows it with a commentary that puts the small local scene into a world perspective. First, read the extract from Jane Austen:

> It was a busy morning with him. Conversation with any of them occupied but a small part of it. He had to reinstate himself in all the wonted concerns of his Mansfield life, to see his steward and his bailiff – to examine and compute – and, in the intervals of business, to walk into his stables and nearest plantations; but active and methodical, he had not only done all this before he resumed his seat as master of the house at dinner, he had also set the carpenter to work in pulling down what had been so lately put up in the billiard room, and given the scene painter his dismissal, long enough to justify the pleasing belief of his being then at least as far off as Northampton. The scene painter was gone, having spoilt only the floor of one room, ruined all the coachman's sponges, and made five of the under-servants idle and dissatisfied . . .
>
> (Austen [1814] 1966: 42)

i) Comment on what you understand to be the significance of this short extract.

ii) Now read the commentary on this same quotation by Said. Are there any similarities between his reading of the text and your own?

The force of this paragraph is unmistakable. Not only is this a Crusoe setting things in order: it is also an early Protestant eliminating all traces of frivolous behaviour. There is nothing in Mansfield Park that would contradict us, however, were we to assume that Sir Thomas does exactly the same things – on a larger scale – in his Antigua 'plantations'. Whatever was wrong there . . . Sir Thomas was able to fix, thereby maintaining his control over his colonial domain. More clearly here than anywhere else in her fiction, Austen here synchronizes domestic with international authority, making it plain that the values associated with such higher things as ordination, law, and property must be grounded firmly in actual rule over and possession of territory.

(Said 1994: 103–4)

Said is careful to explain that the mentions of Antigua in Austen's novel are few and far between, and that Sir Thomas Bertram is not seen at work on his Caribbean plantations in the course of the narrative, and so it is easy to complain that he (Said) is wilfully misreading the novel. In his own defence, he argues:

> I think of [my] reading as completing or complementing others, not discounting or displacing them. And it bears stressing that because *Mansfield Park* connects to the actualities of British power overseas to the domestic imbroglio within the Bertram estate, there is no way of doing such readings as mine, no way of understanding the 'structure of attitude and reference' except by working through the novel . . . But in reading it carefully, we can sense how ideas about dependent races and territories were held both by foreign-office executives, colonial bureaucrats, and military strategists and by intelligent novel-readers educating themselves in the fine points of moral evaluation, literary balance, and stylistic finish.
>
> (Said 1994: 114)

Said here implicates the novel-reading process in other discourses of power that support and perpetuate imperialism. His emphasis on the significance of the novel-reading process in this respect is important to remember.

2 Writing back

One way in which attention is drawn to the Eurocentric bias of literature and literary analysis as it is taught in Western educational institutions is through a process of engaging in a dialogue with canonical texts, showing their omissions and preferences. This can be done in a number of ways:

By criticising with an eye to representation of cultural difference, for instance

By rewriting certain features to satirise the original

By bringing back to prominence characters who are often forgotten.

Literature affects our understanding of cultural identity, although we are often not aware of this, and the tradition of 'writing back' to the cultural heart of the empire, of rewriting literary classics from an alternative point of view illustrates clearly how opinions are formed. An obvious example of this 'writing back' is Jean Rhys' *Wide Sargasso Sea* which reinstates the Caribbean story behind Bertha Mason (see Chapter 6). Another example of a text that has been rewritten is Conrad's *Heart of Darkness*. This novel in itself problematises the colonial relation, and the ironic stance of its narrator means that it has been interpreted both as a critique of colonialism as well as being a product of it. This text has been the focus for many reinterpretations, including Francis Ford Coppola's film *Apocalypse Now*, which puts the Conrad story into the context of the Vietnam war; Margaret Atwood's *Surfacing* rewrites the text in a Canadian context; V.S. Naipaul's *A Bend in the River* is written by a man with Asian-Carribbean origins and Patrick White's *A Fringe of Leaves* replaces the quest for the heart of darkness in Australia.

Another classic text written about colonisation, again from the centre of an empire, is Shakespeare's *The Tempest*, and we are going to use this as a more extended example of the process of 'writing back'. This play has not only been subject to much analysis about its representation of European settlement on an already-inhabited island, but has also been rewritten in various ways. It is a useful text to consider here, since it shows the way in which strategies of resistance to the cultural dominant have been used to subvert one of the most canonised of writers, and how writing out of a different cultural background has become crucial to our interpretation of even the most central texts of Empire. The rewriting of *The Tempest* has been done to highlight the imbalance of power between the magician Prospero – who has taken control of the island and its inhabitants, having been deprived of his own dominions in Europe – and the other characters, notably Caliban, Miranda and Ariel. In particular, attention has been paid to the way in which Caliban is represented, as a shuffling, brutal, bestial character who is bitter and resentful of his subjection to Prospero. This is how Caliban describes his situation in relation to Prospero:

> This island's mine, by Sycorax my mother,
> Which thou tak'st from me. When thou cam'st first,
> Thou strok'st me, and made much of me; wouldst give me
> Water with berries in't; and teach me how
> To name the bigger light, and how the less,
> That burn by day and night: and then I lov'd thee,
> And show'd thee all the qualities o' th' isle,
> The fresh springs, brine-pits, barren place and fertile:
> Curs'd be I that did so! All the charms
> Of Sycorax, toads, beetles, bats, light on you!
> For I am all the subjects that you have,
> Which first was mine own King: and here you sty me
> In this hard rock, whiles you do keep from me
> The rest o' th' island.

> (1.2. 333–45)

Caliban argues here from a position familiar to many people from First Nations (such as North American Indians, or aboriginal peoples from Australia). He argues that Prospero learned from him, and then took advantage of that knowledge to deprive him of his rightful occupancy of his territory, his birthright, effectively confining him to a reservation.

Engagement with *The Tempest* as a way of theorising colonisation perhaps begins with Dominique O. Mannoni's *Prospero and Caliban: The Psychology of Colonization* (1964), which sets up the idea of a 'Prospero complex' that afflicted imperial rulers, making them needful of overarching power, and of a Calibanic relation, or 'dependency complex', which was the lot of the colonial subject, needful of a ruler. Whilst Mannoni's text produced an important psychoanalytic insight into the complicated relationship between coloniser and colonised, and offered understanding of the difficulties of breaking free from the condition of subjection to imperial domination, it has also been criticised forcefully, most notably by Franz Fanon in *Black Skin, White Masks* (1986). This is Fanon's fairly damning critique of Mannoni:

> M. Mannoni takes it upon himself to explain colonialism's reason for existence. In the process he adds a new complex to the standing catalogue: the 'Prospero complex'. It is defined as the sum of those unconscious neurotic tendencies that delineate at the same time the 'picture' of the paternalist colonial and the portrait of the 'racialist whose daughter has suffered an [imaginary] attempted rape at the hands of an inferior being.'
>
> Prospero, as we know, is the main character of Shakespeare's comedy, *The Tempest*. Opposite him we have his daughter, Miranda, and Caliban. Toward Caliban, Prospero assumes an attitude that is well known to Americans in the southern United States. Are they not forever saying that the niggers are just waiting for the chance to jump on white women? . . . If one adds that many Europeans go to the colonies because it is possible for them to grow rich quickly there, that with rare exceptions the colonial is a merchant, or rather a trafficker, one will have grasped the psychology of the man who arouses in the autochthonous [original, native] population the 'feeling of inferiority.'
>
> (Fanon 1986: 107–8)

Fanon is satirising Mannoni's need to excuse the coloniser by giving him this 'Prospero complex'. He points out that the white man's fear of black men raping white women, and their desire for profit, heedless of exploitation, can't be excused so easily. It is this inexcusable behaviour that Fanon sees illustrated by Shakespeare's play.

More recently, in the light of much New Historicist theory (see Chapter 3), Paul Brown has produced a critique of *The*

Tempest which sets it within the context of seventeenth century imperialist projects. His interpretation of the play shows Prospero as coloniser, as in Fanon's version, but both Miranda and Caliban are his *childlike* subjects. Miranda really *is* Prospero's daughter, however, whilst Caliban is a prior inhabitant of the island over which Prospero now rules. Brown also focuses on the question of Caliban as rapist, and, like Fanon, sees this as problematic when one considers what Prospero himself is doing on the island. Brown argues:

> The island itself is an 'uninhabited' spot, a *tabula rasa* peopled fortuitously by the shipwrecked. Two children, Miranda and Caliban, have been nurtured upon it. Prospero's narrative operates to produce them in the binary division of the other, into the malleable and the irreformable . . . [which is] a major strategy of colonialist discourse. There is Miranda, miraculous courtly lady, virgin prospect . . . and there is Caliban, scrambled 'cannibal', savage incarnate. Presiding over them is the cabalist [occultist, mystic] Prospero, whose function it is to divide and demarcate these potentialities, abrogating to the male all that is debased and rapacious, to the female all that is cultured and needs protection.
>
> Such a division of the 'children' is validated in Prospero's narrative by the memory of Caliban's attempted rape of Miranda (I.ii. 347–53), which immediately follows Caliban's own account of his boundless hospitality to the exiles on their arrival (333–46). The issue here is not whether Caliban is actually a rapist or not, since he accepts the charge. I am rather concerned with the political effects of this charge at this moment in the play. The first effect is to circumvent Caliban's version of events by reencoding his boundlessness as rapacity: his inability to discern a concept of private, bounded property concerning his own dominions is reinterpreted as a desire to violate the chaste virgin, who epitomises courtly property. Second, the capacity to divide and order is shown to be the prerogative of the courtly ruler

alone. Third, the memory legitimises Prospero's takeover of power.

i) How do you think Caliban is characterised in the play? (Here are some of the ways he has been thought of: rapist, hospitable native islander, cursing savage, pitiful subjected slave, anti-imperialist insurgent.)
ii) Do you think there are problems with using Caliban as a representative figure for the colonised subject?

Caliban has become a crucial figure for many post-colonial critics. In particular, discussion has focused on his argument with Prospero about language, in which he resists the coloniser's linguistic claim on him, exclaiming:

> You taught me language; and my profit on't
> Is, I know how to curse. The red plague rid you
> For learning me your language!

Language is used as a means of sustaining imperial domination, and literature is obviously implicated in the process of ensuring that ideological structures are communicated alongside linguistic ones. Caliban expresses his resistance to the force of language by 'misusing' it, by using it to swear at Prospero. Although Caliban has been celebrated for his defiance in this scene, his sub-human, aggressive stance is not always a positive symbol for post-colonial writers.

In the instances above, the character of Miranda is given less attention than those of Caliban and Prospero. For a feminist reader, there are clearly problems with the way in which the attempted rape of Miranda is discussed. This is a question that has been taken up by Margaret Laurence's novel, *The Diviners* (1974), which offers analysis of both gender and culture in her reinterpretation of Shakespeare's play. In *The Diviners*, the protagonist, Morag Gunn, is a Canadian novelist of Scottish ancestry. She is struggling with her understanding of her cultural origins, and of those of her country, Canada. The struggles to come to terms with women's inequality, and of cultural identity, are partly explored in Morag's allegorical novel which she calls *Prospero's Child*. In the following extract, the novel synopsis is given by Morag in a letter to a friend:

> It's called *Prospero's Child*, she being the young woman who marries His Excellency, the governor of some island in some ocean very far south, and who virtually worships him and then who has to go to the opposite extreme and reject nearly everything about him, at least for a time, in order to become her own person. It's as much the story of H.E. I've always wondered if Prospero really would be able to give up his magical advantages once and for all, as he intends to do at the end of *The Tempest*. That incredibly moving statement – 'What strength I have's mine own. Which is most faint –' If only he can hang on to that knowledge, that would be true despair within, and that he stands in need of grace like everyone else – Shakespeare did know just about everything. I know it's presumptuous of me to try to put this into some different and contemporary framework and relevance, but I can't help it. Well, hell, maybe it's not so presumptuous at that.
>
> (Laurence 1974: 330)

Consider that, at this stage of Laurence's narrative, her character Morag is married to an English Literature professor who was brought up in India under British rule. Morag is an orphan who has been brought up on the outskirts of a small prairie town, the adopted daughter of a garbage collector.

iii) What is the effect of writing about Prospero's child, rather than about Prospero or Caliban?

iv) Why *rewrite* Shakespeare, rather than just reread him critically?

It is possible to argue that there is no point in spending yet more time on the works of dead white men, when writers could be creating entirely fresh fictions out of their own specific experience, be it Canadian, Caribbean, African American or whatever. However, this would be to miss the point of the 'writing back' process. Canonical English literatures may have marginalised the colonial subject, but nevertheless, canonical English literature was and is very much part of the reading of English-speaking peoples around the world, not just those from Britain. This schooling is not easily forgotten, and many writers have chosen to deal with the ideological assumptions of the traditional literary canon by creating a 'counter-discourse', a form of writing which resists the powerful influence of empire not by denying it but by engaging with it.

Gloria Naylor's novel, *Mama Day* (1990), also reconsiders aspects of *The Tempest*, but the effect is more subtly integrated than in Laurence's novel. The events of Naylor's novel occur in the fictional setting of Willow Springs, 49 square miles of land just off the coast of Georgia and South Carolina, joined to the mainland by a bridge. Miranda Day, who goes by the name Mama Day, is a spiritual healer and figurehead in the local community; her niece Ophelia, nicknamed Cocoa, lives in New York, but she returns to Willow Springs one summer with her new husband, and is caught up in a battle for her life, waged by supernatural forces, directed by Ruby, another Willow Springs matriarch, and deflected by Mama Day. The connection with Shakespeare is not just in the names of the characters. The question of whose forces prevail over the island of Willow Springs is an important one. The novel opens as follows:

> Willow Springs. Everybody knows but nobody talks about the legend of Sapphira Wade. A true conjure woman: satin black, biscuit cream, red as Georgia clay: depending upon which of us takes a mind to her. She could walk through a lightning storm without being touched; grab a bolt of lightning in the palm of her hand; use the heat of lightning to start the kindling going under her medicine pot: depending

upon which of us takes a mind to her. She turned the moon into salve, the stars into a swaddling cloth, and healed the wounds of every creature walking up on two or down on four. It ain't about right or wrong, truth or lies; it's about a slave woman who brought a whole new meaning to both them words, soon as you cross over here from beyond the bridge. And somehow, some way, it happened in 1823: she smothered Bascombe Wade in his very bed and lived to tell the story for a thousand days. 1823: married Bascombe Wade, bore him seven sons in just a thousand days, to put a dagger through his kidney and escape the hangman's noose, laughing in a burst of flames. 1823: persuaded Bascombe Wade in a thousand days to deed all his slaves every inch of land in Willow Springs, poisoned him for his trouble, to go on and bear seven sons – by person or persons unknown.

(Naylor 1990: 3)

Sapphira Wade is Mama Day's great-grandmother, and, however irretrievable the details of the history might be, Mama Day has come to own land on Willow Springs, and wields power there, like her great-grandmother did. There is significance in the way the history is interpreted, clearly. The replacement of the Prospero character by Mama Day as magician and orchestrator of events, openly inverts the power hierarchy of indentured slavery, the resistance of which begins with Sapphira Wade. It radically reinterprets American history of land ownership by writing about an African-American woman as landowner and community leader. The novel also reinscribes African cultural beliefs and traditions, in the representation of struggles against possession by spiritual forces which form the crisis point in the narrative.

The effect of rewriting a story about colonisation has potential to transform the existing traditions of literature by showing new ways of reading, as well as creating a counter-tradition of writing in its own right. Ashcroft *et al.* sum up the process and effects of 'writing back' as follows:

The subversion of a canon is not simply a matter of replacing one set of texts with another. This would be radically to simplify what is implicit in the idea of canonicity itself. A canon is not a body of texts *per se,* but rather a set of reading practices (the enactment of innumerable individual and community assumptions, for example about genre, about literature, and even about writing). These reading practices, in their turn, are resident in institutional structures, such as education curricula and publishing networks. So the subversion of a canon involves the bringing-to-consciousness and articulation of these practices and institutions, and will result not only in the replacement of some texts by others, or the redeployment of some hierarchy of value within them, but equally crucially by the reconstruction of the so-called canonical texts through alternative reading practices.

(Ashcroft *et al.* 1989: 189)

3 Writing and cultural identity

The constitution of identity, and the contribution of such factors as ethnicity, class and gender, are constantly under discussion in current debates (see Chapter 5). Race, ethnicity or culture are not universal or fixed; they are concepts that have variable definitions. In particular, the idea of race as genetic – clearly identifiable by facial features, physical characteristics and skin colour – has been thrown into question by a number of contemporary cultural critics. The current debate is perhaps most clearly illustrated by Diana Fuss (1990), who quotes from Booker T. Washington's autobiography *Up from Slavery* (1901), tell the story of a black man who was travelling in the section of train reserved for Negroes. The traveller was mistaken for a white man by the conductor, who ultimately had to look at the feet of the man of unclear origin, in order to determine whereabouts on the train he was entitled to sit. The absurdity of this situation, that a man is treated in a particular way for no other reason than the way his feet look, is not only an argument against racism, but is also the beginning of an argument about the criteria for racial identity.

Henry Louis Gates Jr explains that the *biological* notion of race is a fiction – he calls things like 'the Jewish race', 'the Aryan race' and the 'black race' misnomers and metaphors. He refuses them as descriptions with any accuracy, or even any meaningfulness, saying:

> the sense of difference defined in popular usages of 'race' has both described and *inscribed* differences of language, belief system, artistic tradition and gene pool, as well as all sorts of supposedly natural attributes such as rhythm, athletic ability, celebration, usury, fidelity and so forth . . . Race has become a trope of ultimate, irreducible difference between cultures, linguistic groups, or adherents of specific belief systems which – more often than not – also have fundamentally opposed economic interests . . . [T]he biological criteria used to determine 'difference' in sex simply do not hold when applied to 'race'. Yet we carelessly use language in such a way as to *will* this sense of *natural* difference. To do so is to engage in a pernicious act of language, one which exacerbates the complex problem of cultural or ethnic difference rather than to assuage or redress it . . . Scores of people are killed every day in the name of differences ascribed only to race. Western writers in French, Spanish, German, Portuguese and English have tried to mystify these rhetorical figures of race, to make them natural, absolute, essential. In doing so, they have *inscribed* these differences as fixed and finite categories which they merely report or draw upon for authority. It takes little reflection, however, to recognise that these pseudoscientific categories are themselves figures. Who has seen a black or red person, a white, yellow, or brown? These terms are arbitrary constructs, not reports of reality.
>
> (Gates 1986a: 5–6)

Gates' position is an important, anti-essentialist one, and something which denies the stability of a 'Black', 'Native' or 'Racially Marked' subject. The arbitrariness of the terms can be seen when people get them wrong. In the case of Aboriginal writer Sally

Morgan, she was brought up to believe that she was Indian, as a conscious act by her family to conceal her native Australian family, to protect her from discrimination. In her autobiography, *My Place* (1988), which also contains the stories of her mother and grandmother, Morgan explains how she was awarded an aboriginal scholarship after she found out her true heritage. However, after studying and succeeding at college, she is summoned to the government department that issues the scholarships:

> 'Mrs Morgan', the senior officer said as I sat down. 'We'll get straight to the point. We have received information, from what appears to be a very reliable source, that you have obtained the Aboriginal scholarship under false pretences. This person, who is a close friend of you and your sister, has told us that you have been bragging all over the university campus about how easy it is to obtain the scholarship without even being Aboriginal. Apparently, you've been saying that anyone can get it.' . . . 'Look', I said angrily, 'when I applied for this scholarship, I told your people everything I knew about my family, it was their decision to grant me a scholarship, so if there's any blame to be laid, it's your fault, not mine. How do you expect me to prove anything? What would you like me to do, bring my grandmother and mother in and parade them up and down so you can all have a look? There's no way I'll do that, even if you tell me to. I'd rather lose the allowance. It's my word against whoever complained, so it's up to you to decide, isn't it?'
>
> (Morgan 1988: 139–40)

What Morgan demonstrates here is the way in which claim to a particular racial heritage is arbitrary but can have significant material consequences. In the case of peoples of First Nations where there are government funds available, to pay for education programmes or as repayment for ancestral land now occupied by settlers, the ability to prove ethnicity becomes an economic issue as well as a matter of personal identity. Precisely how someone of more than one ethnic origin might go about proving her or his claim is shown to be profoundly difficult, and Morgan describes the experience at the scholarship office as 'demeaning', as well as provoking self-doubt about her cultural identity:

> What did it really mean to be Aboriginal? I'd never lived off the land and been a hunter and a gatherer. I'd never participated in corroborees or heard stories of the Dreamtime. I'd lived all my life in suburbia and told everyone I was Indian. I hardly knew any Aboriginal people. What did it mean for someone like me?
>
> (Morgan 1988: 141)

Morgan shows that acculturation, the way in which one is brought up and the people one identifies with, have at least as much effect on her self-identity as her racial label.

Vietnamese film-maker and feminist critic Trinh T. Minh-ha also analyses how it is possible to identify oneself according to a racial grouping. She resists simplistic identification and limiting racial definitions, using the discourse of deconstruction to undo the arguments of racial essentialism:

> *Authenticity* as a need to rely on an 'undisputed origin' is prey to an obsessive *fear*: that of *losing a connection* . . . The *real*, nothing else than a *code of representation* does not (cannot) coincide with the lived or the performed. This is what Vine Deloria Jr accounts for when he exclaims: 'not even Indians can relate themselves to this type of creature who, to anthropologists, is the "real" Indian.'
>
> (Trinh T. Minh-ha 1989: 94)

The people who award aboriginal scholarships need to identify precisely this 'undisputed origin', and they rely on codes of authenticity, but this clear-cut definition does not match up with the lived experience in which ancestry is clouded by the need to protect others from racism, the secrets of illegitimacy and mixed-race, cross-class relationships.

However, the kind of deconstruction of identity and difference that is the practice of Trinh T. Minh-ha and Henry Louis Gates Jr is not a universal practice, and, as for feminism and other theories of representation for marginalised peoples, the problem of giving up race as a ground on which to fight raises the difficulty of getting one's oppression voiced and recognised. It gives away the ground on which to fight against racism and/or blindness to difference. It is very difficult to explain racism if the category of race itself is denied. Thus, some writers and critics celebrate their ethnic identity and cultural heritage and seek to reclaim their subjectivity in this fashion, rather than by trying to dismantle the categories of definition which is the aim of the deconstructionists. They write as a means of exploring their ethnic identity, and as a way of representing themselves. Mary di Michele, an Italian Canadian, explains:

> Doubly distanced, I am distanced again because my *mother tongue*, the only tongue of my primal, early childhood experience, the only language my mother speaks, is Italian . . . I use Italian words [in poetry] to signal difference or to signal that some form of 'translation' is necessary . . . the untranslated word from another language is like an outcrop of bedrock, more physical in its texture than the rest of the text, thick and indecipherable, it is the body of the poet asserting itself to the English mind. On another level it may also marginalise the reader to the text in a similar way to which the writer is marginalised by the language of the tradition in which she writes.
>
> (di Michele 1990: 105)

Di Michele sees her first language as giving her a particular connection with her mother and with her background. But just as she can use an Italian word to draw connections, so she can also use it to deliberately exclude those who don't understand her culture, to make them feel their difference from her, and to force awareness of distinct identities.

4 Post-colonial literary theory

Post-colonial literary theory has only recently been recognised as a designated area within Literary Studies in higher education. Its beginning as a discourse within the academy has disputed origins, but its position within the academy can be recognised now by the publication of a number of student-oriented introductions to the subject, beginning with Ashcroft *et al.*'s student guide to the area, *The Empire Writes Back* (1989). Whatever its origins, it remains a highly contested issue amongst contemporary theorists, and the first area of debate is usually the title given to this group of theories and literatures. This is how Anne McClintock, a white South African now teaching in the United States, describes the problem with the term 'post-colonial':

> How, then, does one account for the curious ubiquity of the preposition 'post' in contemporary intellectual life [post-modern, post-feminist, post-Freudian, etc.], not only in the universities, but in newspaper columns and on the lips of media moguls? In the case of 'post-colonialism', at least, part of the reason is its academic marketability. While admittedly another p-c word, 'post-colonialism' is arguably more palatable and less foreign-sounding to sceptical deans than 'Third World Studies'. It also has a less accusatory ring than 'Studies in Neo-colonialism', say, or 'Fighting Two Colonialisms'. It is more global, and less fuddy-duddy, than 'Commonwealth Studies'. The term borrows, more-over, on the dazzling marketing success of the term 'post-modernism'. As the organizing rubric of an emerging field of disciplinary studies and an archive of knowledge, the term 'post-colonialism' makes possible the marketing of a whole new generation of panels, articles, books and courses.
>
> (McClintock 1994: 299)

McClintock points out the more cynical reasons for the term 'post-colonial' here. She argues that the term has little to do with the literatures being a 'natural' or cohesive grouping; rather, the label has to do with the established practices of teaching and studying literature. Unless a group of texts can be packaged and sold as a course, with a target set of aims and objectives that the student will reach at the end, the course will not be accepted by the institution. Even if the institution accepts the course, it must be 'sold' to a fixed number of students, otherwise it isn't practical to run it. McClintock argues that the 'term-post-colonial' is simply a successful marketing device.

This grouping of literatures, around which critical discourses are focused, may be called post-colonial; they may also be marketed as one of the following, or something else:

Third World literatures
Commonwealth literatures
New literatures written in English
World literatures (written in English)
Migrant writing
Diasporic writing ('dispersed' writing, e.g. Asian-British writing)
Black literatures

It is important to stress that the terms on the above list are not synonymous. The grouping is very loose, and certain terms are more exclusive and more specific (perhaps more meaningful) than others. For instance, 'migrant writing' is a label given to any writers who have written after having moved away from their homeland, either through choice or necessity: obvious examples would be Salman Rushdie and Samuel Beckett. Clearly, this kind of writing does not necessarily have anything to do with racial or ethnic identity, in a way that black writing might have.

Increasingly, the argument is that whatever title is given, it will be too generalised, and that really we should stick to specific labels; of nation, and then perhaps of a sub-group within the nation state. Salman Rushdie argues against even this kind of labelling, and insists that 'Literature written in English' should suffice as a grouping. He contends that any other sub-division enables the traditional British English literature canon to maintain its centrality, ghettoising literatures written in English about other nations. Rushdie's resistance is particularly against the term 'Commonwealth'. He explains that it is particularly difficult to define, and then that, once defined, it can be forgotten:

> The nearest I could get to a definition [of Commonwealth literature] sounded distinctly patronizing: 'Commonwealth literature', it appears, is that body of writing created, I

think, in the English language, by persons who are not themselves white Britons, or Irish, or citizens of the United States of America. I don't know whether black Americans are citizens of this bizarre Commonwealth or not. Probably not. It is also uncertain whether citizens of Commonwealth countries writing in languages other than English – Hindi, for example – or who switch out of English . . . are permitted into the club or asked to keep out . . . [The term] permits academic institutions, publishers, critics, and even readers to dump a large segment of English literature into a box and then more or less ignore it. At best, what is called 'Commonwealth literature' is positioned *below* English literature 'proper' – or . . . it places Eng. Lit. at the centre and the rest of the world at the periphery.

(Rushdie 1991: 63, 66)

However, given that there is, at least for the time being, a critical discourse labelled 'post-colonial' – for pedagogical convenience if nothing else – then it is necessary to look at some definitions of the term and understand how it affects reading practices. Here is a much disputed definition of the subject area by Ashcroft *et al.*:

Generally speaking . . . the term 'colonial' has been used for the period before independence and a term indicating a national writing, such as 'modern Canadian writing' or 'recent West Indian literature' has been employed to distinguish the period after independence.

We use the term 'post-colonial', however, to cover all the culture affected by the imperial process from the moment of colonization to the present day. This is because there is a continuity of preoccupations throughout the historical process initiated by European imperial aggression . . . So the literatures of African countries, Australia, Bangladesh, Canada, Caribbean countries, India, Malaysia, Malta, New Zealand, Pakistan, Singapore, South Pacific Island countries, and Sri Lanka are all post-colonial literatures. The literature of the USA should also be placed in this category. . . What each of these literatures have in common beyond their special and distinctive regional characteristics is that they emerged in their present form out of the experience of colonization and asserted themselves by foregrounding the tension with the imperial power, and by emphasizing their differences from the assumptions of the imperial centre. It is this which makes them distinctively post-colonial.

(Ashcroft *et al.* 1989: 2)

This definition of the term 'post-colonial' is about as broad as it is possible to get, and it is unusual in that it defines the post-colonial moment as beginning with colonisation: other general definitions begin with national independence from the colonisers.

Recently, commentators on the scene, partly in vigorous response to *The Empire Writes Back* (Ashcroft *et al.* 1989), have begun to identify a shift in patterns that characterise post-colonial literatures. South African novelist and literary critic Elleke Boehmer (1995) identifies the migrant writer as producing the definitive form of post-colonial writing, as it is studied in Western universities. She explains that 'extra-territorial' or 'transnational' writers practise a number of literary strategies that make them appealing to current Literature departments. She argues that certain techniques characteristic of much post-modern writing are used extensively in migrant writings, making them particularly amenable to existing analytical techniques. This 'co-mingling' effect – the inclusion of different writing styles, the cut-and-paste techniques of including documentary evidence, historical events combined with fictional characters – is appealing to Western audiences, hence the success of the 'post-colonial' label. The career of the term, along with the careers of other migrant writers, has been promoted, argues Boehmer, by the headline-hitting controversy surrounding the publication of *The Satanic Verses* (1988), and Salman Rushdie's subsequent retreat into hiding in fear of his life. Similarly, the careers of migrant writers have been helped by the fact that most are now living in First-World countries, in proximity to post-colonial critics who can interview them, as well as being available for major publishing tours to support sales of their latest books. The attraction of this kind of post-colonial writing is, claims Boehmer, that 'migrant writers embrace all Western techniques – or techniques familiar to the West – whilst being exotic and "different"'.

It is important to emphasise the connection between features of postmodern literature and post-colonial writing. This similarity is because of the way in which these kinds of literatures resist a dominant discourse. As we have seen, the writing might resist a literary canon, rewrite a particular version of history, or challenge a forceful commonplace view of politics. By emphasising the different ways in which a story might be told, depending on who is speaking, and when, and from where, both postmodern and post-colonial writing destabilise notions of truth and certain knowledge. However, the differences are at least as big as the similarities, and the resistance of the centre by the margins, which operates within postmodern writing, has a particular slant when it is recoded under post-colonialism as the resistance of the empire by the colonised, or the resistance of the First World by the Third World.

The nature of the response to the process of colonisation is not uniform, just as the process of colonisation itself was unique to each area that was taken over. For instance, whilst the writers of white Canadians or white Australians might be ambivalent about the way in which their country was settled, their ancestors were the people doing the colonising, and clearly their relationship with the centre of the empire is going to be different from that of the Native North American Indians or Australian aboriginals, whose land was taken and whose entire culture has been brought to the edge of extinction. This is the argument for maintaining certain distinctions between groups who co-exist under the post-colonial banner, without discarding the label altogether. Analysts argue that the heading is useful so long as it isn't used to over-simplify a diverse range of cultural traditions and their long and variant histories.

5 Freedom, censorship, writing and race

A debate familiar to feminists, and related to questions of essentialism, is also significant in discussions of literature by black
writers. The related debate in feminism is over whether one can
read, or write, as a woman; the corresponding debate in terms of
ethnicity is over whether white writers can accurately represent
black characters in their work. After a history of black characters
receiving no representation at all in white-authored texts, or only
the crudest stereotyped sketch, the white representation of non-
white characters is now an additional problem which is not simply
one of omission or of racist representation. A number of successful fictions by white writers, which feature prominently characters
of a different cultural background to that of the writer, have come
up for scrutiny by critics.

One clear focus for this debate is the representation of
Native North American Indians in white-authored texts. There
are numerous examples: Bill Kinsella has written a whole series of
novels set on an imaginary Indian reservation, and his central
characters are largely represented as comic or drunks; Anne
Cameron represents her Indian protagonists as living traditional
lives of hunters, with privileged knowledge of the natural world
and a distinctive spiritual aspect to their lives. Perhaps a more
familiar Indian character is the narrator of Ken Kesey's *One Flew
over the Cuckoo's Nest* (1962). Chief Bromden is a tall Indian who
all the inmates and staff of the mental asylum suppose to be deaf
and mute, but non-violent. His narrative informs the reader that
this is all a performance, for the Chief's own self-preservation. In
the following extract, he, is looking out of the window of the
institution at night:

> The moon glistened around [the dog] on the wet grass, and
> when he ran he left tracks like dabs of dark paint spattered
> across the blue shine of the lawn. Galloping from one
> particularly interesting hole to the next, he became so took
> with what was coming off – the moon up there, the night,
> the breeze full of smells so wild makes a young dog drunk –

that he had to lie down on his back and roll. He twisted and
thrashed around like a fish, back bowed and belly up, and
when he got to his feet and shook himself a spray came off
him in the moon like silver scales.

He sniffed all the holes over again one quick one, to get
the smells down good, then suddenly froze still with one paw
lifted and his head tilted, listening. I listened too, but I
couldn't hear anything except the popping of the window
shade. I listened for a long time. Then, from a long way off, I
heard a high, laughing gabble, faint and coming closer.
Canada honkers going south for the winter. I remembered
all the hunting and belly-crawling I'd ever done trying to kill
a honker, and that I'd never got one.

(Kesey [1962] 1973: 128–9)

i) How is Bromden characterised in the above extract?

ii) Is there anything that points to the ethnicity of the narrator?

iii) Is there anything that points to the ethnicity of the writer?

Bromden's concern with the outside world, his attention to the
detail of the activity of the dog and the textures of the night are
used to suggest his affinity with the natural world. The portrait of
Bromden is a romanticised version of a 'natural' man. There isn't
perhaps anything explicit that suggests the ethnicity of either the
narrator or the writer.

Native North American writer Lee Maracle explains why she
objects to the telling of stories about Indians by non-native people:

The truth is that you Europeans came here when we had the
land and you had the Bible. You offered us the Bible and took
our land, but I could never steal the soul of you. Occasion-
ally, your sons and daughters reject the notion that Europe
possesses a monopoly on truth and that other races are to be
confined to being baked in pies or contained in reservation
misery. They are an inspiration to me, but they are not
entirely satisfying. Your perception of my Raven, even

when approached honestly by your own imagination, is still European. The truth is that a statement I made at the Third International Feminist Book Fair, objecting to the appropriation of our stories, has nothing to do with censorship. . . . Since then, the debate has focused on censorship and freedom of imagination . . . The truth is that creeping around libraries full of nonsensical anthropocentric drivel, imbuing these findings with falsehood in the name of imagination, then peddling the nonsense as 'Indian Mythology' is literary dishonesty.

(Maracle 1990: 185)

Margaret Atwood, from a different cultural background (and a different economic one, given her international success) opposes any blanket restrictions on the rights of writers to speak from the perspective of characters who are not of their own social and cultural background, insisting that writers must be free to write about what they choose. However, she points out that it can only be done with caution:

I'll say that if you do choose to write from the point of view of an 'other' group, you'd better pay very close attention, because you'll be subject to extra scrutinies and resentments. I'll add that in my opinion the best writing about such a group is most likely to come from within that group – not because those outside it are more likely to vilify it, but because they are likely, these days and out of well-meaning liberalism, to simplify and sentimentalise it, or to get the textures and vocabulary and symbolism wrong.

(Atwood 1990: 23)

Marlene Nourbese Philip documents with rigour and clarity the arguments made by both sides in 'The Disappearing Debate' (in Philip 1992). She concludes that the claim to artistic freedom, in a racist society, is ultimately meaningless, since white writers are able to exercise it and black writers are not. For writers in racist communities, the privilege of being white, 'writing *about* rather than out of another culture virtually guarantees that their work will, in a racist society, be received more readily than the work of writers coming from the very culture' (Philip 1992: 284).

The issue develops then, from a question of writing to one of reception. Gayatri Chakravorty Spivak illuminates the complexities of the problem when she says:

> For me, the question 'Who should speak?' is less crucial than 'Who will listen?' 'I will speak for myself as a Third World person' is an important position for political mobilization today. But the real demand is that, when I speak from that position, I should be listened to seriously; not with that kind of benevolent imperialism, really, which simply says that because I happen to be an Indian or whatever . . . A hundred years ago it was impossible for me to speak, for the precise reason that makes it only too possible for me to speak in certain circles now. I see in that a kind of reversal, which is again a little suspicious. On the other hand, it is very important to hold on to it as a slogan in our time. The question of 'speaking as' involves distancing from oneself. The moment I have to think of the ways in which I will speak as an Indian, or as a feminist, the ways in which I will speak as a woman, what I am doing is trying to generalise myself, make myself a representative, trying to distance myself from some kind of inchoate speaking *as such*. There are many subject positions which one must inhabit; one is not just one thing. That is when a political consciousness comes in. So that in fact, for the person who does the 'speaking as' something, it is a problem of distancing oneself, whatever that self might be. But when the card-carrying listeners, the hegemonic people, the dominant people, talk about listening to someone 'speaking as' something or the other, I think *there* one encounters a problem. When *they* want to hear an Indian speaking as an Indian, a Third World woman speaking as a Third World woman, they cover over the fact of the ignorance that they are allowed to possess, into a kind of homogenization.
>
> (Spivak 1990: 59–60)

Spivak is here arguing about tokenism, and the problem of tokenism is that it is much easier to have a few token figures than to produce real change. It is much easier to have one or two texts by black writers on a Literature course than to redevelop that course and understand it afresh in the light of critiques of empire. In fact, simply adding one token text to the curriculum leads to a limited reading of it, since that work may be taken to stand in for a much wider range.

African-American feminist theorist bell hooks also discusses the difficulty of censorship and appropriation of voice, and she argues that speaking as an act of resistance is often difficult to achieve because:

> [i]n a white-supremacist, capitalist, patriarchal state where the mechanisms of co-optation are so advanced, much that is potentially radical is undermined, turned into commodity, fashionable speech as in 'black women writers are in right now.'
>
> (hooks 1989: 14)

hooks makes a persuasive argument for the way in which such co-optation can be resisted:

> Appropriation of the marginal voice threatens the very core of self-determination and free self-expression for exploited and oppressed peoples. If the identified audience, those spoken to, is determined solely by ruling groups who control production and distribution, then it is easily overdetermined by the needs of that majority group who appears to be listening, to be tuned in. It becomes easy to speak about what that group wants to hear, to describe and define experience in a language compatible with existing images and ways of knowing, constructed within social frameworks that reinforce domination. Within any situation of colonization, domination, the oppressed, the exploited develop various styles of relating, talking one way to one another, talking another way to those who have power to oppress and dominate, talking in a way that allows one to be understood by

someone who does not know your way of speaking, your
language. The struggle to end domination, the individual
struggle to resist colonization, to move from object to
subject, is expressed in the effort to establish the liberatory
voice – that way of speaking that is no longer determined by
one's status as object – as oppressed being. That way of
speaking is characterized by opposition, by resistance. It
demands that paradigms shift – that we learn to talk – to
listen – to hear in a new way.

(hooks 1989: 14–15)

The responsibilities of a white literary critic are to learn to
listen in a new way, to shift paradigms and change critical
approaches. One suggestion of how to proceed is made by Arnold
Krupat who has developed a methodology which he calls 'ethno-
criticism'. This is a literary study based on the findings of
ethnohistoricists (anthropologists who investigate aboriginal
land claims). It is, therefore, rather flawed from the beginning,
in the sense that it is based on Western categories, a practice
which:

cannot help but falsify the lived experience and world view of
any non-western people, *translating* . . . Just as anthropology, in an absolute sense, cannot engage innocently with any
culture – because anthropology . . . turns *people* into *subjects* (of inquiry, at least), *objects* of its knowledge – so too,
can there, in this absolute sense, be no non-violent *criticism*
of the discourse of Others, not even an ethnocriticism. The
question is whether, short of this absolute horizon, it is
worth pursuing certain projects of inquiry in the interest
of a rather less violent knowledge.

(Krupat 1992: 6)

Krupat argues that the understanding of one culture by another
is always going to be imperfect, but he suggests that is not a
reason for not developing appropriate critiques of texts by
writers of another ethnic background, providing the limitations
are recognised.

6 Double colonisation: women and cultural identity

In the same way that feminist criticism began with an assessment of the degree to which women have been excluded from the mainstream of writers, and developed into a recovery project of the unrecognised or underread works by women, so many black feminists have also produced counter-canons, long lists of texts that should be acknowledged. Barbara Christian assesses the situation for African-American women writers:

> Until recently, for most Americans, including Afro-American women, this literature [by African-American women] was unknown, as invisible as working-class women, 'minority' men and women were in our institutions, history, in the American mind-set. When this literature is not neglected, it is denigrated by the use of labels that deny its centrality to American life. It is called 'political', 'social protest', or 'minority' literature, which in this ironic country has a pejorative sound, meaning it lacks craft and has not trans-cended the limitations of racial, sex, or class boundaries – that it supposedly does not do what 'good' literature does: express our universal humanity.
>
> Yet it is precisely because this literature reveals a basic truth of our society, of all societies, that it is central. In every society where there is the denigrated Other, whether that is designated by sex, race, class, or ethnic background, the Other struggles to declare the truth and therefore create the truth in forms that exist for her or him. The creation of that truth also changes the perception of all those who believe they are the norm.
>
> (Christian 1985: 160)

Christian maintains that the literature of the margins can have a transformative effect on the dominant. Hers is an optimistic vision of the effects of cultural exchange. But other writers have written less hopefully about the position of women of colour in white cultures.

Characterisation of black women in fiction by white writers

is seen as taking a particularly limited form. It is possible to look at cultural representations of any people of colour and find startling changes over very short periods of time. Television programmes are a particularly accessible example: reruns of certain episodes of popular series have become impossible to screen after just ten years, because the racism that was tolerated in the past has now become unacceptable. But if there are fixed representations of black people, representations of black *women* have been even more limited:

> For black women in American literature, from the beginning, have been depicted as either sexually loose and therefore tempters of men, or obedient and subservient mammies, loving and tender to the white children they raised and forever faithful to the owners they served.
>
> (McKay 1991: 250)

As an example of the kind of stereotyping McKay is talking about, here is a notorious scene from *Gone With The Wind* (1936) in which Mammy is getting Scarlett ready for a barbecue:

> 'Whut mah lamb gwine wear?'
>
> 'That,' answered Scarlett, pointing at the fluffy mass of green flowered muslin. Instantly Mammy was in arms.
>
> 'No, you ain'. It ain' fittin' fer mawnin'. You kain show yo' buzzum befo' three o'clock an' dat dress ain' got no neck an' no sleeves. An' you'll git freckled sho as you born, an' Ah ain' figgerin' on you gittin' freckled affer all de buttermilk Ah been puttin' on you all dis winter, bleachin' dem freckles you got at Savannah settin' on de beach. Ah sho gwine speak ter yo' Ma 'bout you.'
>
> 'If you say one word to her before I'm dressed I won't eat a bite,' said Scarlett coolly. 'Mother won't have time to send me back to change once I'm dressed.'
>
> Mammy sighed resignedly, beholding herself out-guessed. Between two evils, it was better to have Scarlett wear an afternoon dress at a morning barbecue than to have her gobble like a hog.
>
> (Mitchell 1974: 79)

i) How is the characterisation of Mammy achieved?
ii) How could her relationship to Scarlett be described?

There are, of course, fixed stereotypes of black men, as well as of women, but it is important to recognise the differences between them, and the way in which the realms of experience of black women can be quite distinct to those of men, that they are perceived differently and their experience of being marginalised is not just on the basis of colour or gender but on a connection between the two.

Jane Miller criticises writers such as Frantz Fanon and Edward Said for failing to include the perspectives of women and feminist analyses in their critiques of imperialism and colonialism. She argues:

> Such an omission simultaneously separates, subsumes and subordinates the category of women. It also takes women for granted – paternalistically, no doubt – as undifferentiated elements of a collective humanity: a view which would be easier to accept were that collective humanity not itself, within such theories, under perpetual scrutiny for its splits and conflicts especially. Yet pleas for the inclusion of women within such political theories are likely to be met by objections that they are sectional, sectarian and certainly distracting pleas. The very notion of a testable hypothesis, after all, or of a theory with real explanatory power and usefulness, depends on intellectual traditions which prioritise qualities of thought like coherence or generalisability. So that the invoking of women as absent from such theory and from its making – or as misrepresented by it – can appear to disturb the very foundation and character of serious and valuable academic work.
>
> (Miller 1990: 133)

Miller argues, then, that feminists have been criticised as detracting from anti-racist arguments, when they insist that women must

303

be taken into account as well as, and as distinct from, men in critiques of imperialism, colonisation and racism.

Literature by women of colour is a very successful medium for expressing the particular difficulties of gendered and cultural identity. Consider the following extract from *The Joy Luck Club* by Chinese-American novelist Amy Tan. Tan's novel follows the life stories of four Chinese women and their migration to America. The Chinese women's stories are juxtaposed with the stories of their Chinese-American daughters, whose perspective is often in conflict with that of their mothers. In the quotation below, the narrative voice is that of Lena St Clair, who has a Chinese mother and an American father:

My mother was from Wushi, near Shanghai. So she spoke Mandarin and a little bit of English. My father, who spoke only a few canned Chinese expressions, insisted my mother learn English. So with him, she spoke in moods and gestures, looks and silences, and sometimes a combination of English punctuated by hesitations and Chinese frustration: '*Shwo buchulai*' – words cannot come out. So my father would put words in her mouth.

'I think Mom is trying to say she's tired,' he would whisper when my mother became moody.

'I think she's saying we're the best darn family in the country!' he'd exclaim when she had cooked a wonderfully fragrant meal.

But with me, when we were alone, my mother would speak in Chinese, saying things my father could not possibly imagine. I could understand the words perfectly, but not the meanings. One thought led to another without connection.

'You must not walk in any direction but to school and back home,' warned my mother when she decided I was old enough to walk by myself.

'Why?' I asked.

'You can't understand these things,' she said.

'Why not?'

'Because I haven't put it in your mind yet.'

'Why not?'

'Aii-ya! Such questions! Because it is too terrible to consider. A man can grab you off the streets, sell you to someone else, make you have a baby. Then you'll kill the baby. And when they find this baby in the garbage can, then what can be done? You'll go to jail, die there.'

(Tan 1990: 106)

iii) What features mark the ethnicity of Ying-Ying St. Clair (the mother)?

iv) How is Ying-Ying's relationship with her husband represented?

v) Try to imagine that the writer of the text is a white American man, rather than a Chinese-American woman. Does it affect your interpretation?

Glossary

black: This term has been reclaimed from being a pejorative label, and can be used to create identification between any people of colour, although mostly it is claimed by people of African descent. Other people of colour sometimes do, and sometimes don't, identify themselves with this term.

colonisation: The process of displacing one population and resettling the land with another, sometimes by force, and maintained by a variety of coercive measures.

Commonwealth: Nations whose head of state remains the British monarch are members of the Commonwealth, although Britain itself is not usually what is being referred to when talking of Commonwealth nations.

diasporic. Meaning 'scattered' or 'dispersed', the term can refer to migrants, or to people with more than one culture or country of origin.

empire: An extensive territory ruled over by an emperor or sovereign state.

ethnicity: Distinct from racial (biological) identity, a person's ethnicity includes all features of his or her cultural origin, including religion, cooking traditions, philosophies, etc.

First Nations: Peoples whose land is now populated by settlers: North American Indians, Inuit, Australian aboriginals, New Zealand Maoris, South Pacific Islanders, etc.

imperial: Pertaining to those political, ideological or military practices used to establish or maintain an empire.

migrant: A person who has moved from his or her place of origin.

native: One born in a place. It can be used as a derogatory term to mean primitive or pagan, but it is also a term often preferred by First Nations (North American Indians, for example, often refer to themselves as Native).

neo-colonial: Newly colonial or currently colonial; used to refer to nations who may have gained their independence but are still subject to domination by European or US capitalism and culture.

other: Person of a different race or ethnicity; often used to mean 'non-white', or colonised subject (See also Other/other in Chapter 5).

post-colonial: Generally used to refer to a once-colonised nation that has gained independence, although Ashcroft *et al.* (1989) use the term to refer to any period from the moment of colonisation onwards.

race: Used to refer to characteristics governed by genetics such as skin colour, hair colour and texture, facial features. The biological foundation of the term has been contested as being arbitrary.

settler culture: Includes the white populations of Australia, Canada and New Zealand, where colonising cultures have established themselves as the dominant population. White South Africans are also generally included in this category, although they are not the majority population.

Select bibliography

1 Challenging the canon

Edward Said's acclaimed *Culture and Imperialism* (1994) is an erudite discussion of the way in which discourses of imperialism figure in the kind of literary texts that are regular features of English degree courses. His discussion is detailed, witty and controversial, and it provides significant fresh readings of some familiar fictions. Robyn Warhol and

Diane Price Herndl's collection, *Feminisms* (1991), contains a number of essays on the subject of race and the canon: note especially Paul Lauter's 'Class, Caste and Canon', Nellie McKay's 'Reflections of Black Women Writers: Revising the Literary Canon' and Barbara Christian's 'Trajectories of Self-Definition: Placing Contemporary Afro-American Women's Fiction' (Williams and Chrisman 1994).

2 Writing back

There is a section on 'post-colonialism as a reading strategy' – which is devoted to writing back – included in *The Empire Writes Back* (Ashcroft *et al.* 1989), which explores some case-studies. Diana Brydon has written about the complex literary heritage of the post-colonial subject in several essays: 'Re-Writing *The Tempest*' (1984a), 'The Thematic Ancestor' (1984b) and 'Commonwealth or Common Poverty?' (1989). There are also some relevant essays in Adam and Tiffin's (eds) *Past the Last Post* (1991).

3 Writing and cultural identity

A text which combines sophisticated post-colonial discourse with questions about the stability of 'race' as a category is Henry Louis Gates Jr's wide and varied collection of essays, *'Race', Writing and Difference* (1986b). Gates's introductory essay has become the standard text for this debate, but the other essays in his collection are also much referred to. Diana Fuss's *Essentially Speaking* (1990) is clearly written whilst retaining sophistication; she covers the general area of subjectivity, and she has a chapter on African-American critics, as well as one on identity politics. Jonathan Rutherford has edited a collection of essays, *Identity: Community, Culture, Difference* (1990) on various areas of cultural representation, not just literature, and, as with Fuss's text, the essays explore identity in a broad sense, inclusive of ethnicity but not solely about it.

4 Post-colonial literary theory

The Empire Writes Back (Ashcroft *et al.* 1989) has become the standard beginners' guide for post-colonial theory. In this fast-developing area, it is rapidly becoming out of date, but it remains a clearly organised reference text for those new to post-colonial literature, with lucid discussion and historical contextualisation, and it has a good bibliography of critical sources, divided up into national areas. The authors of *The Empire Writes Back* have also collected together a large collection of some of the most well-known essays and some less established work in a volume of over 500 pages entitled *The Post-Colonial Studies Reader* (1994). This looks like becoming the standard text for literary studies in this area for some time to come. Another good introductory text is *Colonial Discourse and Post-Colonial Theory* (Williams and Chrisman 1994), a collection of essays by a variety of critics, which present many of the key debates currently raging in the field. Another general introduction, which gives a good idea of the different kinds of literatures as well as the theoretical issues that come under the post-colonial umbrella, is Elleke Boehmer's *Colonial and Post-Colonial Literature* (1995). There are several excellent journals that cover the field, and provide a good source of up-to-date information. These include: *World Literatures Written in English*, *The Journal of Commonwealth Literature*, *Kunapipi* and *Ariel*.

5 Freedom, censorship, writing and race

Marlene Nourbese Philip's collection, *Frontiers: Essays and Writings on Racism and Culture* (1992) draws on a wide range of cultural representations and situations, and has extremely clear, direct discussions of racism and how to argue against it. *Language in Her Eye* (L. Scheier *et al.* 1990) contains essays by women writing in Canada; many of the essays address issues of multiculturalism and publishing conditions for black writers. Salman Rushdie writes movingly of his experience of censorship in his essays 'In Good Faith', 'Is Nothing Sacred' and 'One Thousand Days in a Balloon', all collected together under the title *Imaginary Homelands* (1991). A collection of essays also on the effect of *The Satanic Verses* has been edited by Lisa Appignanesi and Sara Maitland, titled *The Rushdie File* (1989).

6 Double colonisation: women and cultural identity

There are now many, many collections of essays by black women writers, all with specific focus points. Barbara Christian's *Black Feminist Criticism* (1985) and Sandi Russell's *Render Me My Song* (1990) are two texts which offer analyses of African and African-American women's writing; Christian's work also contains some more generalised essays on black women's writing. For committed essays on more general issues for black women, the work of bell hooks is broad-based, radical and entertaining. She has a number of publications which include: *Ain't I a Woman? Black Women and Feminism* (1982), *Feminist Theory: From Margin to Center* (1984) and *Talking Back: Thinking Feminist – Thinking Black* (1989).

Gayatri Chakravorty Spivaks *In Other Worlds* (1987) is a challenging collection of essays which combines the approaches of deconstruction, Marxism and feminism together with a sharp eye for the continuing effects of imperialism in literary studies. Spivak is widely acknowledged as one of the most brilliant critics to develop the theories of Jacques Derrida, and her work is often inaccessible for the novice. However, a number of interviews with her have been collected under the title *The Post-Colonial Critic* (1991), and this provides a gentler introduction to her thinking.

Vron Ware's *Beyond the Pale: White Women, Racism and History* (1992) is one of the few texts to consider the specific collaboration of white women in the projects of empire. She also considers the need to define white identity – in the same way as women of colour have defined a black identity – rather than accepting white as 'neutral'.

Bibliography

Abrams, M. (1952) *The Mirror and the Lamp*, Oxford: Oxford University Press.

Adam, I. and Tiffin, H. (eds) (1991) *Past the Last Post*, Hemel Hempstead: Harvester Wheatsheaf.

Althusser, L. (1976) *Essays on Ideology*, London: Verso.

Andrews, B.C. (1994) 'Bomb Then, Bomb Now' in P. Hoover (ed.) *Postmodern American Poetry: A Norton Anthology*, New York: Norton.

Appignanesi, L. and Maitland, S. (eds) (1989) *The Rushdie File*, London: Fourth Estate.

Appignanesi, R. and Zarate, O. (1992) *Freud for Beginners*, Cambridge: Icon Books.

Ashcroft, B., Griffiths, G. and Tiffin, H. (1989) *The Empire Writes Back: Theory and Practice in Post-Colonial Literatures*, London and New York: Routledge.

Ashcroft, B., Griffiths, G. and Tiffin, H. (1994) *The Post-Colonial Studies Reader*, London and New York: Routledge.

Atwood, M. (1979) *Surfacing*, London: Virago.

Atwood, M. (1989) *Cat's Eye*, London: Bloomsbury.

Atwood, M. (1990) 'If You Can't Say Something Nice,

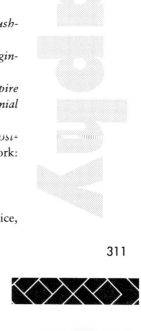

Don't Say Anything at All' in L. Scheier, S. Sheard and E. Wachtel (eds), *Language in Her Eye: Writing and Gender*, Toronto: Coach House Press.

Austen, J. (1966) *Mansfield Park*, London: Penguin.

Austin, J.L. (1962) *How to do Things with Words*, Oxford: Oxford University Press.

Babb, H. (ed.) (1972) *Essays in Stylistic Analysis*, New York: Harcourt Brace Jovanovich.

Bal, M. (1985) *Narratology: Introduction to the Theory of Narrative*, Toronto and London: University of Toronto Press.

Barrell, J. (1988) *Poetry, Language and Politics*, Manchester: Manchester University Press.

Barrie, J.M. (1987) *Peter Pan*, New York: Signet Classics.

Barthes, R. (1972a) *Critical Essays*, trans. R. Howard, Illinois: Northwestern University Press.

Barthes, R. (1972b) *Mythologies*, London: Pan Books.

Barthes, R. (1974) *S/Z*, trans. Richard Miller, New York: Hill and Wang.

Barthes, R. (1975) *The Pleasure of the Text*, trans. Richard Miller, Jonathan Cape: London.

Barthes, R. (1977) *Image/Music/Text*, trans. S. Heath, London: Fontana.

Belsey, C. (1980) *Critical Practice*, London: Methuen.

Belsey, C. and Moore, J. (eds) (1989) *The Feminist Reader: Essays in Gender and the Politics of Literary Criticism*, Basingstoke: Macmillan.

Bernheimer, C. and Kahane, C. (eds) (1985) *In Dora's Case*, London: Virago.

Berry, M. (1977) *An Introduction to Systemic Linguistics*, 2 vols, London: Batsford.

Best, G. (1979) *Mid-Victorian Britain 1851–1875*, London: Weidenfeld and Nicolson.

Birch, D. (1989) *Language, Literature and Critical Practice*, London: Routledge.

Blake, N. (1991) *An Introduction to the Language of Literature*, London: Macmillan.

Blake, W. (1986) *Poetical Works*, Oxford: Oxford University Press.

Blakemore, D. (1992) *Understanding Utterances*, Oxford: Blackwell.

Blau DuPlessis, R. (1993) 'Reader, I Married Me' in G. Greene and C. Kahn (eds), *Changing Subjects: The Making of Feminist Literary Criticism*, London and New York: Routledge.

Blonsky, M. (ed.) (1985) *On Signs*, Oxford: Basil Blackwell.

Bloomfield, L. (1935) *Language*, London: George Allen and Unwin.

Bloor, T. (1986) 'University Students' Knowledge about Language', Committee for Linguistics in Education, Working Papers No. 8. *British Association of Applied Linguistics*.

Bly, R. (1991) *Iron John*, Dorset: Element Books.

Boehmer, E. (1995) *Colonial and Post-Colonial Literature*, Oxford: Oxford University Press.

Bond, E. (1965) *Saved*, London: Methuen.

Boone, J. and Cadden, M. (eds) (1990) *Engendering Men: The Question of Male Feminist Criticism*, New York and London: Routledge.

Bordo, S. (1992) 'Postmodern Subjects, Postmodern Bodies' (review essay), *Feminist Studies*, 18, 1, 159–75.

Bowie, M. (1991) *Lacan*, Fontana Modern Masters Series, London: Fontana.

Brennan, T. (ed.) (1989) *Between Feminism and Psychoanalysis*, London: Routledge.

Brontë, C. (1966) *Jane Eyre*, London: Penguin.

Brooks, C. (1968) *The Well-Wrought Urn*, New York: Harcourt and Brace.

Brown, G. and Yule, G. (1983) *Discourse Analysis*, Cambridge: Cambridge University Press.

Brown, P. (1985) ' "This Thing of Darkness I Acknowledge Mine": *The Tempest* and the Discourse of Colonialism' in J. Dollimore and A. Sinfield (eds), *Political Shakespeare: New Essays in Cultural Materialism*, Manchester: Manchester University Press.

Brydon, D. (1984a) 'Re-Writing *The Tempest*', *World Literatures Written in English*, 23, 1, 75–88.

Brydon, D. (1984b) ' "The Thematic Ancestor": Joseph Conrad, Patrick White and Margaret Atwood', *World Literatures Written in English*, 24, 2, 386–97.

Brydon, D. (1989) 'Commonwealth or Common Poverty? The New Literatures in English and the New Discourse of Marginality' in S. Slemon and H. Tiffin (eds), *After Europe*, Sydney: Dangaroo Press.

Butler, J. (1992) 'Contingent Foundations: Feminism and the Question of "Postmodernism" ', in J. Butler and J.W. Scott (eds) *Feminists Theorize the Political*, London: Routledge.

Butler, J. and Scott, J.W. (eds) (1992) *Feminists Theorize the Political*, London: Routledge.

Cameron, D. (1985) *Feminism and Linguistic Theory*, Basingstoke: Macmillan.

Cameron, D. (ed.) (1990) *The Feminist Critique of Language: A Reader*, London: Routledge.

Cameron, D. (1992) 'New Arrivals: The Feminist Challenge in Language Study' in G. Wolf (ed.), *New Departures in Linguistics*, New York: Garland Press, 215–35.

Carr, E.H. (1961) *What is History?*, London: Pelican.

Carter, P. and Simpson, P. (1989) *Language, Discourse and Literature: An Introductory Reader in Discourse Stylistics*, London: Unwin Hyman.

Carter, R. (ed.) (1983) *Language and Literature: An Introduction to Stylistics*, London: Unwin Hyman.

Caudwell, C. (1957) *Illusion and Reality*, London: Lawrence and Wishart.

Chapman, R. (1988) 'The Great Pretender: Variations on the New Man Theme' in R. Chapman and J. Rutherford (eds) *Male Order: Unwrapping Masculinity*, London: Lawrence and Wishart.

Chapman, R. and Rutherford, J. (eds) (1988) *Male Order: Unwrapping Masculinity*, London: Lawrence and Wishart.

Chatman, S. (1978) *Story and Discourse: Narrative Structure in Fiction and Film*, Ithaca: Cornell University Press.

Chatman, S. and Levin, S. (1967) *Essays on the Language of Literature*, Boston: Houghton Mifflin.

Chomsky, N. (1957) *Syntactic Structures*, The Hague: Mouton.

Chopin, K. (1979) *The Awakening*, London: The Women's Press.

Christian, B. (1985) *Black Feminist Criticism: Perspectives on Black Women Writers*, New York: Pergamon Press.

Christian, B. (1994) 'Trajectories of Self-Definition: Placing Contemporary Afro-American Women's Fiction' in P. Williams and L. Chrisman (eds), *Colonial Discourse and Post-Colonial Theory*, Hemel Hempstead: Harvester Wheatsheaf.

Cixous, H. (1981) 'The Laugh of the Medusa' in E. Marks and I. de Courtivron (eds), *New French Feminisms*, Sussex: Harvester Press.

Cixous, H. and Clément, C. (1986) *La Jeune Née (The Newly Born Woman)*, Manchester: Manchester University Press.

Coates, J. (1986) *Women, Men and Language*, London: Longman.

Cohen, D. (1990) *Being a Man*, London: Routledge.

Cook, G. (1992) *The Discourse of Advertising*, London: Routledge.

Coulthard, M. (ed.) (1994) *Advances in Written Text Analysis*, London: Routledge.

Coward, R. (1984) *Female Desire*, London: Grafton Books.

Crystal, D. and Davy, D. (1969) *Investigating English Style*, London: Longman.

Culler, J. (1974) 'Introduction to F. de Saussure', *Course in General Linguistics*, London: Fontana.

Culler, J. (1975) *Structuralist Poetics*, London: Routledge and Kegan Paul.

Culler, J. (1976) *Saussure*, London: Fontana.

Culler, J. (1980) *Barthes*, London: Fontana.

Culler, J. (1981) *The Pursuit of Signs: Semiotics, Literature, Deconstruction*, London: Routledge and Kegan Paul.

Culler, J. (1983) *On Deconstruction*, London: Routledge and Kegan Paul.

Davis, R. Con (ed.) (1983) *Lacan and Narration: The Psychoanalytic Difference in Narrative Theory*, Baltimore: Johns Hopkins University Press.

Davis, S. (ed.) (1991) *Pragmatics: A Reader*, Oxford: Oxford University Press.

De Man, P. (1979) *Allegories of Reading*, New Haven: Yale University Press.

De Man, P. (1983) *Blindness and Insight*, London: Methuen.

Di Michele, M. (1990) 'Conversations with the Living and the Dead' in L. Scheier, S. Sheard and E. Wachtel (eds), *Language in Her Eye: Writing and Gender*, Toronto: Coach House Press.

Derrida, J. (1978) *Writing and Difference*, London: Routledge and Kegan Paul.

Derrida, J. (1982) *Margins of Philosphy*, Hertfordshire: Harvester.

Dollimore, J. and Sinfield. A. (eds) (1985) *Political Shakespeare: New Essays in Cultural Materialism.* Manchester: Manchester University Press.

During, S. (1992) *Foucault and Literature: Towards a Genealogy of Writing*, London: Routledge.

Eagleton, T. (1976a) *Criticism and Ideology*, London: Verso.

Eagleton, T. (1976b) *Marxism and Literary Criticism*, Methuen: London.

Eagleton, T. (1983) *Literary Theory: An Introduction*, Oxford: Blackwell.

Eagleton, T. (1990) *The Ideology of the Aesthetic*, Oxford: Blackwell.

Eagleton, T. (1991) *Ideology: An Introduction*, London: Verso.

Easthope, A. (1984) *Poetry as Discourse*, London: Methuen.

Eco, U. (1979) *The Role of the Reader: Explorations in the Semiotics of Texts*, Hutchinson: London.

Eco, U. (1985) *The Name of the Rose*, London: Picador.

Eichenbuam, B. (1965) 'The Theory of the "Formal Method"' in L. Lemon and M. Reis (eds), *Russian Formalist Criticism: Four Essays*, Lincoln and London: University of Nebraska Press, 99–140.

Eksteins, M. (1990) *Rites of Spring: The Great War and the Birth of the Modern Age*, London: Black Swan.

Eliot, G. (1965) *Middlemarch,* London: Penguin.

Eliot, T.S. (1975) *Selected Prose of T.S. Eliot*, ed. Frank Kermode, London: Faber and Faber.

Emmott, C. (1994) 'Frames of Reference: Contextual Monitoring and the Interpretation of Narrative Discourse' in M. Coulthard (ed.), *Advances in Written Text Analysis*, London: Routledge, 157–66.

Erlich, V. (1955) Russian Formalism: *History-Doctrine*, The Hague: Mouton.

Fabb, N. and Durant, A. (1990) *Literary Studies in Action*, London: Routledge.

Fabb, N., Attridge, D., Durrant, A. and McCabe, C. (eds) (1987) *The Linguistics of Writing: Arguments Between Language and Literature*, Manchester: Manchester University Press.

Faderman, L. (1981) *Surpassing the Love of Men: Romantic Friendship and Love Between Women from the Renaissance to the Present*, New York: William Morrow.

Faderman, L. (1992) *Odd Girls and Twilight Lovers: A History of Lesbian Life in Twentieth-Century America*, London: Penguin Books.

Faludi, S. (1991) *Backlash: The Undeclared War Against Women*, London: Chatto and Windus.

Fanon, F. (1986) *Black Skin, White Masks*, trans. Charles Lam Markmann, London: Pluto Press.

Felman, S. (ed.) (1982) *Literature and Psychoanalysis. The Question of Reading: Otherwise*, Baltimore: Johns Hopkins University Press.

Fillmore, C. (1982) 'Towards a Descriptive Framework for Spatial Deixis' in R.J. Jarvella and W. Klein, *Speech, Place and Action*, London: John Wiley, 31–59.

Fish, S. (1975) *Is There a Text in this Class: The Authority of Interpretive Communities*, Cambridge, Mass.: Harvard University Press.

Fish, S. (1980) 'Affective Stylistics' in J. Tomkins (ed.), *Reader Response Criticism*, Baltimore: John Hopkins University Press.

Flaubert, G. (1982) *Madame Bovary,* London: Penguin.

Fleming, I. (1978) *Thunderball*, London: Pan.

Forgas, D. (1986) 'Marxist Literary Theories' in A. Jefferson and D. Robey (eds) *Modern Literary Theory: A Comparative Introduction*, London: Batsford, 166–203.

Forster, E. (1971) *Aspects of the Novel*, London: Penguin.

Foucault, M. (1979) *Discipline and Punish: The Birth of the Prison*, trans. A. Sheridan, London: Penguin.

Foucault, M. (1986) *The Foucault Reader*, ed. P. Rainbow, Harmondsworth: Penguin.

Foucault, M. (1987) *Death and the Labyrinth*, London: Athlone Press.

Fowler, R. (ed.) (1966) *Essays on Style and Language*, London: Routledge and Kegan Paul.

Fowler, R. (ed.) (1968) *Essays in the Language of Literature*, Oxford: Oxford University Press.

Fowler, R. (1971) *The Languages of Literature: Some Linguistic Contributions to Criticism*, London: Routledge and Kegan Paul.

Fowler, R. (1986) *Linguistic Criticism*, Oxford: Oxford University Press.

Fowles, J. (1963) *The Collector*, London: Jonathan Cape.

Fowles, J. (1977) *The Magus*, revised version, London: Jonathan Cape.

Freud, S. (1957) *Collected Papers vol. V*, ed. J. Strachey, London: The Hogarth Press.

Freud, S. (1969) *Collected Papers vol. II*, trans. Joan Rivière, London: The Hogarth Press.

Freud, S. (1973a) 'The Dream-Work' in S. Freud, *Introductory Lectures on Psychoanalysis*, trans. J. Strachey, Pelican Freud Library, London: Penguin Books.

Freud, S. (1973b) 'Femininity' in S. Freud, *New Introductory Lectures*, trans. J. Strachey, Pelican Freud Library, London: Penguin Books.

Freund, E. (1986) *The Return of the Reader: Reader Response Criticism*, London: Methuen.

Frow, J. (1986) *Marxism and Literary History*, Oxford: Blackwell.

Frye, N. (1957) *Anatomy of Criticism*, Princeton: Princeton University Press.

Fuss, D. (1990) *Essentially Speaking: Feminism, Nature and Difference*, London: Routledge.

Gallop, J. (1992) *Feminism and Psychoanalysis: The Daughter's Seduction*, Basingstoke: Macmillan.

Galloway, D. (1971) *The Absurd Hero in American Fiction*, Texas: University of Texas Press.

Garber, M. (1993) *Vested Interests: Cross-Dressing and Cultural Anxiety*, London: Penguin Books.

Gaskell, M. (1981) *North and South*, London: Penguin.

Gates, H.L., Jr (1986a) 'Writing "Race" and the Difference it Makes' in H.L. Gates, Jr (ed.), *'Race', Writing, and Difference*, Chicago: University of Chicago Press.

Gates, H.L., Jr (ed.) (1986b) *'Race', Writing, and Difference*, Chicago: University of Chicago Press.

Gearhart, S. (1985) *The Wanderground*, London: The Women's Press.

Geertz, C. (1973) *The Interpretation of Cultures*, New York: Basic Books.

Genette, G. (1982) *Figures of Literary Discourse*, trans. Alan Sheridan, New York: Columbia University Press.

Gilbert, S. and Gubar, S. (1979) *The Madwoman in the Attic*, New Haven: Yale University Press.

Glaser, M. (1985) 'I Listen to the Market' in M. Blonsky (ed.), *On Signs*, Oxford: Basil Blackwell.

Goldmann, P. (1975) *Towards a Sociology of the Novel*, London: Methuen.

Greenblatt, S. (1980) *Renaissance Self-Fashioning*, Chicago: Chicago University Press.

Greenblatt, S. (1988) *Shakespearean Negotiations: The Circulation of Social Energy in Renaissance England*, Oxford: Oxford University Press.

Greenblatt, S. (1989) 'Towards a Poetics of Culture' in H.A. Veeser (ed.), *The New Historicism*, London: Routledge.

Greene, G. and Kahn, C. (eds) (1993) *Changing Subjects: The Making of Feminist Literary Criticism*, London and New York: Routledge.

Greer, G. (1993) *The Female Eunuch*, London: Paladin.

Greimas, A.J. (1983) *Structural Semantics: An Attempt at Method*, Lincoln: Nebraska University Press.

Grimm, J. and Grimm, W. (1973) *The Complete Grimm's Fairy Tales*, London: Routledge and Kegan Paul.

Halliday, M.A.K. (1973) *Explorations in the Functions of Language*, London: Edward Arnold.

Halliday, M.A.K. (1987) *An Introduction to Functional Grammar*, London: Edward Arnold.

Halliday, M.A.K. and Hasan, R. (1976) *Cohesion in English*, London: Longman.

Harland, R. (1993) *Beyond Superstructuralism: The Syntagmatic Side of Language*, London: Routledge.

Harris, R. (1980) *The Language Myth*, London: Duckworth.

Harris, R. (1987) *Reading Saussure*, London: Duckworth.

Hawkes, T. (1977) *Structuralism and Semiotics*, London: Methuen.

Hawthorn, J. (ed.) (1985) *Narrative: From Malory to Motion Pictures*, London: Edward Arnold.

Healy, T. (1992) *New Latitudes: Theory and English Renaissance Literature*, London: Edward Arnold.

Hemingway, E. (1981) *The Essential Hemingway*, London: Jonathan Cape.

Hernadi, P. (1972) *Beyond Genre*, Ithaca: Cornell University Press.

Hill, C. (1961) *The Century of Revolution, 1603–1714* , London: Nelson.

Hirsch, E.D. Jr. (1967) *Validity in Interpretation*, Chicago: University of Chicago Press.

Hirsch, E.D. Jr. (1976) *The Aims of Interpretation*, Chicago: University of Chicago Press.

Hodge, R. and Kress, G. (1979) *Language as Ideology*, London: Routledge.

Holdcroft, D. (1991) *Saussure: Signs, Systems, Arbitrariness*, Cambridge: Cambridge University Press.

Holland, N. (1975) *5 Readers Reading*, New Haven: Yale University Press.

Holland, N. (1980) 'Unity Identity Text Self' in J. Tomkins (ed.), *Reader Response Criticism*, Baltimore: Johns Hopkins University Press.

Holub, R. (1984) *Reception Theory: A Critical Introduction*, London: Methuen.

hooks, b. (1982) *Ain't I a Woman? Black Women and Feminism*, London: Pluto Books.

hooks, b. (1984) *Feminist Theory: From Margin to Center*, Boston: South End Press.

hooks, b. (1989) *Talking Back: Thinking Feminist – Thinking Black*, London: Sheba Feminist Publishers.

Howard, P. (1984) *The State of the Language*, London: Hamish Hamilton.

Humm, M. (ed.) (1992) *Feminisms*, Hemel Hempstead: Harvester Wheatsheaf.

Hutcheon, L. (1988) *A Poetics of Postmodernism: History, Theory, Fiction*, London and New York: Routledge.

Ingarden, R. (1973) *The Literary Work of Art*, Evanston: Northwestern University Press.

Ingarden, R. (1978) *The Cognition of the Literary Work of Art*, Evanston: Northwestern University Press.

Irigaray, L. (1985) *This Sex Which is Not One*, trans. Catherine Porter, Ithaca: Cornell University Press.

Iser, W. (1974) *The Implied Reader: Patterns of Communication in Prose Fiction*, Baltimore: Johns Hopkins University Press.

Iser, W. (1978) *The Act of Reading: A Theory of Aesthetic Response*, Baltimore: Johns Hopkins University Press.

Iser, W. (1980) 'Interaction Between Text and Reader' in S.R. Suleiman and I. Crosman (eds), *The Reader in the Text: Essays on Audience and Interpretation*, Princeton: Princeton University Press, 106–19.

Jackson, L. (1991) *The Poverty of Structuralism: Literature and Structuralist Theory*, London: Longman.

Jakobson, R. (1967) 'Linguistics and Poetics' in S. Chatman, and S. Levin, (eds), *Essays on the Language of Literature*, Boston: Houghton Mifflin.

Jameson, F. (1972) *The Prison-House of Language: A Critical Account of Structuralism and Russian Formalism*, Princeton: Princeton University Press.

Jardine, A. and Smith, P. (1987) *Men in Feminism*, London: Methuen.

Jarvella, R.J. and Klein, W. (1982) *Speech, Place and Action*, London: John Wiley.

Jauss, H.R. (1982a) *Aesthetic Experience and Literary Hermeneutics*, Minneapolis: University of Minnesota Press.

Jauss, H.R. (1982b) *Toward an Aesthetic of Reception*, trans. Timothy Bahti, Minneapolis: University of Minnesota Press.

Jefferson, A. and Robey, D. (eds) (1986) *Modern Literary Theory: A Comparative Introduction*, London: Batsford.

Jeffries, L. (1994) 'Language in Common: Apposition in Contemporary Poetry by Women' in K.. Wales (ed.) *Feminists Linguistics in Literary Criticism*, Cambridge: D.S. Brewer.

Jespersen, O. (1922) *Language: Its Nature, Development and Origin*, London: Allen and Unwin.

Joyce, J. (1964) *Finnegan's Wake*, London: Faber and Faber.

Kaplan, C. (1986) *Sea Changes: Culture and Feminism*, London: Verso.

Kermode, F. (1968) *Continuities*, London: Routledge and Kegan Paul.

Kesey, K. (1973) *One Flew over the Cuckoo's Nest*, London: Pan Books.

Kinney, A.F. and Collins, D.S. (eds) (1987) *Renaissance Historicism*, Amherst: University of Massachusetts Press.

Kolodny, A. (1986) 'Dancing Through the Minefield' in E. Showalter (ed.), *The New Feminist Criticism: Essays on Women, Literature and Theory*, London: Virago.

Kristeva, J. (1981) 'La Femme, ce n'est jamais ça' in E. Marks and I. de Courtivron (eds), *New French Feminisms*, Sussex: Harvester Press.

Krupat, A. (1992) *Ethno-Criticism: Ethnography, History, Literature*, Berkeley: University of California Press.

Lacan, J. (1977) *Écrits – A Selection*, trans. Alan Sheridan, London: Tavistock Publications.

Lakoff, G. (1987) *Women, Fire and Dangerous Things*, Chicago: Chicago University Press.

Lakoff, R. (1975) *Language and Women's Place*, New York: Harper and Row.

Lane, M. (ed.) (1970) *Structuralism: A Reader*, London: Jonathan Cape.

Larkin, P. (1988) *Collected Poems*, ed. A. Thwaite, London: Faber and Faber.

Laurence, M. (1974) *The Diviners*, Toronto: McClelland and Stewart.

Lauter, P. (1991) 'Caste, Class, and Canon' in R. Warhol and D. Price Herndl (eds), *Feminisms: An Anthology of Literary Theory and Criticism*, New Jersey: Rutgers University Press.

Lawrence, D.H. (1967) *Selected Literary Criticism*, London: Heineman Educational Books.

Lawrence, D.H. (1980) *Sons and Lovers*, London: Penguin.

Lecercle. J.J. (1990) *The Violence of Language,* London: Routledge.

Lecercle, J.J. (1993) 'The Trouble with Stylistics', *European English Messenger*, 2,1, 14–18.

Lee, D. (1992) *Competing Discourses*, London: Longman.

Leech, G. (1969) *A Linguistic Guide to English Poetry*, London: Longman.

Leech, G. and Short, M. (1981) *Style in Fiction: A Linguistic Introduction to English Fictional Prose*, London: Longman.

Legouis, E. and Cazamian, L. (1964) *A History of English Literature*, London: Dent.

Lehman, D. (1991) *Signs of the Times: Deconstruction and the Fall of Paul de Man*, London: André Deutsch.

Lemon, L. and Reis, M. (eds) (1965) *Russian Formalist Criticism: Four Essays, Lincoln and London: University of Nebraska Press.*

Lentriccia, F. (1980) *After the New Criticism, Chicago: Chicago University Press.*

Lévi-Strauss, C. (1970) *The Raw and the Cooked*, London: Jonathan Cape.

Levinson, S. (1983) *Pragmatics*, Cambridge: Cambridge University Press.

Lodge, D. (1966) *The Language of Fiction*, London: Routledge and Kegan Paul.

Lodge, D. (1977) *The Modes of Modern Writing*, London: Edward Arnold.

Lodge, D. (1980) *Working with Structuralism*, London: Routledge and Kegan Paul.

Lodge, D. (1989) *Nice Work*, London: Penguin.

Longhurst, D. (ed.) (1989) *Gender, Genre and Narrative Pleasure*, London: Unwin Hyman.

Lukàcs, G. (1962) *The Historical Novel*, London: Merlin.

Lukàcs, G. (1978) *Writer and Critic and Other Essays*, London: Merlin.

Lyndon, N. (1993) *No More Sex War: The Failures of Feminism*, London: Sinclair Stevenson.

Lyons, J. (1977) *Semantics*, 2 vols, Cambridge: Cambridge University Press.

MacCannell, J. Flower (1986) *Figuring Lacan: Criticism and the Cultural Unconscious*, London: Croom Helm.

McClintock, A. (1994) 'The Angel of Progress: Pitfalls of the Term "Post-Colonialism"' in P. Williams and L. Chrisman (eds), *Colonial Discourse and Post-Colonial Theory: A Reader*, Hemel Hempstead: Harvester Wheatsheaf.

McGann, J. (ed.) (1985) *Historical Studies and Literary Criticism*, London: University of Wisconsin Press.

McHale, B. (1987) *Postmodernist Fiction*, London: Methuen.

McKay, N. (1991) 'Reflections of Black Women Writers: Revising the Literary Canon' in R. Warhol and D. Price Herndl (eds), *Feminisms: An Anthology of Literary Theory and Criticism*, New Jersey: Rutgers University Press.

Macherey, P. (1978) *A Theory of Literary Production*, London: Routledge and Kegan Paul.

Mair, G.H. (1969) *English Literature 1450-1900*, Oxford: Oxford University Press.

Mannoni, D. O. (1964) *Prospero and Caliban: The Psychology of Colonization*, New York: Praeger.

Maracle, L. (1990) 'Native Myths: Trickster Alive and Crowing' in L. Scheier, S. Sheard and E. Wachtel (eds), *Language In Her Eye: Writing and Gender*, Toronto: Coach House Press.

Marks, E. and de Courtivron, I. (eds) (1981) *New French Feminisms*, Sussex: Harvester Press.

Marlatt, D. (1988) *ana historic*, Toronto: Coach House Press.

Marlatt, D. (1991) *Salvage*, Alberta: Red Deer College Press.

Marshall, B. (1992) *Teaching the Postmodern: Fiction and Theory*, London: Routledge.

Martin, W. (1986) *Recent Theories of Narrative*, Ithaca: Cornell University Press.

Masson, J. (1992) *The Assault on Truth: Freud and Child Sexual Abuse*, London: Fontana.

Mey, J. (1994) *Pragmatics: An Introduction*, Oxford: Blackwell.

Miller, A. (1983) *For Your Own Good: The Roots of Violence in Child-Rearing*, London: Faber and Faber.

Miller, J. (1990) *Seductions: Studies in Reading and Culture*, London: Virago.

Mills, S., Pearce, L., Spaull, S. and Millard, E. (1989) *Feminist Readings, Feminists Reading*, Hemel Hempstead: Harvester Wheatsheaf.

Mitchell, J. and Rose, J. (eds) (1985) *Feminine Sexuality: Jacques Lacan and the 'École Freudiénne'*, trans. Jacqueline Rose, New York: Norton.

Mitchell, M. (1974) *Gone with the Wind*, London: Macmillan.

Modleski, T. (1991) *Feminism Without Women*, London: Routledge.

Moers, E. (1976) *Literary Women*, London: W.H. Allen & Co.

Moi, T. (1985) *Sexual/Textual Politics*, London and New York: Methuen.

Montgomery, M., Fabb, N., Durant, A., Furniss, T. and Mills, S. (1992) *Ways of Reading: Advanced Reading Skills for Students of Literature*, London: Routledge.

Morgan, S. (1988) *My Place*, London: Virago.

Morris, C. (1946) *Signs, Language, Behavior*, New York: George Brazilier.

Morris, P. (ed.) (1994) *The Bakhtin Reader*, London: Edward Arnold.

Mühlhaüsler, P. and Harre, R. (1990) *Pronouns and People*, Oxford: Basil Blackwell.

Mulhern, F. (ed.) (1992) *Contemporary Marxist Literary Criticism*, London: Longman.

Murray, D. (ed.) (1989) *Literary Theory and Poetry*, London: Batsford.

Nash, W. (1992) *An Uncommon Tongue: The Uses and Resources of English*, London: Routledge.

Naylor, G. (1990) *Mama Day*, London: Vintage.

Norris, C. (1982) *Deconstruction: Theory and Practice*, London: Methuen.

Peirce, C.S. (1932) *Collected Papers*, Cambridge: Harvard University Press.

Perkins, D. (1992) *Is Literary History Possible?*, Baltimore: Johns Hopkins University Press.

Petry, S. (1990) *Speech Acts and Literary Theory*, London: Routledge.

Philip, M. Nourbese (1992) *Frontiers: Essays and Writings on Racism and Culture*, Stratford, Ontario: The Mercury Press.

Phillips, A. (1993) *On Kissing, Tickling and Being Bored*, London: Faber and Faber.

Piaget, J. (1971) *Structuralism*, London: Routledge and Kegan Paul.

Pinker, S. (1994) *The Language Instinct: The New Science of Language and the Mind*, London: Allen Lane, Penguin.

Poulet, G. (1969) 'Phenomenology of Reading', *New Literary History*, 1, 1, 53–68.

Pratt, M.L. (1977) *Towards a Speech Act Theory of Literary Discourse*, Bloomington: Indiana University Press.

Prince, G. (1980) 'Introduction to the Study of Narrative' in J. Tomkins (ed.) (1980) *Reader Response Criticism*, Baltimore: Johns Hopkins University Press.

Propp, V. (1958) *Morphology of the Folktale*, Bloomington: Indiana University Press.

Rabinow, P. (ed.) (1986) *The Foucault Reader*, London: Peregrine.

Ray, W. (1984) *Literary Meaning*, Oxford: Blackwell.

Reynolds, M. (ed.) (1993) *The Penguin Book of Lesbian Short Stories*, London: Viking.

Rhys, J. (1988) *Wide Sargasso Sea*, London: Penguin.

Riffatere, M. (1978) *The Semiotics of Poetry*, Bloomington: Indiana University Press.

Rimmon-Kenan, S. (1983) *Narrative Fiction: Contemporary Poetics*, London: Methuen.

Robinson, L. (1986) 'Treason Our Text: Feminist Challenges to the Literary Canon' in E. Showalter (ed.), *The New Feminist Criticism: Essays on Women, Literature and Theory*, London: Virago.

Roiphe, K. (1994) *The Morning After: Sex, Fear and Feminism*, London: Hamish Hamilton.

Rose, J. (1984) *The Case of Peter Pan: The Impossibility of Children's Literature*, Basingstoke: Macmillan.

Rushdie, S. (1988) *The Satanic Verses*, London: Viking.

Rushdie, S. (1991) *Imaginary Homelands: Essays and Criticism 1981–1991*. London: Granta Books.

Russ, J. (1984) *How to Suppress Women's Writing*, London: The Women's Press.

Russell, S. (1990) *Render Me My Song: African-American Women Writers from Slavery to the Present*, London: Pandora.

Rutherford, J. (ed.) (1990) *Identity: Community, Culture, Difference*, London: Lawrence and Wishart.

Said, E. W. (1994) *Culture and Imperialism*, London: Vintage.

Sapir, E. (1963) *Language*, London: Rupert Hart-Davis.

Saussure, F. de (1974) *Course in General Linguistics*, London: Fontana.

Scheier, L., Sheard, S. and Wachtel, E. (eds) (1990) *Language in Her Eye: Writing and Gender*, Toronto: Coach House Press.

Schiffrin, D. (1993) *Approaches to Discourse*, Oxford: Blackwell.

Scholes, R. (1974) *Structuralism in Literature: An Introduction*, New Haven: Yale.

Searle, J. (1969) *Speech Acts*, Cambridge: Cambridge University Press.

Sebeok, T. (ed.) (1961) *Style in Language*, Cambridge, Mass.: MIT Press.

Sedgewick, E.K. (1985) *Between Men: English Literature and Male Homosocial Desire*, New York: Columbia University Press.

Segal, L. (1990) *Slow Motion: Changing Masculinities, Changing Men*, London: Virago.

Seidler, V. (ed.) (1992) *Men, Sex and Relationships: Writings from Achilles Heel*, London: Routledge.

Sell, R. (ed.) (1991) *Literary Pragmatics*, London: Routledge.

Sellers, S. (1991) *Language and Sexual Difference: Feminist Writing in France*, Basingstoke: Macmillan.

Shklovsky, V. (1965) 'Art as Technique' in L. Lemon and M. Reis (eds), *Russian Formalist Criticism: Four Essays*, Lincoln and London: University of Nebraska Press.

Showalter, E. (1977) *A Literature of Their Own: British Women Novelists from Brontë to Lessing*, Princeton: Princeton University Press.

Showalter, E. (ed.) (1986) *The New Feminist Criticism: Essays on Women, Literature and Theory*, London: Virago.

Silverman, K. (1983) *The Subject of Semiotics*, Oxford: Oxford University Press.

Simpson, P. (1993) *Language, Ideology and Point of View*, London: Routledge.

Slemon, S. and Tiffin, H. (eds) (1989) *After Europe*, Sydney: Dangaroo Press.

Smith, P. (1987) 'Men in Feminist Theory' in A. Jardine and P. Smith (eds), *Men in Feminism*, London: Methuen.

Smith, P. (1988) *Discerning The Subject*, Minneapolis: University of Minnesota Press.

Smith, P. (1991) 'Vas' in R. Warhol and D. Price Herndl (eds), *Feminisms*, New Jersey: Rutgers University Press.

Spillane, M. (1973) *I, the Jury*, New York: New American Library.

Spivak, G.C. (1987) *In Other Worlds*, New York and London: Methuen.

Spivak, G.C. (1990) *The Post-Colonial Critic: Interviews, Strategies, Dialogues*, ed. S. Harasym, London and New York: Routledge.

Stierle, K. (1980) 'The Reading of Fictional Texts' in S.R. Suleiman and I. Crosman (eds), *The Reader in the Text: Essays on Audience and Interpretation*, Princeton: Princeton University Press.

Stimpson, C. (1991) 'Zero Degree Deviancy: The Lesbian Novel in English', in Price Herndl and Warhol (eds), *Feminisms*, New Jersey: Rutgers University Press.

Strickland, G. (1981) *Structuralism or Criticism? Some Thoughts on How We Read*, Cambridge: Cambridge University Press.

Suleiman, S.R. and Crosman, I. (eds) (1980) *The Reader in the Text: Essays on Audience and Interpretation*, Princeton: Princeton University Press.

Sweetser, E. (1990) *From Etymology to Pragmatics*, Cambridge: Cambridge University Press.

Tallis, R. (1988) *Not Saussure*, Basingstoke: Macmillan.

Tan, A. (1990) *The Joy Luck Club*, London: Minerva.

Tillyard, E.M. (1972) *The Elizabethan World Picture*, London: Pelican.

Todorov, T. (1971) *The Poetics of Prose*, Oxford: Blackwell.

Todorov. T. (1981) *Introduction to Poetics*, London: Harvester.

Tomashevsky, B. (1965) 'Thematics' in L. Lemon and R. Reis (eds), *Russian Formalist Criticism: Four Essays*, Lincoln and London: University of Nebraska Press.

Tomkins, J. (ed.) (1980) *Reader Response Criticism*, Baltimore: Johns Hopkins University Press.

Toolan, M. (ed.) (1992) *Language, Text and Context*, London: Routledge.

Traugott, E. and Pratt, M. (1980) *Linguistics for Students of Literature*, New York: Harcourt Brace.

Trinh T. Minh-ha (1989) *Woman, Native, Other: Writing Postcoloniality and Feminism*, Bloomington and Indianapolis: Indiana University Press.

Turner, L. (1994) *The Love of Dugan Magee*, Surrey: Silhouette Books.

Van Herk, A. (1989) *No Fixed Address*, London: Virago.

Van Peer, W. (ed.) (1986) *Taming the Text: Explorations in Language, Literature and Culture*, London: Routledge.

Veeser, H.A. (ed.) (1989) *The New Historicism*, London: Routledge.

Walder, D. (1991) *Literature and the Modern World: Critical Essays and Documents*, Open University: Oxford University Press.

Wales, K. (1989) *A Dictionary of Stylistics*, London: Longman.

Wales, K. (1992) *The Language of James Joyce*, London: Macmillan.

Wales, K. (ed.) (1994) *Feminist Linguistics in Literary Criticism*, Cambridge: D.S. Brewer.

Ware, V. (1992) *Beyond the Pale: White Women, Racism and History*, London: Verso.

Warhol, R. and Price Herndl, D. (eds) (1991) *Feminisms: An Anthology of Literary Theory and Criticism*, New Jersey: Rutgers University Press.

Warland, B. (ed.) (1991) *Inversions: Writings by Dykes, .Queers and Lesbians*, London: Open Letters.

Washington, Booker T. (1901) *Up from Slavery.* In *Three Negro Classics* (1965), New York: Avon Books.

Weedon, C. (1987) *Feminist Practice and Post-Structuralist Theory*, Oxford: Blackwell.

White, H. (1973) *Metahistory: The Historical Imagination in Nineteenth-Century Europe*, Baltimore: Johns Hopkins University Press.

Whitford, M. (1989) 'Re-Reading Irigaray' in T. Brennan (ed.), *Between Feminism and Psychoanalysis*, London: Routledge.

Widdowson, H.G. (1975) *Stylistics and the Teaching of Literature*, London: Longman.

Widdowson, H.G. (1979) *Explorations in Applied Linguistics*, London: Longman.

Williams, P. and Chrisman, L. (eds) (1994) *Colonial Discourse and Post-Colonial Theory: A Reader*, Hemel Hempstead: Harvester Wheatsheaf.

Williams, R. (1976) *Keywords*, London: Croom Helm.

Williams, R. (1977) *Marxism and Literature*, Oxford: Oxford University Press.

Williamson, J. (1978) *Decoding Advertisements*, London: Marion Boyars.

Wimsatt, W.K. and Beardsley, M. (1954) *The Verbal Icon: Studies in the Meaning of Poetry*, Lexington: Kentucky University Press.

Wolf, G. (ed.) (1992) *New Departures in Linguistics*, New York: Garland Press.

Wolf, N. (1993) *Fire with Fire: The New Female Power and How it Will Change the 21st Century*, London: Chatto and Windus.

Woolf, V. (1980) *To the Lighthouse* London: Penguin.

Wright, E. (1984) *Psychoanalytic Criticism: Theory in Practice*, London: Methuen.

Wright, E. (ed.) (1992) *Feminism and Psychoanalysis: A Critical Dictionary*, Oxford: Blackwell.

Yeats, W.B. (1987) *The Collected Poems*, ed. R. Finneran, London: Macmillan.

York, R.A. (1987) *The Poem as Utterance*, London: Methuen.

Zimmerman, B. (1991) 'What Has Never Been: An Overview of Lesbian Feminist Literary Criticism' in R. Warhol and D. Price Herndl (eds), *Feminisms: An Anthology of Literary Theory and Criticism*, New Jersey: Rutgers University Press.

Index

329